A KID'S GUIDE TO
ASIAN AMERICAN HISTORY

MORE THAN 70 ACTIVITIES

VALERIE PETRILLO

CHICAGO
REVIEW
PRESS

To Mike:

Amazing artist, amazing son

Follow your dreams, nurture your

creativity

The best is yet to come

Library of Congress Cataloging-in-Publication Data
Petrillo, Valerie.
   A kid's guide to Asian American history : more than 70 activities
/ Valerie Petrillo. — 1st ed.
      p. cm.
   Includes bibliographical references and index.
   ISBN-13: 978-1-55652-634-3
   ISBN-10: 1-55652-634-2
   1. Asian Americans—History—Juvenile literature. 2. Asian
Americans—History—Study and teaching—Activity programs—
Juvenile literature. I. Title.

   E184.A75P48 2007
   973'.0495—dc22

                                          2006031673

Cover and interior design: Gail Rattray
Interior illustrations: Gail Rattray and Michael Petrillo

© 2007 by Valerie Petrillo
All rights reserved
First edition
Published by Chicago Review Press
814 North Franklin Street
Chicago, Illinois 60610
ISBN-13: 978-1-55652-634-3
ISBN-10: 1-55652-634-2
Printed in the United States of America
5 4 3 2 1

• Contents •

Acknowledgments   vi

Time Line   viii

Introduction   xi

1 · FROM EAST TO WEST

Pack an Immigrant Trunk   3

Create a Japanese Folding Fan   4

2 · CHINESE AMERICANS

Make Honeydew Bubble Tea   11

Create a Tiger Hat   13

Construct an Evil Spirit Apron   15

Do Chinese Opera Face Painting   16

Make a Shoulder Yoke   19

Write Chinese Characters   23

Say It in Chinese (Mandarin)   25

Create a Chinese Brush Painting Greeting Card   26

Craft a Lacquer Box   28

Try Chinese Paper Cutting   30

Practice Feng Shui   32

Cook an Authentic Chinese Nian Gao for Chinese New Year   35

Wrap Chinese Jiaozi   38

Make a Lai See: Chinese Red Envelope   40

Create a Tray of Togetherness: A Sweet Tray   42

Make a Chinese Lion   43

Perform the Lion Dance   45

Make a Pot Cover Gong   46

Paint a Chinese Calligraphy Banner   47

Light Up a Dragon Lantern   48

Arrange a Moon Festival Picnic   51

Put on a Chinese Shadow Puppet Show   52

Design a Double Happiness Signature Cloth   56

Practice Tai Chi   57

Chase the Dragon's Tail   59

Construct a Chinese Abacus   60

Use an Abacus   61

Try the Chinese Ribbon Dance   63

3 · JAPANESE AMERICANS

Make a Bento Lunch 67

Create an Otedama Beanbag Game 68

Paint a Daruma Doll 73

Prepare Miso Soup 75

Craft a Furoshiki 77

Make Rice Balls 78

Say It in Japanese 80

Fold an Origami Dog and Cat 81

Write Haiku 82

Practice Taiko Drumming 83

Create Gyotaku: Japanese Fish Printing 84

Paint Your Face Like a Kabuki Actor 86

Make a Kadomatsu to Place at Your Front Door 88

Join in a Bon Odori Dance 90

Make a Carp Streamer for Children's Day 91

Enjoy Chanoyu: The Japanese Tea Ceremony 94

Build a Japanese Rock Garden 100

Create Ikebana: A Traditional Japanese Cut Flower Arrangement 101

Play Jan, Ken, Pon: The Original Rock, Paper, Scissors Game 103

Make a Milk-Cap Game 104

4 · KOREAN AMERICANS

Say It in Korean 108

Make a Korean Flag 109

Join in Tuho: Arrow Throwing 111

Have Fun with Jegi-chagi: Tassel Kicking 112

Set Up a Tol: A Fortune-Telling Birthday Party 119

Try a Front Kick in Taekwondo 121

Create a Colorful Pojagi: Korean Wrapping Cloth 122

Prepare Ttok-kuk Soup 125

Make a Jumoni: Good Luck Bag 126

Enjoy Yut: A Game Played with Sticks 127

Construct a Korean Kite 129

5 · FILIPINO AMERICANS

Filipino Shell Crafts: Make a Picture Frame 139

Say It in Filipino 141

Prepare Halo-Halo: A Fruity, Icy Filipino Treat 142

Join in Tumbang Preso: Kick the Can Game 144

Try Sungka: A Cowrie Shell Game 145

Put Together a Balikbayan Box 147

Make a Parol: A Star Lantern 149

Cook Up Bibingka: A Sweet Rice Dessert 151

Practice the Pandango Sa Ilaw 152

Create Your Own Jeepney 156

6 · Asian Indian Americans

Wrap a Sari   165

Say It in Hindi   166

Make Ghungroos: Asian Indian Dancing Bells   167

Try Yoga   168

Make Banana Lassi: A Yogurt Drink   170

Play Snakes and Ladders   171

Make a Diya for Diwali   176

Create a Chalk Rangoli: An Asian Indian Welcome   177

Do Mehndi: Asian Indian Hand Painting   178

7 · Southeast Asian Americans

Make a Sponsor Box   186

Vietnamese in America   188

Prepare a Bowl of Vietnamese Beef Noodle Soup   190

Create a Foam Dragon for Tet   192

Laotians in America   195

Play Pov Pob: A Hmong Ball-Toss Game for
     New Year's   196

Color a Hmong Flower Cloth: Paj Ntaub   197

Design a Storytelling Cloth   199

Cambodians in America   201

Cambodian Court Dance: Learn the Hand Gestures   202

Mold a Khmer Theater Mask   203

Say It in Khmer   205

Make Cambodian Spring Rolls   206

Conclusion   207

Design a Poster to Celebrate Asian Pacific American
     Heritage Month   211

Resources   213

Asian American Quick Facts   213

Glossary   215

Bibliography   221

Asian American Museums   225

Suggested Reading List for Kids   230

Asian American Movies and Videos   231

Web Sites   232

Teacher's Guide   234

History Standards and Learning Objectives   237

Index   239

• Acknowledgments •

I am especially grateful to Judy Lau for sharing so much of her family's Chinese heritage with me. Her knowledge of Chinese, as well as Chinese American culture, her rich and detailed explanations of Chinese traditions, and her willingness to answer countless questions helped me to bring the book alive. Thank you also to Fee Har Chin for her wonderful recipe for Nian Gao, written down for the first time for this book! I also would like to thank Anna Lau and Sandie Lau for graciously reading the manuscript and helping me translate some of the Chinese words.

Thanks also to Chand Sripad for helping to enrich and clarify the chapter on Indian culture. Chand has been instrumental in bringing Indian classical dance and music to our Andover, Massachusetts community, as well as to help found a Hindu religious education program here.

Thanks and appreciation to my sister Norma Cahill who dropped everything when needed to help with artistic and technical issues.

Special thanks go to Lisa Rosenthal, my wonderful editor who I will miss dearly as she pursues her own writing career. I also want to thank my current project editor, Michelle Schoob, who has done a top notch job; Devon Freeny, a most meticulous copy editor; Scott Rattray for a great design; illustrators Mike Petrillo and Gail Rattray for their marvelous artwork; and Cynthia Sherry for the wonderful opportunity to write this book.

Finally, I am most grateful to my husband Hank who offered endless support and encouragement through many months of research and writing, who came with me to Asian museums, ethnic neighborhoods, and immigration ports so that I could step however briefly into the shoes of immigrants coming to America. I also want to thank my three children, Mike, Nick, and Noelle who have tried everything from ttok-kuk soup to bibingka, and who continue to delight me with their own talents and creativity.

◆ Time Line ◆

1763	Filipinos jump ship from Spanish galleons and settle in New Orleans.
1849	Gold is discovered in California. First wave of Chinese immigrants arrive to mine for gold.
1852	First 195 Chinese contract workers arrive in Hawaii to work on sugar and pineapple plantations.
1868	First 150 Japanese laborers travel to Hawaii to work on sugar and pineapple plantations.
1869	Chinese workers help complete the transcontinental railroad.
1882	Chinese Exclusion Act is passed.
1898	U.S. Supreme Court case is won by Wong Kim Ark. The court declares that all children of immigrants born in the United States are American citizens.
1899	First Asian Indians immigrate from the Punjab area of India.
1903	First Korean workers arrive in Hawaii.
	Filipino students, pensionados, arrive in the United States.
1906	San Francisco earthquake destroys all Chinese immigration records. Many Chinese enter the country as "paper sons."

1907	First group of Filipino laborers come to Hawaii.
1908	Gentlemen's Agreement between the United States and Japan prevents Japanese laborers from entering the United States. A provision allows the wives of Japanese in the United States to immigrate. Hundreds of "picture brides" enter the United States between 1910 and 1920.
1910	Angel Island Immigration Station opens.
1913	California Alien Land Act is passed, making it illegal for aliens to own land.
1917	Asiatic Barred Zone is created, excluding citizens from most of Asia from immigrating to the United States.
1923	United States Supreme Court decides in *United States vs. Bhagat Singh Thind* that Asian Indians are not eligible to become naturalized citizens.
1924	United States Immigration Act of 1924 shuts down nearly all immigration from Asia.
1934	Tydings-McDuffie Act is passed, changing the status of Filipinos from "nationals" to "aliens."
1941	Japan attacks Pearl Harbor.
1942	Japanese Americans are imprisoned in internment camps after Executive Order 9066 is signed by President Franklin D. Roosevelt.
1943	Congress repeals all Chinese Exclusion Acts, allows citizenship for Chinese living in the United States, and allows a small quota of immigration from China per year.
1945	War Brides Act allows the wives of American servicemen to immigrate to the United States.

1946	Luce-Celler Act grants naturalization rights to Filipinos and Asian Indians and also allows for a small immigration quota from the Philippines and India each year.
1952	McCarran-Walter Act eliminates race as a requirement for naturalization. A small quota from each Asian country is allowed per year.
1956	Alien Land Laws are repealed in California.
1965	Immigration Act of 1965 abolishes immigration quotas based on national origins.
	United States sends troops to Vietnam to fight against the North Vietnamese.
1973	United States withdraws from Vietnam.
1975	The North Vietnamese take over South Vietnam, the Pathet Lao take over Laos, and Pol Pot and the Khmer Rouge overtake Cambodia. Thousands of refugees flee to the United States.
1978	Thousands of boat people escape from Southeast Asia.
1987	Amerasian Homecoming Act of 1987 is passed.
1988	President Ronald Reagan signs the Civil Liberties Act of 1988, providing reparations to Japanese Americans.
1990	Immigration Act of 1990 allows for higher quotas from all countries and gives preference to certain skilled professions.
	President George H. W. Bush designates May of each year as Asian Pacific American Heritage Month.

◆ Introduction ◆

Do you know what Tiger Woods the golfer, Jerry Yang the inventor of the Internet company Yahoo!, and Gary Locke the governor of Washington have in common? They are all *Asian Americans*. Asian Americans are people who *immigrated* (moved from one country to another where they were not native) to the United States from Asia, or who have a parent, grandparent, or great-grandparent from Asia.

Most people don't realize that many of the things we use every day originally came from Asia. Think Asia when you sip a cup of tea, take a karate class, shake pepper on your food, or enjoy fireworks on the Fourth of July. Asia brought us paper, the wheelbarrow, the compass, ramen noodles, the walkman, karaoke, futons, and sushi.

In *A Kid's Guide to Asian American History* you are invited on a journey to explore the diversity of Asian American culture through more than 90 activities. In chapter 1 we will look at the voyage from Asia and the challenge of moving into the unknown a half a world away. We will pack a trunk and imagine how it felt to be an Asian immigrant deciding what to bring and what to leave behind.

In chapter 2 we will find out about Chinese Americans and learn about their part in building the American West:

they toiled as railroad workers, gold miners, and laborers, but until recently they were largely absent from history books. We will walk through the streets of Chinatown, learn how to write in Chinese, construct our own abacus, and make a gong and Chinese lion for Chinese New Year.

In chapter 3 we'll move on to the contributions of Japanese Americans, from their hard labor on Hawaii's sugar plantations to the brave all–Japanese American 442nd Regimental Combat Team and 100th Battalion, who fought in World War II. We will learn about the dark period in Japanese American history when Japanese Americans were forced to live in internment (holding) camps, because Japan was at war with America. We will build a Japanese rock garden, create a Japanese cut flower arrangement called ikebana, and enjoy a simmering cup of miso (soybean paste) soup.

Korean Americans will follow in chapter 4. We'll hear about how a Korean American, Harry Kim (Kim Hyung-soon), created the "fuzzless peach" known as the Sun Grand nectarine, and how Korean Americans succeed by building small businesses. We will try a move in taekwondo, Korea's own martial art; construct a Korean kite for Seol, the Korean New Year; and make a pojagi, a Korean wrapping cloth.

The history of Filipino Americans will be covered in chapter 5. It may be a surprise to you to learn that the first Asians to settle in the United States were Filipino sailors who jumped off Spanish ships in the 1700s and made their homes in the Louisiana Territory, or that the Philippines was a territory of the United States from the turn of the 20th century until 1946. Come along and play sungka, a Filipino game made with the cowrie shells that line the beaches of the Philippines; cook up some bibingka, a Filipino sweet rice dessert; and create your own jeepney, a uniquely Filipino vehicle made from old United States Army jeeps.

Chapter 6 will explore Asian Indian Americans. We will see how early Asian Indian immigrants labored in the lumber yards, forests, and farmlands of the West, and appreciate the contributions of Asian Indian Americans today such as Subrahmanyan Chandrasekhar, who won the Nobel Prize for Physics; Kalpana Chawla, an Asian Indian American astronaut; and Sabeer Bhatia, who created a free form of e-mail called Hotmail. Join us as we learn how to wrap a sari, the traditional costume of Asian Indian Americans; make a lamp for the Asian Indian festival of Diwali; and paint our hands with henna like an Asian Indian American bride.

In chapter 7 we will study the somber refugee experience of the Southeast Asians who fled Vietnam, Laos, and Cambodia because of the effects of war and persecution there. We will learn about the boat people who escaped Southeast Asia in small overcrowded boats, risking drowning, starvation, and pirate attacks. We will see the strides Southeast Asians have made in the years since the wars and learn about their culture. We'll make a storytelling cloth as Laotians do to tell about their journey as refugees, learn to mold a Khmer theater mask to help honor and preserve the culture of Cambodia, and prepare pho, the beef noodle dish that Vietnamese Americans enjoy.

In conclusion, we will explore the differences between Asian and American culture and how Asian Americans have adapted to these differences. We'll celebrate Asian Pacific American Heritage Month by designing a meaningful poster.

Throughout the book there are sidebars with a lot of fun facts about Asian American culture such as "Why are so many Chinese things red?" and "What is a picture bride?" alongside biographies of Asian Americans who have made important contributions both inside the United States and around the world. The resource section includes wonderful books, Web sites, and movies about Asian American culture. There is also a list of Asian American museums that offer hands-on workshops and lively celebrations of Asian American culture. The teacher's guide is a helpful resource, too, for use in the classroom.

So join in this celebration of Asian American cultures and peoples as you learn about the important contributions that have enriched the fabric of America.

1
From East to West

Who Are Asian Americans?

Asian Americans are as diverse as the vast country we live in. They are Chinese American descendants of the gold rush pioneers who work as stockbrokers on Wall Street, and they are restaurant workers in Chinatown who arrived only weeks ago. They are Korean greengrocers and Asian Indian software engineers, Filipino business owners and Vietnamese fishermen, Japanese students and Cambodian writers. Many are American citizens. They are all an important part of the world's only nation of immigrants, the United States of America.

It takes a certain type of courage to leave what is comfortable and secure for the promise of the unknown. When the first Asian immigrants reached America by boat, they must have thought that they were entering another world. They left countries that had been devastated by famine or war and they were pulled to the United States with prom-ises of jobs. When they arrived they were confronted with a confusing new language, different foods and customs, exhausting work, prejudice, and the loneliness of knowing that an entire ocean separated them from their families.

The Voyage

The first Asian Americans typically came by steamship, and the trip took weeks. They usually bought third-class tickets in steerage (below decks quarters) because they were cheaper than buying first- or second-class tickets. Beds were bunked in tight rows and there was little fresh air or sunlight. Steerage passengers were allowed on the deck in fair weather, but if there was a storm at sea they were sent back below. They suffered from gut-wrenching seasickness and hunger. Disease spread rapidly because they were living in such close quarters. The conditions on board were unsanitary—there were no bathrooms, there was no clean water to wash, and they had to eat a meager diet of rice and water.

Today, steamships have largely been replaced by airplanes for immigrants who come to the United States. The journey is kinder—without the risks of disease, seasickness, and hunger—but it doesn't guarantee a welcome mat, and such a quick trip makes it harder to prepare yourself mentally. A long sea trip physically separates you from your homeland. You have time to think about the home you are leaving; and the country for which you are bound. For immigrants coming by airplane, breakfast in the Far East and supper in the United States can be a sudden change.

Pack an Immigrant Trunk

For the early immigrants, their whole lives had to be packed into a single trunk and brought to America. Most immigrants never returned to Asia. In packing the trunk they had to decide what to bring for practical reasons, things like clothing and pots and pans, and what to bring for sentimental reasons, items such as family jewelry, photographs, and letters. This activity will help you imagine what the process was like for those who had to leave so much behind.

What You Need

Acrylic brown paint

Paintbrush

Heavyweight cardboard box with
   removable top (the box that computer
   paper comes in works well)

Items you would choose to bring if you
   were to immigrate to a new country:
   money, clothing, religious items,
   pictures of your family, a favorite
   blanket, books, clothing, a childhood
   toy, etc.

What You Do

1. Paint the top and bottom of the box with the brown paint. Two coats may be needed. Let dry.
2. Fill the box with what you feel you will need for the journey ahead.
3. Think about these questions: What did you leave out? Did you include any items that tell someone who you are as a person? Any that reflect on your culture? Discuss this activity with someone else and detail the items each of you included in your box. What would the other person pack? Are his or her choices different from yours? Why?

Create a Japanese Folding Fan

The first Japanese immigrants who came to America aboard ships usually brought folding fans with them. The folding fan was created in Japan, then spread to China and eventually to the rest of the world.

Japanese folding fans were traditionally used by both men and women as accessory items. They were used for decorative purposes, as well as for keeping cool. Historically the *samurai* (members of the ruling warrior class in Japan) used fans made with separate iron pieces (also called "ribs"), and royalty had their own special folding fans. Fans were also preserved on screens as artwork. There are special fans for the Japanese tea ceremony, for a form of Japanese theater called Noh, and for traditional Japanese dance. Fans, like designer pocketbooks today, often told about the social or economic class of their owner.

Historians study these fans in order to understand the culture of the time and learn what the immigrants valued. They do the same with other items that the immigrants brought with them. These types of artifacts are being collected by places such as the Ellis Island Immigration Museum in New York.

What You Need

1 piece 18-by-25-inch wrapping paper with wilderness designs (or paper with your own designs drawn on it)

Stapler

What You Do

1. Fold the paper in half the long way with the design facing out. Keep the folded part on top.
2. Fold the paper accordion style, back and forth.
3. Staple the ends together at the bottom. Now you're ready to keep cool with your fan.

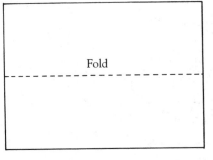

Fold

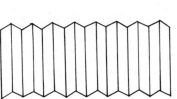

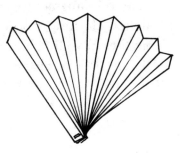

Angel Island

The first stop for many Asian immigrants entering the United States was called *Angel Island*. It was a processing center for immigrants in San Francisco, California, that opened in 1910. A similar center, *Ellis Island*, processed mostly European immigrants on the East Coast, in New York City.

Unlike on Ellis Island, where most immigrants were usually admitted to the country within hours, on Angel Island immigrants were detained for days, months, even years. At the time, the nation feared that too many Asians were entering the country, so they made entering the country as difficult as possible. Immigrants were subjected to hours of interrogation, and often imprisoned without cause.

Angel Island was closed in 1940, but the scars of what Asian immigrants endured there are scratched on the walls in Chinese poetry. The Angel Island Immigration Station has been preserved as a museum in honor of Asian immigrants. The poems are still visible on the walls.

Here is a poem by a Chinese immigrant who was detained at Angel Island:

There are tens of thousands of poems on these walls
They are all cries of suffering and sadness
The day I am rid of this prison and become successful
I must remember that this chapter once existed
I must be frugal in my daily needs
Needless extravagance usually leads to ruin
All my compatriots must remember China
Once you have made some small gains,
you should return home early

> —Written by one from Heungshan
> From *Island: Poetry and History of Chinese Immigrants on Angel Island, 1910–1940* by Him Mark Lai, Genny Lim, and Judy Yung

Although the poem is bleak, there is still a tone of hopefulness, of the good that is to come. It is this spirit, this hopefulness and confidence in the promise of America, that continues to draw people from all over the world.

2
Chinese Americans

When you think of the Wild West days you probably think of gold miners and cowboys. Did you know that the Chinese contributed a great deal to the development of the West? They worked in the gold mines, on the transcontinental railroad, on the sugar-cane plantations of Hawaii, in the creation of California's farmlands, and in general they provided a vast labor force to a growing country.

Chinese Americans are the largest Asian American group in the United States. Starting in the late 1840s thousands of Chinese, mostly men, left their homeland in order to find work to provide for themselves and their families. When gold was discovered in California in 1848, it attracted hundreds of Chinese *sojourners* (soh-jurn-ers). A sojourner is a person who leaves home to seek fortune in another place, with the intention of returning home within a short time.

Ticket brokers handed out colorful leaflets in Chinese seaports, encouraging farmers to come to America with promises of plentiful jobs and streets lined with gold. The name that the Chinese used for California was *Gam Saan*, which means "Gold Mountain." The way these poor farmers were able to afford the high fare to cross the ocean was through the *credit-ticket system*. The farmer was given a ticket by a broker in China, and when he began to earn money in America he would pay the broker back along with interest (additional money).

Immigrants began their trip by traveling by *junk* (Chinese sailboat) across the Pearl River Delta from Guangdong (a province of China) to Hong Kong or Macao. From there they traveled to America by means of an American or British steamship to San Francisco, California. The trip was difficult, lasting one to two months. The Chinese followed hordes of Americans as well as other foreigners to California for gold. Hopeful miners

WHY DID THEY LEAVE CHINA?

China at the time of the gold rush had been involved in wars with other countries as well as internal wars. The government placed the burden of paying for these wars on the village farmers, by charging them high taxes on their crops. The farmers could not pay the taxes and still have enough money left over to feed their families. Natural disasters, including floods that ruined crops and a population explosion in certain areas, led to widespread hunger and poverty. Problems such as these encouraged some Chinese to *emigrate* (to leave one's country and move elsewhere). The word *emigrate* is used when you talk about leaving a country. You say *immigrate* when talking about your new country or destination.

staked claims in places where gold was likely to be found. To *stake a claim* meant to hammer a wooden stake into the ground and declare that you owned the gold mined there.

In the gold mines, the Chinese were treated unequally from the white miners right from the beginning. The best mines were usually claimed by white men, and only when the mines had been picked over were the Chinese allowed to go in and mine.

Even so, the thoroughness and patience of the Chinese led them to have moderate success at mining. The easy way to mine for gold is to drill through the ground for it, but this requires the purchase of expensive equipment. The Chinese practiced a more economical but painstaking form of mining called *placer mining*, in which you sift sand and water to find gold nuggets and dust. The Chinese worked in cooperative groups and devised clever methods to find small pieces of gold that had been left behind. In China, many had learned how to build dams and change the direction of streams and rivers. This valuable knowledge helped them find gold that was previously underwater.

Some of the Chinese mining groups became successful enough to form companies and purchase the land they mined. Concerned that they were losing income to the Chinese miners, native-born Americans became jealous and fearful of them. Speeches were made and newspaper articles written that fostered these fears in others. Eventually the state of California responded by enacting a law that required foreign miners to pay a heavy tax to the state each month. The purpose of the law was to eliminate competition from all foreigners engaged in mining and to discourage Chinese immigration to California. This made it almost impossible for the Chinese miners to earn a decent living.

In the early years, many Chinese immigrants also became farmworkers. The Chinese made great contributions to California's success in farming, even though most of them worked as tenant farmers. *Tenant farmers* have an arrangement with landowners who let them farm the land in exchange for part of the profits. Chinese farmers used irrigation techniques (watering methods) they had learned from farming along the Yellow and Yangtze Rivers in China, and transformed thousands of acres of California swamps and marshes into profitable farmland.

In Hawaii, the Chinese were responsible for the development of rice as a crop. We can thank Ah Bing, a Chinese immigrant to Oregon, for producing a new type of fruit that we know as the Bing cherry, and Lue Gim Gong for developing a frost-resistant orange that became vitally important to Florida's success in the citrus industry. Despite their demonstrated abilities, the Chinese worked for half the amount of pay that white workers earned.

In the years following the gold rush, many Chinese chose to leave California for other parts of the United States. They worked as farmers, factory workers, railroad workers, fishermen, miners, laundry workers, and merchants.

Chinatowns

The first Chinatown emerged in San Francisco as the result of the gold mining boom. It was a place where mostly male Chinese immigrants lived in crowded rooms in tenements (low-cost rental apartments in the city that are often run-down and barely meet basic living standards) that looked over busy streets and alleys. Over the years Chinatown grew from a simple mining town in the 1850s to a family neighborhood and tourist attraction after World War II.

Chinatowns in San Francisco and Sacramento, and then in New York, Boston, Chicago, and other cities in America, mimicked life in China. Walking through the streets you could hear the sounds of Chinese with its high and low tones, see the men with long braids called *queues* (kyooz),

and smell the cooking aromas of ginger and garlic from restaurants with names such as "The House of Many Fortunes" and "Great Prosperity."

There were *scribes*, or professional letter writers, who could write in Cantonese and address the letters properly so that the men, many of whom could not read and write in their own language, could communicate with their families in China. The letters to these wives left behind always spoke of promises to return to China. Letters from their families back home often pleaded or demanded that the men return, something few could ever afford to do.

In Chinatown they could read newspapers in Cantonese, gamble in the many gambling houses, linger over tea, and buy familiar Chinese foods such as roasted duck, salted fish, sea cucumber, pickled plums, and shark's fin soup.

If sick, they would visit the herbalist, who recommended age-old Chinese remedies. As families settled in Chinatowns, many Chinese Americans worked in the factories, laundries, and restaurants. In their free time they attended Chinese plays at the opera houses, meditated in Chinese temples, and sent their children to Chinese schools to learn Chinese.

Today you can still visit Chinatowns in cities across America. It is very enjoyable to take a tour of the city, enjoy an authentic Chinese meal, and shop in the many stores that offer beautiful framed calligraphy, statues of Buddha, tea sets, fans, incense, Chinese porcelain, jade, and 24-karat gold.

Grocery stores in Chinatown are busy, bustling markets where people yell their orders in Chinese to butchers and fish sellers, where shelves are stocked from floor to ceiling with imported Chinese foods such as dried cuttlefish, duck's feet, dried seaweed, pig snouts, whole fish, live frogs and turtles, and a spectacular selection of teas. Outside, boxes and baskets of bok choy, Chinese broccoli, bitter melon, lo bok, and other Chinese fruits and vegetables spill onto the sidewalk.

Chinese bakeries are sprinkled throughout Chinatown, where delicious aromas from moon cakes, pork buns, sticky rice cookies, and red bean paste cakes waft out to the street.

In Chinatown there is something for everyone. It's like visiting a slice of China right here in America.

TEA

Tea is very important to Chinese Americans, and it is served at every meal. Chinese tea has been exported all over the world for hundreds of years, and is still the most important crop in China. The magnificent clipper ships built by Americans in the 19th century were specifically designed for speed in delivering tea from China.

There are three major categories of tea— green, black (called red in China), and oolong tea, but there are hundreds of varieties of each. In Chinatown, many shops carry 50 or more varieties of tea!

Chinese Americans usually prefer loose tea, rather than tea bags.

Buddhism

Many Chinese Americans are Buddhists and attend Buddhist temples. Buddhism began in India in the fifth century B.C.E. and spread to many areas of Asia and the rest of the world. Its founder is Siddhartha Buddha, a Hindu prince. Buddhism is based on the teachings of Buddha, which are called the *Four Noble Truths*. The truths are that life is suffering, that ignorance and desire causes suffering, that understanding this (called finding *enlightenment*) leads to *nirvana* (nir-vah-nah), an end to suffering, and that by following Buddhist teachings you can learn the way to achieve nirvana.

Chinese Clothing

The formal clothing and dress of the early Chinese immigrants was very beautiful and ornate. Chinese Americans looked very different from the typical American at the time. A man wore a silk jacket and trousers, with an American gray or black felt hat with a rim (raised edge that goes around the hat) and a low crown (the top of the hat). On his feet he wore white stockings and cloth shoes that had cork or pigskin soles.

The men wore their hair in long queues, braids that stretched down the length of their backs, and kept the top front part of their heads shaved. They had been forbidden to cut these braids while living under Manchu rule in China, and eventually it became the Chinese style. The Manchus were nomadic people from the north of China who took over the capital of Beijing from the Han people

Make Honeydew Bubble Tea

For the newest twist on China's oldest drink, enjoy a glass of bubble tea. You can buy it in a bakery or teahouse in Chinatown or make your own at home. Bubble tea is green Chinese tea that is mixed with cream, ice, and your choice of a variety of flavors. If you buy it in Chinatown you can ask for it with black tapioca pearls, which are chewy and eaten through a wide straw like a dessert.

Here's a delicious recipe without the tapioca pearls.

4 servings

What You Need
Adult supervision required
1 teabag of green tea
½ cup sugar
2 cups chopped honeydew melon
2 cups ice
1 cup half-and-half cream
Blender
4 tall glasses
Optional: straws

What You Do
1. Brew 1 cup of green tea, following directions on the package, and add the sugar.
2. Put the tea aside to cool or place in the refrigerator.
3. Place the melon, ice, cooled tea, and half-and-half cream in the blender.
4. Blend until bubbly.
5. Pour into glasses, add a straw, and enjoy!

RED

If you visit Chinatown one of the first things you will notice is the color red. Red is the luckiest of all colors in Chinese culture. It represents good fortune, light, the sun, fire, life, and energy. Chinese Americans use red in clothing, art, buildings, even food!

They wore beautifully ornate tiny slippers called *lotus shoes*. Women with bound feet were thought to be more attractive. Unfortunately the practice was very painful and caused the women to move with great difficulty. Foot binding was outlawed in China in 1911.

in 1644 (most of the people living in China were Han) and set up the Qing Dynasty, which lasted for 250 years.

While working outdoors in the mines and fields, the men wore cotton blouses and short, loose pants. They wore round, umbrella-type hats made of bamboo or grass that were shaped into a cone at the top. This was to allow the long queue to be wrapped up into the hat. On their feet they wore sandals or American work boots.

Chinese American women, of which there were few in those early days, wore similar silk blouses and trousers, sometimes secured with a sash around the waist. Chinese women arranged their hair in lovely twists and knots, which they often decorated with jewelry and flowers. White face powder distinguished their makeup from what American women wore.

Some of the first women had *lily feet*, or bound feet, which was a thousand-year-old custom in China. Little girls would have their feet bound in tight bandages to prevent them from growing more than three or four inches long.

VERA WANG (1949–)
Fashion Designer

Vera Wang is a Chinese American fashion designer who made her name by creating sophisticated, elegant wedding gowns. Wang became a bridal designer when at 40 years old she got married for the first time and could only find fussy, frilly wedding dresses without much style. Vera Wang also designs beautiful, stylish evening gowns for celebrities as well as clothing, jewelry, gifts, and her own line of perfume.

Create a Tiger Hat

When the first Chinese families arrived in America, some of the children, especially boys, would be seen wearing elaborately embroidered *tiger hats*. The purpose of these hats was to frighten off bad spirits and attract good luck to the child. Some say that the tiger hats (and tiger shoes) gave the child an extra set of eyes when he was learning how to walk.

The hats were made of silk and embroidered with symbols such as bats to represent happiness, lotus flowers to show purity, butterflies for long life, and fish to symbolize plenty or surplus. On the top of the hat was the Chinese character for "king" known as wang (wong). The wang character was used because it resembled the markings of a tiger. The hats also had small bells that swung as the children moved, to scare away bad spirits. Tiger hats are still worn by children in China today.

What You Need
Large brown paper grocery bag
Scissors
Sheets of felt in different colors such as
    black, white, yellow, brown, red, green,
    and deep pink or purple (any colors
    may be substituted for the colors listed)
Glue
1 pipe cleaner
Pencil
2 pieces 16-inch-long thin ribbon or string
2 small bells that jingle (available in craft
    stores)

What You Do
1. Flatten the bag and cut in half right down the middle. Set one half aside to make a second tiger hat or throw away.
2. Open the bag. What was the flat bottom of the bag will now be the tiger's face. Cut along the front, sides, and back as shown in the diagram.
3. Cut shapes out of the felt: yellow for the wang character and butterfly bellies, white for the tiger's eyes and teeth, black for the middle of the eyes, brown for the whiskers, green for the eyebrows and bats, red for the mouth, orange for the ears and nose, pink or purple for the butterfly wings. Follow the drawings on the picture or design your own.
4. Glue the felt pieces onto the bag. To make the nose pop out, pull the middle up a bit, and glue just the edges. Do the same to the butterfly wings to make the butterflies look three-dimensional.

5. Cut the pipe cleaner in half to make the butterfly antennae. Right above each butterfly, carefully poke 2 holes using the pencil and thread the pipe cleaner through. Be careful not to rip the bag.

6. Above the bat on one side of the bag, use the pencil to gently poke two holes close together. Thread the ribbon through both holes so that the ribbon hangs outside the bag. Pull the ribbon through the top of one of the bells and tie.

7. Repeat on the other side.

8. Wear your tiger hat proudly!

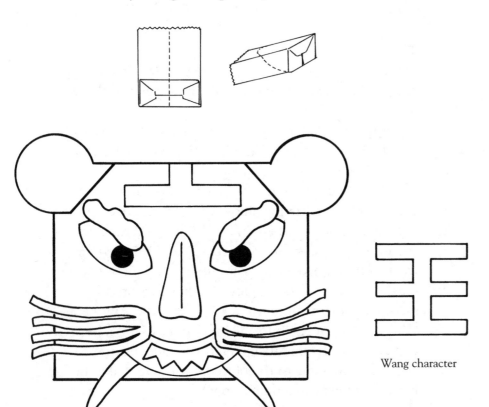

Front of hat

Wang character

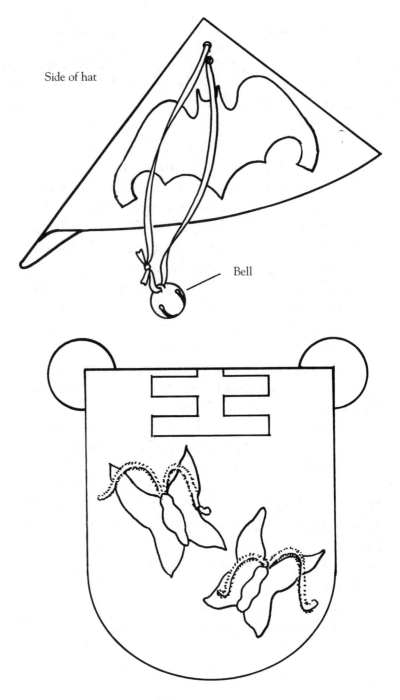

Side of hat

Bell

Back of hat

Construct an Evil Spirit Apron

Special aprons were embroidered for children, especially boys, to wear on the fifth day of the fifth month of the Chinese calendar. It was believed that bad spirits were most likely to emerge at that time, and that the apron would scare them away. Early Chinese American families took great care to keep their sons safe. This was because in China, sons were responsible for maintaining the family's wealth and caring for their parents in old age. After marriage, a girl "belonged" to her husband's family and was expected to look after them instead of her own family.

The evil spirit apron is made up of red and black blocks of fabric embroidered with five poisonous animals: the spider, scorpion, centipede, snake, and lizard.

What You Need
Large brown paper grocery bag
Scissors
Pencil
Ruler
Black and red colored markers (paint may
   be used instead)
Red, green, brown, and black pieces of felt
Hole puncher
4 long ribbons, strings, or shoelaces

What You Do
1. Hold the paper bag upside down with the side that has writing on it in the back. Cut off the top of the bag and the side that has writing on it. Lay the bag flat.
2. Cut an armhole on each side of the bag as shown in the diagram. Use your pencil if desired to draw the lines.
3. Use your ruler and pencil to block out the different sections.
4. Draw the insects as shown on the felt and cut out with scissors. Glue down.
5. Color the red and black blocks with markers or paint.
6. Punch holes where shown and tie ribbons into each hole.
7. Tie and wear.

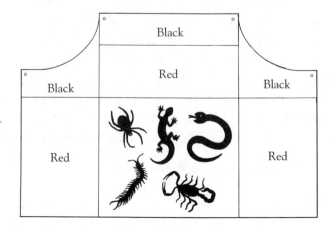

Do Chinese Opera Face Painting

Chinese operas started as entertainment for the many bachelors in Chinatown, but as immigration laws changed and women moved in, operas became family occasions. Traveling acting groups performed familiar folktales with colorful costumes to the sounds of gongs and cymbals. Families brought baskets of food and arrived at all different times of the evening. The later you arrived, the less money it cost. Children were free to move about, and adults socialized with friends and relatives during the performance. It was a noisy, bustling evening enjoyed by all.

Chinese operas have four main types of roles: the sheng, or male role; dan, the female role (male *and* female roles were played by men until the 1920s); chou, the clown or comic relief role; and fa mein, the painted face role. The literal translation of "fa mein" is "flower face." The colors of the painted face give clues to the nature of the character. Red faces symbolize loyalty, courage, and devotion; blue shows ferocity; yellow indicates cleverness; purple means the character is upright; and white shows a scheming nature. Silver- and gold-painted faces are reserved for the gods.

We will use face paint to create the character of Meng Liang from the opera *Mu Ke* (Stockaded Village). Before you start, remember: any mistakes can be washed away with soap and water!

What You Need

Newspaper work surface
Mirror
Watercolor paintbrush
Paper cup filled halfway with water
Water-based black, white, and red face paint (available in craft stores)

What You Do

1. Lay out the newspaper work surface and place the mirror so you can see yourself.
2. Dip the brush into the water and then the white paint. Paint all the white areas first, as shown.
3. Wash the brush in water. Dip the brush in black and paint the black markings.
4. Wash the brush and paint the red designs. The red parts are over the forehead and above the black moustache.
5. Wash the brush in water. Let it dry before using for your next opera.

Chinese Build the Transcontinental Railroad

Thousands of Chinese immigrants worked from dawn to dusk under grueling conditions to build the *transcontinental* (across the continent) railroad. They swung picks and axes to chop away at mighty mountains, lowered enormous support beams into the ground to support trestles (stilt-like bridges), laid rail, and used heavy sledgehammers to pound spikes into tracks. Along the way men were injured and killed in blasting accidents, lost fingers and toes to frostbite, and were trapped and sometimes lost in blinding snow and avalanches.

In 1863 a plan was made to build a railroad that would extend from one coast to another across the whole country, a transcontinental railroad. At the time, the only ways to get all the way across the United States were overland by stagecoach, which was very slow, and by sea, which took weeks. Once the railroad was built, it would be possible to make the passage in just a few days.

It was decided that the Central Pacific Railroad would build its track from Sacramento, California, and head east, and the Union Pacific Railroad would start its track in Omaha, Nebraska, and head west. They would meet at Promontory Summit in Utah.

By this time, the gold rush was over and Chinese immigrants were looking for new ways to make money. The Chinese, despite their small size, were excellent laborers who worked hard in teams of 12 to 20 men. They had their own foremen, as well as cooks who made traditional Chinese food.

POLLY BEMIS (1853–1933)
Chinese American Frontier Woman

Polly Bemis was born Lalu Nathoy in Shanghai, China, in 1853. At 19 she was kidnapped by Chinese criminals who smuggled her into America and sold her illegally to a Chinese American saloon owner in Idaho named Hong King. She was abused and treated badly by Hong King. Her luck changed when Lalu, now called Polly, was lost in a poker game to another saloon owner, Charlie Bemis.

Charlie Bemis was a kindhearted man who released Polly to freedom. She ran a successful boarding house in Warrens, Idaho, and maintained a close relationship with Charlie. After Charlie was shot in the head, Polly healed him with traditional Chinese medicines. They eventually married and became homesteaders along the Salmon River in Idaho. Throughout their life there, and in the years following Charlie's death, Polly was a helpful and beloved member of her community.

The greatest challenge facing the railroaders was the mountains of the Sierra Nevada. Several tunnels had to be carved out of them for the railroad to pass through. Here the Chinese suggested a blasting technique they had learned in China. First they wove reeds into a basket strong enough to hold a person. Then a worker was put in the basket and

FLOWERS FROM CHINA

Some of the most beautiful flowering plants that grow on American soil were imported here from China in the 19th century. Azaleas, magnolias, chrysanthemums, rhododendrons, hibiscus, camellia, and the flower that the Chinese consider the "king of flowers," the peony, are all here thanks to the Chinese.

they began to use a new explosive called *nitroglycerine*. Nitroglycerine does not need to be lit, but it is extremely dangerous because it explodes on impact. Just shaking it could and did blow up entire crews.

Finally on May 10, 1869, the Central Pacific met the Union Pacific Railroad in Promontory, and there was a great celebration in honor of the "meeting of the rails." A golden spike was hammered into the final rail. Despite the years of hard work and dedication, not one Chinese railroader was invited to the celebration.

lowered over the side of the cliff, where he pounded a hole in the rock, filled it with dynamite, and lit the fuse. Immediately the men above pulled furiously until the worker in the basket was up and out of danger.

At the end of the day, the Chinese relaxed in small camps that they set up with lightweight tents. They enjoyed hot baths by boiling water and pouring it into whiskey barrels. Most Americans at the time did not bathe often and thought that this Chinese custom was strange. The Chinese workers ate foods prepared by their cook such as dried cuttlefish, dried mushrooms, seaweed, salted cabbage, meat, and rice.

The Chinese drank boiled tea, which had the fortunate side effect of keeping the men healthy—because the tea was made from boiling water, it killed any germs that were in it. Non-Chinese workers drank water directly from ponds and streams and often got sick.

When the bosses decided the usual black-powder explosive was not powerful enough to blast through the tunnels,

THE CHINESE LAUNDRYMAN

Chinese immigrants found a way to be business owners in a field where they faced little discrimination—laundry cleaning. This was an industry where the hours were long, the pay low, and the work hot and tiresome, but the Chinese enjoyed the freedom of finally being able to be their own bosses. It didn't take a lot of money to start a laundry business either—you needed only a stove to heat water, wash basins, an iron, and a little bit of English.

The Chinese laundryman was a uniquely American occupation. In China, doing laundry was considered women's work. Most Chinese men had never washed or ironed clothes before moving to America. From gold mines to logging towns to cities large and small, the Chinese laundryman became a familiar figure.

Make a Shoulder Yoke

Chinese immigrants had an efficient way of carrying goods—a device called a *shoulder yoke*. They stretched a stick across their shoulders and hung a basket on each end of it. In this way they transported gold, food, hot tea, laundry, and anything else that needed to be moved. Because the weight was evenly distributed across their shoulders, it allowed them to carry heavier loads.

This activity works best outside.

What You Need

2 pieces 4-foot-long rope
2 heavyweight baskets with handles
Sturdy 4-foot-long stick
Something you need to carry, such as the
    laundry, mail, or newspapers

What You Do

1. Tie a rope to each side of one basket. Repeat with the other rope and basket.
2. Loop the top of one rope around the stick twice on one end.
3. Repeat with the other end.

4. Lift and carry by putting the stick behind your neck and resting it on your shoulders. Hold the stick at the ends.
5. Lower the baskets to the ground and put some items in each side to carry. Do not make them too heavy.
6. Try carrying the same amount in your arms. Is it harder to balance?

19

"The Chinese Must Go!": Racism and Discrimination

The Chinese suffered from many forms of racism and discrimination in the United States. In the beginning they were welcomed and admired for their hard work and polite behavior, but by the end of the 19th century those feelings would change. After the gold rush ended, jobs grew scarce in the West and people had trouble making enough money to take care of their families. White Americans became increasingly jealous of the success that the Chinese were able to achieve because of their hard work and persistence. The feeling was that the Chinese were taking jobs away from native-born Americans and had to be stopped.

Politicians running for office used the Chinese as scapegoats and created campaigns with slogans such as "The Chinese must go!" to gain support and votes. Angry mobs burned down Chinese homes, beat up Chinese workers, and even stuffed them into railroad cars in an effort to drive them out. Hundreds of Chinese fanned out across the country to cities such as Chicago, New York, and Boston to flee the escalating hostility in California. Some even returned to China, leaving behind their dreams of a better life in America.

The anti-Chinese movement led to laws making it illegal for nonwhites to testify in court (1854), to become citizens (1855), or to own land (California 1913). Eventually, most of these laws were overturned, but in 1882, the Chinese Exclusion Act prevented all Chinese from immigrating to America with the exception of merchants, diplomats, and students. It slammed the door of immigration on just the Chinese! It was particularly unfair because at that time in America, millions of immigrants still flowed in freely from Europe and other parts of the world.

More restrictive immigration laws followed. The Scott Act of 1888 permanently banned all Chinese laborers from immigrating to America. It also banned the return of Chinese laborers who had gone back to China to visit. Twenty thousand Chinese who had left on temporary visits were denied reentry into America.

The Immigration Act of 1924 completely prohibited Chinese as well as most other Asians from immigrating, and placed severe quotas on immigration from other countries. Immigration from any country could not be more than 2 percent of the current population in the United States from that country. The law favored immigrants from Great Britain, Ireland, and Northern Europe, because they had greater numbers of people already here.

It wasn't until the middle of the next century that the door to America would swing open again for the Chinese. In 1943 Congress repealed the Chinese Exclusion Act, largely in response to the fact that China had been our ally in World War II. President Roosevelt described the act as a "mistake."

The Immigration Act of 1965 was created in order to reunite families that had been separated during World War II and to attract skilled professionals from around the world to keep the American economy strong. The law had the unexpected effect of throwing off all the shackles of the previous laws and freeing thousands of Asian Americans to immigrate.

PAPER SONS:
How an Earthquake Helped the Chinese

After the Chinese Exclusion Act of 1882 and the Scott Act of 1888 were passed, it was nearly impossible to immigrate here unless you were the son or daughter of an American-born Chinese parent. The Chinese population was 100,000 in 1880, and dropped to 60,000 by 1920.

In 1906, an amazing thing happened. A devastating earthquake hit San Francisco, California, causing a wave of fires to erupt throughout the city. Whole blocks of homes and businesses burned down, and one of the buildings destroyed contained the government offices that held all the immigration records. This allowed young men in China to pretend that they had been born in San Francisco to Chinese women without having to provide birth records. They paid Chinese men in the United States to sign papers saying that they were their fathers. These papers permitted them the priceless opportunity to immigrate to the United States as American citizens, along with their wives and children. These men became known as *paper sons*.

The following quote by a Chinese man illustrates how common this practice was: "Exactly how many Chinese men falsely claimed citizenship as paper sons will never be known, but if every claim to citizenship were true, each of the Chinese women who lived in San Francisco before 1906 would have had to have borne 800 children!" (from *Strangers from a Different Shore* by Ronald Takaki).

The American authorities soon caught on to the scam and became suspicious of these paper sons. They interrogated them at the Angel Island Immigration Station before allowing them to enter the country. Angel Island was a far more forbidding place than the Ellis Island Immigration Station in New York. Here the objective was to find a reason to send them back, rather than at Ellis Island where the objective was to process them through the system. They tried to catch them in the deception by asking detailed questions about the village that their "father" came from. One of the questions asked was, "How many water buffaloes does your village have? How many are male and how many are female?"

Although the numerous paper sons were grateful for the ability to become American citizens, many lived in fear of being caught. They were sometimes blackmailed by fellow Chinese or white Americans who were looking for money, or exposed by other paper sons who had to inform on them to avoid being sent back to China themselves.

21

China Today

China is the largest country in Asia and the third-largest country in the world. It borders 14 other countries, with a coastline along the Yellow Sea, East China Sea, and South China Sea. It is a *Communist country*, meaning the government owns all the property and businesses and makes most of the decisions for the people. In recent years, the government has allowed more private business, but strictly controls what people are able to say and do in public.

The most amazing thing about China is the number of people who live there. There are 1.3 billion people who live in China. (Compare to Canada, which is a bigger country in size but is home to only 30 million people.) That means about one in every four people on Earth lives in China! Because it is hard to feed so many people, the Chinese government encourages families to have only one child.

It Started in China!

China has probably contributed more to world civilization than any other country in history. It is home to the longest continuous civilization, which is more than 5,000 years old! Paper, one of China's greatest inventions, was created about 2,000 years ago from tree bark and cloth fibers. Paper became an effective way to communicate because it allowed information to be spread from village to village and then eventually from country to country. The Chinese were also the first to invent movable type, which they created out of clay in the 11th century. Movable type is when you move individual letters (as in English) or characters (in Chinese) to form a page, which is then printed on paper. Wood block printing was used even earlier, when entire pages were cut into wood and then used for printing a page of paper. The first book was printed using this method in 868 B.C.E.

The compass was invented in the third century by a Chinese man named Zheng who used it to navigate ocean voyages. The Chinese were the first to invent gunpowder, which was also used to make fireworks. The first wheelbarrow was invented in China about 1,700 years ago.

Porcelain originated in China. We sometimes refer to porcelain dishes as "china," which makes it easy to remember where it came from. Sericulture, the process of cultivating silkworms to produce raw silk, was discovered by the Chinese more than 4,000 years ago. The secret was guarded so fiercely that anyone caught smuggling a silkworm out of the country could be sentenced to death.

Acupuncture is a centuries-old practice from China. Practitioners use very thin needles to redirect energy, or qi (chee), within the body. Thousands of Americans each year receive acupuncture treatments to heal everything from asthma to headaches.

Tea was discovered in China hundreds of years ago and has spread to become the most popular beverage in the world. Legend has it that tea drinking began when wild tea leaves blew into a pot of water being boiled by Emperor Shen-Nung in the year 2737 B.C.E.

Write Chinese Characters

In the Chinese language, symbols known as *characters* rather than letters are used to communicate. While letters match particular sounds, Chinese symbols represent whole words or ideas. This means you can't sound out words; you have to memorize the characters. You must know between 3,000 and 5,000 characters just to read the newspaper! Most Chinese people do not memorize all the characters because there are just too many, more than 40,000.

Chinese symbols began about 3,000 years ago with picture inscriptions on bones. Over the years the pictures have become more like symbols. Some still look like pictures of what they represent, but many do not.

Try making some of the Chinese characters below.

What You Need
Thick black marker
Paper

What You Do
1. Draw the characters below. Follow the arrows for the direction of the lines.

2. Combine characters to make a new character with a different meaning. Draw these characters.

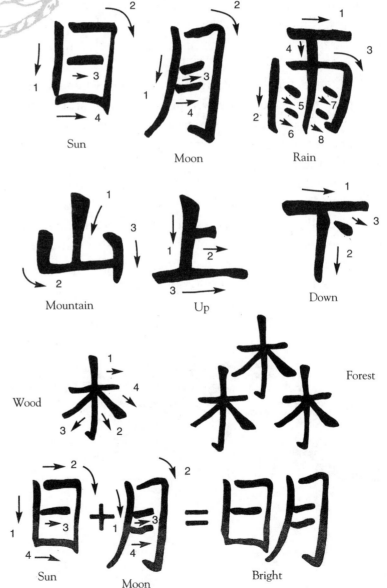

Sun

Moon

Rain

Mountain

Up

Down

Wood

Forest

日 + 月 = 明
Sun   Moon   Bright

23

Confucianism

To understand Chinese values such as filial piety (respect for one's parents), humaneness (acting as a good member of society), respect for ritual (being polite and having good manners), and loyalty, one must look to *Confucianism*. Confucianism is not a religion but a philosophy that guides one's life. The founder of Confucianism was a teacher named Confucius, who was born in 551 B.C.E.

Confucius taught that an orderly society depends on each person being educated in moral behavior and knowing his or her responsibilities, which are based on his or her position on the ladder of social status (the person's importance or rank in relation to others). Confucius said that the subject should respect the ruler, that the son should respect the father, that wives should respect their husbands, that a younger sibling should pay respect to an older sibling, and that friends should treat each other with respect. In every relationship the person in the higher social position has a responsibility to be kind, honorable, and fair.

BACHELOR SOCIETIES

Most of the first Chinese immigrants in the 1800s were male. A great majority of these men left their wives and children behind with the idea that they would soon return to China after accumulating their fortunes in the United States. Another reason the women stayed behind was because Confucianism required women to take care of the children and the parents of her husband, as well as the graves of his ancestors.

The men lived in stark boarding houses with bunks lined up against the walls, dormitory style. They congregated in Chinatowns to eat traditional Chinese food, talk, and gamble. They visited in the back rooms of tiny Chinese stores to play games such as Chinese chess, mah-jong (a game played with tiles like scrabble), and fan tan (played with chips).

For unmarried men, the prospect of finding a wife in America was slim. There were almost no unmarried Chinese women, and in some states there were laws that prohibited interracial marriage. Men who were already married spent little on themselves in order to send money home to China. A small amount of American money was worth much more in China. Sadly, most of the men ended up living lonely lives in America, unable to accumulate the fortune they were seeking in order to return to China.

Say It in Chinese (Mandarin)

Mandarin is the official language of China. It is a *tonal language*, which means that the same word can have different meanings depending on how you say it. The word "ma" in Mandarin can mean "mother," "hemp," "horse," or "scold," depending on which tone you use. Try saying the word "ma" using the four different tones below. There is also a neutral tone. (Although Mandarin is the official language in China, Cantonese, another Chinese dialect, is more commonly spoken by Chinese Americans.)

1. High and even.
2. Rising as if you're asking a question.
3. Falling and rising again.
4. Falling.
5. Neutral.

Practice these words in Mandarin. The numbers will tell you which tone to use.

Welcome:	*huan ying* (wan 1, ying 3)
Hello:	*ni hao* (nee 3, how 3)
Good-bye:	*zai jian* (zi 4, jen 4)
Thank you:	*xie xie* (syeh 4, syeh 4)

WONG KIM ARK (1873–?)
Civil Rights Activist

Wong Kim Ark was the son of Chinese immigrants. He was born in San Francisco in 1873. After returning to the United States after a trip to China in 1895, he was shocked to find himself barred from reentering the country by customs officials.

American customs officials declared that Ark could not return because the laws at the time did not allow Chinese immigrants to reenter the country once they left. The problem was that Wong Kim Ark, despite his Chinese looks and Chinese name, was an American who had been born in San Francisco, and he should have been treated just like any other American citizen.

Ark used the U.S. courts to fight for the American citizenship he believed he was entitled to. On March 28, 1898, the Supreme Court made a historic ruling. They declared that under the 14th Amendment not only was Mr. Wong Kim Ark a citizen of the United States, but *all* children of immigrants, provided the children are born in the United States, are citizens as well. This ruling remains the law of the land today.

Create a Chinese Brush Painting Greeting Card

Chinese brush painting is an ancient art brought to America by Chinese Americans. In brush painting, the balance of empty space in the composition is as important as the drawing itself. The Chinese believe that in order to capture nature on paper, you must become part of nature. The following is a quote by a painter named Wang Wei who lived in the eighth century.

The wind rises from the green forest, and the foaming water rushes in the stream. Alas! Such painting cannot be achieved by physical movements of the brush but only by the spirit entering it.

For our card we will paint a plum blossom, which is a symbol of hope. The blossoms, which sometimes appear when snow is still on the ground, promise the return of spring.

What You Need
Thick newspaper work surface
Rice paper or manila paper
Watercolor paintbrush
Paper cup filled halfway with water
Black watercolor paint

What You Do
1. Go outside and quietly observe the outdoors. Pretend you are placing a frame around some small part of what you see, such as a snow-covered branch or a leaf falling to the ground. Look closely to see the details that you didn't see at first from a distance. Now you are ready to paint.
2. Lay out the newspaper work surface.
3. Fold your paper in half. You will paint your plum blossom on the front.
4. You control the darkness of the paint by dipping the brush in the water and the black paint and testing the shade of black on the newspaper. More water makes

the color lighter; more paint makes it darker. Paint the branches first using a medium-dark paint.

5. Add more water to the brush to make the flower petals lighter than the branches.

6. Add paint to the brush to make the paint darker than the flowers or the branches. Paint a circle in the middle of each flower. Add short, sharp strokes around each circle and moss dots on the branches.

GIANT PANDA BEAR

The first giant panda bear came to the United States from China in 1936. His name was Su-Lin and he was brought from China by a Manhattan socialite turned adventurer named Ruth Harkness. She gave the giant panda to the Brookfield Zoo in Chicago, where he was adored by Americans.

Giant pandas are among the most endangered species in the world. There are only about 1,600 that live in the wild and only about 20 that live in zoos outside of China. There are several reasons why the pandas are endangered. Their natural forest habitat has shrunk because of overdevelopment, the bears eat only bamboo and will starve if it is not available, they have a very low reproductive rate, and they are vulnerable to being hunted for their valuable furs. The government has tried to reverse the process by setting aside natural reserves for the pandas to live and the bamboo to grow. Anyone caught poaching (illegally killing for its fur) a giant panda bear in China receives the death sentence.

Pandas have odd eating habits. In the wild, they eat almost exclusively bamboo, and they eat for 10 to 12 hours each day. They can eat up to 40 pounds of it in a single day! An adult panda bear can grow up to about five feet tall and weigh between 175 and 300 pounds. Pandas typically live to be about 30 years old.

Craft a Lacquer Box

Chinese lacquerware has been admired by Americans for centuries. The first pieces to arrive from China must have looked quite exotic, their highly polished red-and-black finishes decorated with dragons, flowers, carvings, and precious stones such as mother of pearl, jade, and ivory.

Lacquer is a hard, shiny coating that has been used in China for hundreds of years. The first lacquer was made from the sap of the Asian lacquer tree. It was painted in as many as 40 thin layers over a structure made of materials such as wood, bamboo, leather, and metal.

Chinese-lacquered furniture, umbrellas, musical instruments, jewelry boxes, sewing boxes, screens, and decorative items were eagerly purchased by Americans in the 17th and 18th centuries. It was during a time known as the China Tea Trade, when goods from China were highly desired, especially silk, porcelain, and tea.

Lacquerware continues to be popular in America, where synthetic (man-made) lacquer is used as well.

We will use acrylic enamel for our box, instead of lacquer, but it will give our box the same highly polished look.

What You Need

Adult supervision required

Thick newspaper work surface

Small, unpainted wooden hinged box (available in craft stores)

Gloss black acrylic enamel (available in craft stores)

Gloss red acrylic enamel (available in craft stores)

2 paper cups (to pour the paint into)

Thick paintbrush

Thin paintbrush

Optional: polyurethane gloss varnish and cup (available in craft stores)

What You Do

1. Lay out the newspaper work surface.
2. Paint the outside of the wood box with the black enamel using the thick paintbrush. Be careful not to paint the box closed. Let dry 4 hours. Paint the inside of the box and let dry.
3. Repeat step 2 to add a second coat of paint.
4. Paint a red dragon on the front using the thin paintbrush. Use the picture here as a guide, or design your own. Let dry. Repeat with a second coat if necessary.

5. Optional: Paint varnish on the outside of the box with the thick paintbrush. Let dry 10 minutes. Paint the inside of the box, and let dry. For more shine, apply another coat.

MAYA LIN (1959–)
Architect, Sculptor

In 1981, Maya Lin, a 21-year-old architectural student from Yale University, won a national competition to design the Vietnam Veterans Memorial in Washington, D.C. At the time, many Americans criticized the choice of Maya Lin. They thought a young Chinese American girl would not be capable of making an appropriate American memorial. Others criticized the stark, contemporary look of the memorial, which was very different from traditional statues. Despite the criticism, the Vietnam Veterans Memorial has become one of the most visited tourist sites in the United States.

The Vietnam Veterans Memorial, also known as "the Wall," features two shiny black granite walls arranged in a V shape. Inscribed on the walls are the names of every one of the soldiers who were missing or who died in Vietnam, 58,000 names in total.

Try Chinese Paper Cutting

Chinese paper cutting is a centuries-old folk art practiced all over China and brought to the United States by Chinese immigrants. A *folk art* is an art or craft made by ordinary people as well as artists that reflects the country or region where these people live.

Paper cutting can be simple or quite ornate. The type we will learn here is made with paper and scissors and can be placed in a window to allow the light to pass through. In this activity you'll make goldfish, symbols of wealth and abundance in China that are often presented in pairs.

What You Need

Photocopier
2 pieces colorful paper (origami paper works well but
    ordinary computer paper is fine)
Small scissors with pointed ends
Hole puncher
Tape

What You Do

1. Make photocopies of the goldfish pattern onto the 2 pieces of colored paper.
2. Start cutting around the outline of one goldfish, starting at the head and moving over the back and around. You should be cutting away the black ink. Use one hand to cut and the other hand to guide the paper.
3. Use the hole puncher to make the eye.
4. Repeat steps 2–3 for the other goldfish pattern.
5. Tape the goldfish in a window to allow the light to show through.

AMY TAN (1952–): Author

Amy Tan is a Chinese American novelist who has written award-winning novels based on the relationships between Chinese American daughters and their Chinese mothers. *The Joy Luck Club* and *The Kitchen God's Wife* are her most well-known novels. Amy Tan also writes children's books.

I. M. Pei (1917–): Architect

I. M. Pei is considered one of the most gifted, innovative architects in the world—he designed the glass pyramid at the entrance of the world-famous Louvre art museum in Paris, France. Pei was born in Guangzhou, China, and left to study architecture in the United States at 17 years old. Pei's modern designs also include the East Wing expansion of the National Gallery in Washington and the Rock and Roll Hall of Fame and Museum in Cleveland, Ohio. In 1983, Pei won architecture's highest award, the Laureate of the Pritzker Architecture Prize.

Yin and Yang

An important concept in understanding Chinese American culture is the belief in yin and yang. In all things, yin and yang must be balanced. *Yin* is feminine, dark, negative, cold, and passive. *Yang* is masculine, light, positive, warm, and active. The balance between yin and yang affects everything in the universe. Harmony depends on the proper balance between the two. Everything in life is composed of varying amounts of yin and yang, opposites that together make a whole. The yin-yang symbol shows the relationship between these two forces.

Yin and yang are always considered when treating the health of a person. Traditional Chinese medicine is used to balance the forces of yin and yang within the body.

Herbal Shops

A store that can always be found in Chinatown is the Chinese herbal shop. The walls of the shop are lined with tiny wooden drawers filled with different dried herbs, flowers, nuts, and seeds. Glass bottles and jars stand in cabinets. The Chinese doctor checks your pulse and then recommends what is needed to keep the energy balanced within the body. The herbs are then sliced with a knife or ground with a mortar and pestle so that the customer can boil them into soups or teas to keep the body healthy. Chinese Americans use these herbs not only to cure illness, but also to *prevent* illness.

Here are some unusual things you can buy in a Chinese herb shop: dried seahorses for skin problems, shredded bamboo skin for low energy, chrysanthemum tea for vision problems, black fungus for blood circulation, tiger balm for sore muscles, and shark's fin for healthy skin.

Chinese Zodiac and Lunar Calendar

The Chinese use the same calendar we do for day-to-day life, but they use the Chinese calendar for traditional holidays and to decide when events such as weddings should occur. It is a combination lunar/solar calendar. The years are according to the sun, and the months according to the moon.

The Chinese lunar calendar follows the cycles of the moon, with each month beginning on the darkest day. Each year is named after one of 12 animals, which is supposed to represent the characteristics of the person born in that animal's year. According to legend, Buddha called a meeting of

Practice Feng Shui

People who follow the principles of *feng shui* (fung shwey) believe that there are two types of energy in the world: chi, a gentle and helpful form of energy that travels in winding ways, and sha, a negative, bad energy that can only move in straight lines. Feng shui originated in China more than 3,000 years ago and has become very popular in the United States. There are many principles involved in understanding feng shui. Here are some interesting ones:

Good Feng Shui

Displaying fresh flowers in the living room. They bring good energy into the home, but when they start to wilt they should be thrown away.

Hanging a small bell on the outside of the front door. This invites good fortune in.

Keeping an odd number of goldfish in an aquarium in the family or living room for good fortune. At least one of the goldfish should be black.

Hanging metal wind chimes in the north part of your house for good luck.

Bad Feng Shui

Pointing a finger at someone. This directs bad energy toward that person.

Mops and brooms in plain sight. They should be hidden away in a closet when not in use because they symbolize the sweeping away of good fortune.

Giving clocks or watches as gifts. This is the opposite of wishing someone a long life. It is a symbol that their life on earth is limited and ticking away.

Cactus plants and other thorny plants in the home. The sharp thorns give off tiny amounts of bad energy.

all the animals in the world and only 12 attended. To honor them, Buddha named a year after each animal in the order in which they arrived. It is the year of that animal once every 12 years.

It's fun to look up what Chinese year you were born in. Match the year you were born to the animal on its right. Many Chinese Americans believe that the year you are born can determine general aspects of your personality.

1960, 1972, 1984, 1996, 2008, 2020 Year of the Rat:
    ambitious, intelligent, and happy
1961, 1973, 1985, 1997, 2009, 2021 Year of the Ox:
    dependable, patient, and fair minded
1962, 1974, 1986, 1998, 2010, 2022 Year of the Tiger:
    sensitive, sincere, and optimistic
1963, 1975, 1987, 1999, 2011, 2023 Year of the Rabbit:
    talented, quiet, and calm
1964, 1976, 1988, 2000, 2012, 2024 Year of the Dragon:
    enthusiastic, bold, and generous
1965, 1977, 1989, 2001, 2013, 2025 Year of the Snake:
    wise, charming, and mysterious
1966, 1978, 1990, 2002, 2014, 2026 Year of the Horse:
    friendly, energetic, and adventurous
1967, 1979, 1991, 2003, 2015, 2027 Year of the Sheep:
    compassionate, gentle, and creative
1968, 1980, 1992, 2004, 2016, 2028 Year of the Monkey:
    clever, playful, and witty
1969, 1981, 1993, 2005, 2017, 2029 Year of the Rooster:
    confident, determined, and reliable

YO-YO MA (1955–): Cellist

Yo-Yo Ma is considered to be one of the world's most accomplished cellists. His father, Hiao-Tsiun Ma, was a music teacher who taught at China's Nanjing University. Yo-Yo's father taught him how to break up complicated pieces of music in order to master them. In this way, Yo-Yo was able to give a concert at the University of Paris at only five years old! The family left Paris for New York in 1962. Today Yo-Yo Ma delights audiences with his music all over the world.

1970, 1982, 1994, 2006, 2018, 2030 Year of the Dog:
    honest, faithful, and straightforward
1971, 1983, 1995, 2007, 2019, 2031 Year of the Pig:
    sincere, caring, and strong

Chinese New Year

Chinese New Year is the biggest Chinese American holiday and is celebrated for 15 days at the end of January or the beginning of February depending on the Chinese calendar. (Since the Chinese calendar is based on the phases of the moon, it always begins on the first new moon of the year.) The holiday celebrates the beginning of spring and the importance of family. There is a lot of preparation leading up to the new year. First the house must be cleaned inside and out, bills paid, and hair cut. This cleaning symbolizes sweeping away the bad fortune of the past in order to have a fresh start.

The house is decorated with bowls of fresh flowers and platters of oranges, tangerines, and dried sweet fruit. The color red is everywhere—in clothing, in red paper greetings on the walls, and in the red envelopes of money given as gifts. It is a custom to not wash your hair on New Year's Day so that you don't wash away the good fortune of the coming year. Food is chopped up before New Year's Day so that knives cannot "cut away" the happiness and good luck to come.

In traditional Chinese American homes the Kitchen God is honored. A picture of the Kitchen God hangs over the family's stove, watching all that is good or bad throughout the year. At the end of the old year, the Kitchen God reports to the Jade Emperor, who is the ruler of all gods, about how the family has behaved. To ensure a good report, the family sends the Kitchen God on his journey by presenting a feast of cakes, such as *nian gao* (a sticky rice cake), honey, and candied fruit. Sometimes honey is smeared on the Kitchen God's lips so that he will send a "sweet" report. Then the old picture is destroyed and a new picture of the Kitchen God is hung over the stove.

MICHAEL CHANG (1972–)
Tennis Player

In 1989, Michael Chang became the youngest player ever to win the French Open, one of the four most important contests in tennis, known as "grand slam events." The other grand slam events are the Australian Open, Wimbledon, and the U.S. Open.

Earlier, at 15, Michael was the youngest male to win a singles match at the U.S. Open. The next year he became the youngest to play at Wimbledon in England. During his career, Chang won 34 professional titles. He retired from the professional tennis tour in 2003.

MICHELLE KWAN (1980–)
Figure Skating Champion

Michelle Kwan was born in California and is one of America's most well-known figure skaters. She has won five World Championships, nine U.S. National Championships, the silver medal at the 1998 Olympics, and the bronze medal at the 2002 Olympics. She began skating at age five and always wears a Chinese good luck charm around her neck, a gift from her grandmother.

Cook an Authentic Chinese Nian Gao for Chinese New Year

The rising of the cake symbolizes advancement in the coming year. Stores and bakeries are piled high with these New Year's cakes before the holiday.

This is a recipe from Fee Har Chin, who immigrated to the United States in 1958 from the Guangdong province of China. She makes this recipe for her children and grandchildren for Chinese New Year, using only a wok and chopsticks!

What You Need

Adult supervision required

Round 9- to 10-inch cake pan, about 2 inches deep

Small amount of oil to grease pan

Small pot

4 slabs brown rock sugar candy (available in Asian food stores)

3 cups cold water for recipe, additional water for steaming

Mixing bowl

1 pound glutinous rice flour (available in Asian food stores)

2 teaspoons wheat starch (available in Asian food stores)

Mixing spoon

Small rack to use as a steamer rack (the type of rack you put cookies on to cool)

Large pan and cover (big enough to hold the steamer rack)

Toothpick

Knife

Small bowl

1 egg

Wire whisk

Spatula

What You Do

1. Grease cake pan with a little oil.
2. Put sugar candy and ½ cup of the water in the pot, and melt over low heat. Turn off the stove and let stand.

3. In a mixing bowl, put in the flour, wheat starch, and remaining water. Mix thoroughly until smooth.

4. Pour in the warm, melted sugar candy, and quickly mix well.

5. Place the steamer rack at the bottom of the large pan. Pour water into the pan and fill up to the bottom of the steamer rack. Cover and bring to a boil.

6. Pour the flour mixture into the cake pan. Note: This should only be done after the water has come to a boil.

7. Put the cake pan on top of the steamer rack. Cover and steam on high heat for 30 minutes. Stick in a toothpick and if it comes out clean, then it is done. Otherwise continue to cook for another 5 minutes and test again until it's done.

8. Remove from the steamer and let cool. Put in the refrigerator until firm.

9. Just before eating, cut into thin slices (about ¼ inch thick). In a small bowl, whisk an egg and dip each slice in the egg mixture. Place slices on a nonstick frying pan over medium heat until the pieces are soft. Flip the slices occasionally.

10. Enjoy!

On New Year's Eve the family dresses in all-new clothes, usually with a lot of red for good luck. They pay their respects to their ancestors and the gods by leaving out offerings of tea, incense, and food. Next the entire family— grandparents, parents, children, aunts, uncles, and cousins— sit down to a feast of many delicious courses. The food that is served is symbolic of the good fortune the family wishes for in the coming year. Shark's fin soup is eaten for prosperity. A vegetarian dish called *jai choy* or Buddha's Delight represents all the wishes for the new year. The dish includes fat choy (sea moss that looks like stringy black hair and represents prosperity) and fun see (bean threads which symbolize longevity, or long life). Ho-see (dried oysters), though not vegetarian, are included in jai choy recipes from Southern China (where most Chinese Americans are from) because the Chinese word for them sounds like "good things."

Fish and chicken are served whole with head and feet attached to symbolize the wholeness of the family. Also, the Chinese word for "fish," "yu," sounds similar to the word for "plenty," and the chicken resembles the mythical bird known as the phoenix, which is the bird of wealth. Foods with long strands such as Chinese broccoli and uncut noodles symbolize the wish for longevity. At midnight a steamed dumpling known as *jiaozi* (gee-ow-za), which looks like gold money (yuen bow), is eaten.

New Year's Day in the Chinese American community sees a steady stream of family and friends visiting each other's homes. When you visit on New Year's Day it is customary to bring oranges and tangerines, which represent good luck and health. The tangerines must have the leaves attached to them, because it symbolizes the attachment of you to the person or family you are visiting. Everyone is on his or her best behavior, because negative or unhappy behavior on New Year's Day might make the coming year unlucky. Guests are treated to nian gao. Other snacks include the *tray of togetherness*, which is an eight-section

HAVE YOU EATEN YET?

Food and socializing is so central to Chinese American culture that a traditional greeting among Chinese immigrants is "Sik jor fan mei ah?" which means, "Have you eaten yet?"

Chinese Americans cut up the meat and vegetables *before* the meal, so that it is not necessary to use a knife at the table. This centuries-old tradition of chopping food into small pieces and cooking it quickly at high temperatures is called *stir-frying*. In China, where cooking fuel such as wood is scarce, people found that they could conserve fuel by cooking this way. The large, curved cooking pot that is used for stir-frying is called a *wok*.

Steamed white rice is served at almost every meal. Today most Chinese American families have automatic rice cookers. Rice is served in a small bowl, which is picked up and held close to the mouth while the rice is eaten with chopsticks.

In the planning of meals, Chinese cooking strives for a balance between yin and yang foods. Yin foods are considered cold, and yang foods, hot. Some yin foods are bean sprouts, tofu, and water. Rice, mushrooms, and chicken are considered yang foods. Even the way food is cooked has yin and yang qualities; boiling is yin, roasting is yang. If you are tired you may need more yang foods. Excited, upset? Yin foods will help to calm you down.

platter that holds various sweet dried fruits and seeds such as coconut, ginger, and sweet lotus seed.

The Chinese New Year Parade is the grand finale of Chinese New Year and is enjoyed by both Chinese and non-Chinese Americans in Chinatowns from San Francisco to Boston. The sounds of firecrackers and drums pierce the air to ward off bad spirits; street vendors sell sweet dried fruits, flowers, and candy; and a spectacular dragon, half a city block long, weaves its way through the crowded streets, its body propped up by dozens of dancers.

Wrap Chinese Jiaozi

These dumplings are commonly made for Chinese New Year by Chinese Americans from the north of China, where wheat is a larger crop than rice. Their round, golden appearance symbolizes gold ingots, ancient Chinese money. It is a wish for wealth and prosperity in the coming year. Filling the jiaozi is a festive occasion in which the family sit and talk while they make towering platters in anticipation of the holiday.

Make this delicious Chinese dumpling a group activity like Chinese Americans do. It's messy but delicious!

About 50 dumplings

What You Need
Adult supervision required

To Make Wrappers and Filling
14-ounce package frozen dumpling
    wrappers (available in Asian food
    stores)
Mixing bowl and fork
5–6 cups finely chopped Chinese cabbage
    (also called Napa cabbage)
1½ cups finely chopped green onions (also
    called scallions)

1½ pounds ground pork
1 tablespoon sesame oil (vegetable oil may
    be substituted)
1 tablespoon rice vinegar
3 tablespoons soy sauce
1 teaspoon salt
½ teaspoon black pepper
Bowl with warm water
Cookie sheet
Large cooking pot and cover
Slotted cooking spoon
Shallow glass serving platter

To Make Dipping Sauce
½ cup soy sauce
½ cup rice wine vinegar
½ cup finely chopped green onions
Small bowl

What You Do
1. Thaw wrappers by putting them in the refrigerator for a few hours.
2. To make the filling: using the fork, stir the Chinese cabbage and green onions in the mixing bowl with the

ground pork, sesame oil, rice vinegar, soy sauce, salt, and black pepper.

3. Take a dumpling wrapper and wet just the edges with the warm water on both sides. This will allow the dumpling to seal after it is stuffed.

4. Place a strip of the filling down the middle of the wrapper using the fork. Fold the wrapper in half and seal the edges by pressing them together tightly. The dumpling should look like a semicircle. As you finish each dumpling, lay it on the cookie sheet.

5. Fill the cooking pot a little more than halfway with water. Add about a tablespoon of salt to the water.

6. After the water comes to a boil, gently place the dumplings one at a time into the water. You can cook about 20–25 at a time. Gently stir the dumplings so that they don't stick together.

7. When the water comes to a boil for a second time, add ½ cup cold water to the pot. Let it come to a boil a third time and add another ½ cup cold water. This is to prevent the dumplings from bursting. Now remove the pot from the burner and cover. Let sit for 10 minutes.

8. Gently remove each dumpling with the slotted cooking spoon and allow to drain. Place on serving platter.

9. Repeat steps 6–8 for the rest of the dumplings.

10. To make the dipping sauce: mix soy sauce and rice wine vinegar; add green onions. Pour into small bowl.

11. Dip and eat!

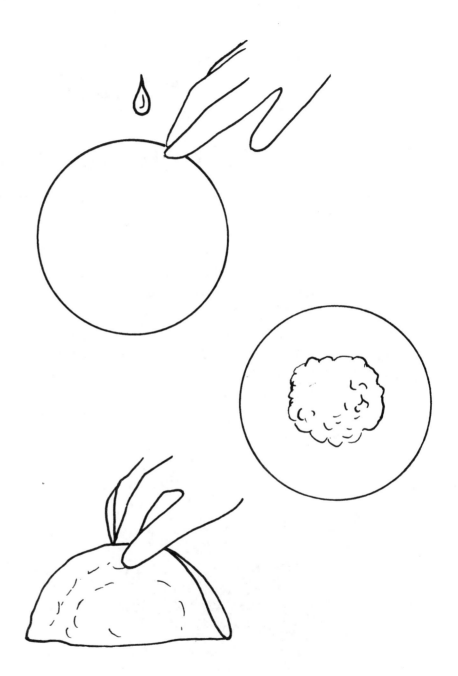

Make a Lai See: Chinese Red Envelope

Chinese New Year would not be complete without Chinese red envelopes, or *lai see* (ly see). Children and unmarried young people greet adults by saying, "Gong hay fat choy," which means "Wishing you prosperity and wealth," and in return the adults give them little red envelopes decorated with symbols for luck and wealth with money inside. It is an old tradition from China by which adults wished children good luck in growing up healthy. In modern times it means good luck in the coming year.

1 envelope (but you'll probably want to make more!)

What You Need
1 piece red paper
Pencil
Scissors
Glue stick
Gold paint pen, marker, or colored pencil

What You Do
1. Copy the outline of the envelope below onto the red paper. Fold in on the dotted lines.
2. Use the glue stick to glue the side and bottom together.
3. Draw the fancy form of the Chinese symbol for prosperity on the front with the gold pen as shown.
4. Fill the envelope with coins or slips of paper with good wishes written on them.
5. Seal the top with the glue stick.
6. Give to friends and family.

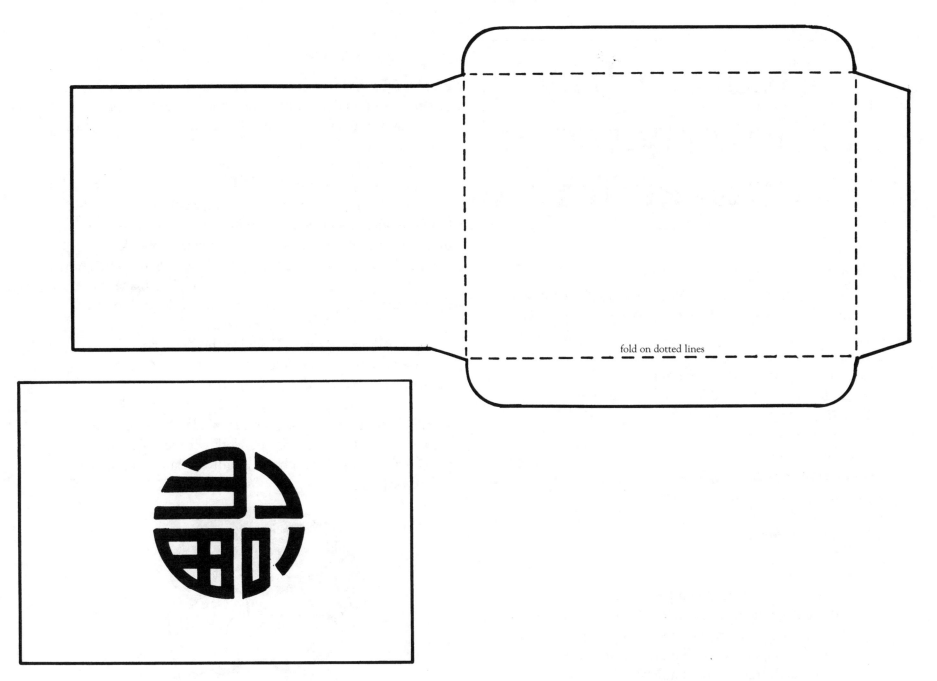

fold on dotted lines

41

Create a Tray of Togetherness: A Sweet Tray

You may need to visit an Asian market to buy some of these ingredients, but most can be purchased in supermarkets that have an Asian food section.

What You Need

A round tray or platter with dividers
Sweet lotus seeds for children and a long family lineage
Candied melon for good health
Coconut strips for togetherness
Red dates for prosperity
Red melon seeds for happiness
Lichee nuts for strong family ties
Peanuts for longevity
Longan for many sons

What You Do

1. Arrange each treat in a different section of the tray.
2. Place the tray next to the front door for visitors to enjoy. The candy represents sweetness for the new year and the circular tray celebrates togetherness.
3. Share with friends and family!

The Lion Dance

Lion dancers are a colorful and delightful part of Chinatown celebrations and demonstrations. Lions are seen as protectors in traditional Chinese life. They dance down the streets of Chinatown to bring good fortune and whisk away bad spirits. The lion dance is a 1,000-year-old tradition!

Lion dancers are usually members of martial arts programs who work to learn the steps and perform for crowds. Chinese lion dancers wear a heavy head made of papier-mâché that is decorated with colorful paint and fake fur. The lead dancer must be able to lift the heavy head up and over his head several times, and pull strings to make the eyes blink and the mouth open and close. Behind the lead dancer are one or two others who wear a colorful silk costume over their bent backs to form the lion's body. They must be very agile to be able to follow the lead dancer's movements in a hunched position.

The lion dances down the street accompanied by the sounds of Chinese drums, gongs, cymbals, and sometimes fireworks. It is then "fed" for its work with lettuce attached to lai see envelopes, which are usually donated to the martial arts schools.

Make a Chinese Lion

What You Need

8½-by-11-inch red, white, green, and black paper

Pen

Scissors

Paper grocery bag

Glue

Small piece aluminum foil

1 package any color craft fur (type of yarn available in craft stores) or cotton balls

Paper party streamers in green, red, yellow, orange, pink, and blue

What You Do

1. Fold the red paper in half. Use the template shown to make the lion's mouth.
2. Turn the grocery bag upside down.
3. Use the red lion's mouth to trace onto the paper bag as shown in the drawing. Also draw additional lines as shown.
4. Cut along the dotted lines on the paper bag, pull the flap upward, and fold.
5. Open the red lion's mouth. Cut small pieces of white paper to make teeth. Glue all around.
6. Glue the part of the lion's mouth (above the fold) "A" to the inside of the flap you made on the paper bag. Let part "B" (below the fold) hang freely.
7. Decorate the lion as desired. Some ideas are:

   - Make a circle of aluminum foil to glue on the forehead between the eyes. Traditional lion masks have mirrors that are supposed to reflect and bounce bad spirits from the lion.
   - Cut and glue circles of black and white paper to make the eyes, green paper to make the nose, and yellow paper for the ears.
   - Make a small cone of black paper to make the horn and glue to the top of the head.
   - Glue craft fur or cotton balls around the eyes and nose.
   - Glue different colored streamers over all sides of the bag and beneath the mouth to look like a beard. Let hang freely.

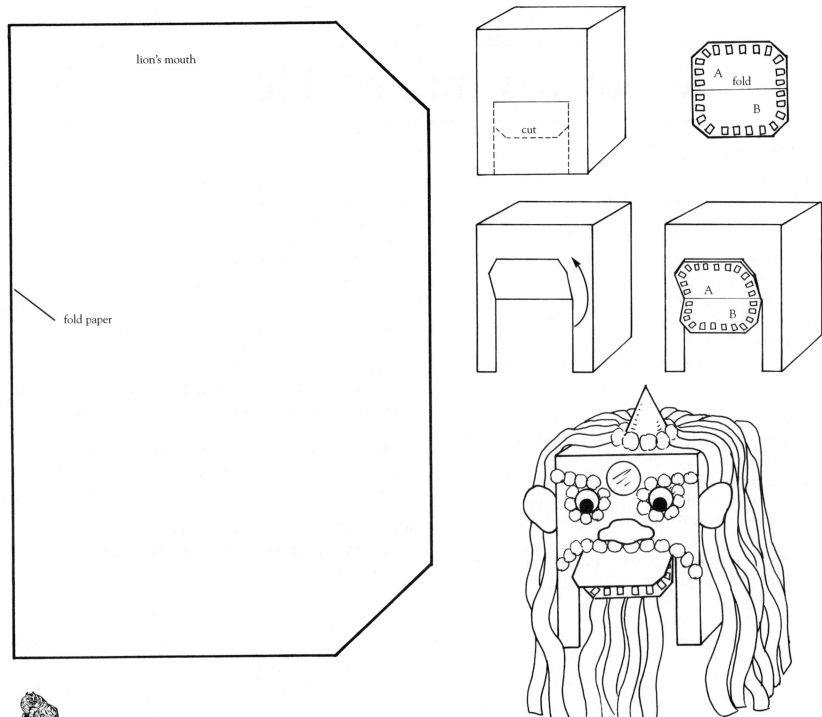

lion's mouth

fold paper

cut

A
fold
B

A
B

Perform the Lion Dance

This performance is called "the awakening of the lion."

What You Need

Chinese lion mask

An audience

Lettuce or other greens

Pot cover gong (see next activity for
   direction on making this)

What You Do

1. Place the lion mask over your head. You will be able to see through the "beard."
2. Begin by bowing three times to the audience as a sign of respect.
3. Make different movements to imitate those of a real lion: sleeping, stretching, coming out of your cave, eating, playing, jumping, and scratching.
4. Afterward the lion is rewarded by someone in the audience with lettuce or other greens, which symbolize wealth and prosperity. Approach the lettuce carefully to be sure that it is not a trap. Pretend to eat the lettuce and then throw it to your left, right, and to the middle of the performing area. This symbolizes the spreading of prosperity and good luck to all.
5. End your lion dance by again bowing three times.

Make a Pot Cover Gong

This is a simple but authentic-sounding gong you can make with a pot cover.

What You Need
Ask to borrow a metal pot cover out of the
    kitchen, 10 inches wide or larger
3 feet strong thin ribbon
Large metal spoon

What You Do
1. Find the middle of the ribbon and tie a knot around the pot cover handle.
2. Tie the ends of the ribbon together and allow the pot cover to hang down from it.
3. Bang the spoon against the outer edge of the pot cover—the edges make the best sound.
4. Use the gong to accompany the lion dance, and also the ribbon dance (see p. 63).

Paint a Chinese Calligraphy Banner

In China, calligraphy is considered the highest art of what are known as the *Three Perfections*. The other two perfections are brush painting and poetry.

Chinese Americans use calligraphy to create many types of "lucky papers" that display wishes for good luck in the new year. These include long red scrolls with traditional Chinese wishes or poems painted on them. Banners are hung in pairs, to the left and right of a door. Other lucky papers include red diamond-shaped pages painted with the characters for fortune, prosperity, longevity, and good luck.

People label things in their homes—for instance, by taping a note that says "always full" to a container of rice or candy. Pictures of children, fish, and flowers hang in Chinese businesses.

What You Need

Newspaper work surface
2 paper cups, one filled with water
Black paint
Thick paintbrush, pointed at the end
Red squares of paper

What You Do

1. Lay out the newspaper work surface.
2. Fill the empty cup with an inch or so of paint, and lay the brush in front of you.
3. The Chinese believe that through calligraphy you can achieve inner harmony and fully develop your potential as a human being. To begin an exercise in calligraphy you should first clear your mind of all stray thoughts.
4. Concentrate on breathing slowly in and out.
5. When you feel calm and ready, begin by holding the paintbrush in an up-and-down position. It should feel comfortable in your hands. Practice making the character below on a scrap of newspaper, following the arrows for the correct way to paint it.
6. Position the red square of paper so that it looks like a diamond.
7. Paint the character onto the diamond. This is "fook," the character for good fortune.

Light Up a Dragon Lantern

In China, the New Year's celebration lasts for two weeks, ending with an event known as the Lantern Festival. It celebrates the beginning of spring after the long winter. Brightly colored lanterns in every size and material parade through the village, fireworks fill the air, and families engage in riddle-guessing contests and eat jiaozi dumplings and sweet rice flour balls in syrup, called tang yuan. The highlight of the holiday is the arrival of the large dragon that winds its way through the streets bringing good luck. Although not as common as in China, lantern festivals are still held in large Chinatowns in America. Here is a colorful lantern you can make that really lights up!

What You Need

Adult supervision required

Knife or sharp scissors (for adult to cut holes in water bottles)

3 empty 16-ounce water bottles, labels removed, with caps removed on 2 bottles, and all completely dry

White glue

Paper cup

Water

Aluminum foil work surface

Several sheets yellow and green tissue paper

Scissors (for cutting tissue paper and foam)

Thick paintbrush

1 sheet green craft foam

Pencil

Pipe cleaners in different colors

Black marker

10 clear battery-operated lights (These are the same type of lights used on a Christmas tree. They can be found year round in craft stores.)

2 C batteries (or whatever size battery the lights require according to the package)

What You Do To Make the Dragon's Body

1. Ask an adult to cut a hole about the size of a nickel in the bottom of each of the three bottles.
2. Squeeze a squirt of glue in the paper cup, add in an equal amount of water, and mix.
3. Place a sheet of aluminum foil down as a work surface.
4. Rip several strips of yellow tissue paper. Cut about 15 small triangles out of the green tissue paper with scissors.
5. Paint glue all over the outside of one bottle. Stick strips of yellow paper over it to cover. The fewer the strips of paper you use, the better the light will show

through when you are done. Paint glue over the top of each strip as you press it down. Repeat with the other two bottles.

6. Press the green triangle tissue in a line as shown, as if they were the spiny part of the dragon's back. Some of the paper should stick up. Repeat with the other two bottles. Set them upright on the aluminum foil to dry for several hours.

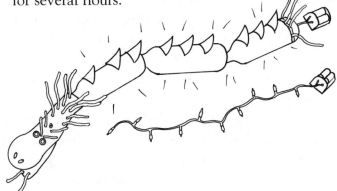

To Make the Dragon's Head

1. On the green craft foam, draw the shape of the dragon's head in pencil using the diagram as a guide. Repeat for the dragon's mouth. Cut out the shapes.

2. Use a small piece of green pipe cleaner to attach the mouth to the head. Use the sharp end to poke a hole and then pull the pipe cleaner through.

3. Use a half piece of pipe cleaner and pull through 2 holes to make the horns.

4. Use a half piece of red pipe cleaner to pull through the bottom of the mouth to look like fire.

5. Pull several pipe cleaners in different colors through to make the dragon's mane.

6. Draw the eyes, eyebrows, and nostrils with the black marker. Set aside the head.

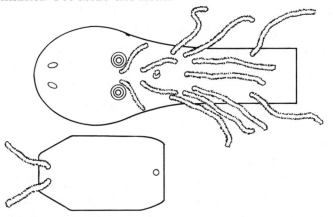

To Assemble the Dragon's Head and Body

1. When the bottles are dry, attach them to each other by stringing the lights through the holes in the bottles. There should be 3 or 4 bulbs in each bottle. The first bottle should be the only one with the cap left on.

2. Attach the dragon's head by wrapping a pipe cleaner around the craft foam and the bottle cap.

3. Wrap a pipe cleaner around the very end of the last bottle. This is what the dragon's "tail" will be attached to.

4. Attach several pipe cleaners in different colors as shown to make a multicolored tail.

5. Insert the batteries and light up your dragon lantern! It looks best at night with all the lights off. Make sure to turn the lantern off when you are not using it.

49

CHINESE DRAGONS

Chinese dragons have the head of a camel, the eyes of a demon, the antlers of a stag, the ears of an ox, the body of a snake, the belly of a frog, the scales of a carp, and the claws of an eagle. Unlike dragons in Western folktales, Chinese dragons bring good luck and are the guardians of gentle rains and blessings. They were the symbol of royalty for many centuries in China.

During the Chinese New Year Parade in San Francisco's Chinatown, the golden dragon that weaves its way through the streets is over 200 feet long and carried by more than 100 people. Its colorful bamboo-and-rattan body is adorned with hundreds of lights, rabbit fur, and silver, and topped with a dramatic six-foot head. The highlight of the parade, it makes its appearance through clouds of exploding firecrackers.

Moon Festival

The Moon Festival is on the 15th day of the eighth month of the Chinese calendar, which usually falls in August, though sometimes it falls in September. It is thought that the moon is rounder on this day than at any other time of the year. There are many legends that explain the origins of the Moon Festival, but the most popular is the story of Lady Chang Er. Thousands of years ago, Lady Chang Er was married to an archer, Hou Yi, who saved the earth by shooting arrows and knocking down 9 out of 10 suns that threatened to scorch the earth. Hou Yi was rewarded by a goddess with a pill that would allow him to live forever. Lady Chang Er took the pill herself and floated up to the moon, where she will live forever.

The Moon Festival is celebrated by eating *moon cakes* and looking at the moon with loved ones outside. Moon cakes are usually purchased in Chinese bakeries. They are made with a variety of fillings such as salted egg yolk, sweet bean paste, and coconut. The outside is inscribed with the Chinese insignia of the baker.

Moon cakes are said to have helped the Chinese overthrow their Mongol invaders. After China was taken over by the Mongols in the 13th century, the Chinese people plotted to overthrow them by passing messages in moon cakes.

50

Arrange a Moon Festival Picnic

Celebrate the Moon Festival by having a night picnic. It should occur on the full moon in August or early September.

What You Need

Blanket

Moon cakes (can be purchased in Chinese bakeries, or use round cookies or cakes instead)

Round plates filled with round fruit to resemble the moon: grapes, peaches, apples, pomegranates, melons, and pomelos

Thermos of tea

Cups

What You Do

1. Set up your food and drinks on the blanket.
2. See if you can see the outline of the beautiful moon goddess Chang Er on the face of the moon. Can you see other faces on the moon?

Put on a Chinese Shadow Puppet Show

Shadow puppet theater is an inexpensive form of traditional theater that Chinese Americans brought with them to their new country. The figures are made from leather that is dyed and cut into colorful shapes that resemble Chinese paper cuttings. (see p. 30)

Shadow puppet plays are usually adaptations of Chinese folktales. Make your own shadow puppet play based on the Chinese folktale called *The Magic Paintbrush*:

There was a kind young boy named Ma Liang who had an old man come to him in a dream and present him with a magic paintbrush. When he awoke the brush was really in his room. Everything Ma Liang painted with the paintbrush came to life. When he saw people who needed help, he painted things to help them. He painted rice bowls for the hungry, cows to help the farmers till their lands, oil lamps for unlit homes, and more. He filled his village with hope.

One day the bad Emperor heard about Ma Liang and his magic paintbrush and demanded that he paint gold and riches just for him. When Ma Liang refused, the Emperor sent him to prison. There the Emperor demanded that Ma Liang paint a ship to travel to a mountain of gold. Ma Liang was smart and developed a secret plan. He quickly painted a mountain and ship. When the Emperor got on the ship, Ma Liang painted a huge wave that crashed into the ship and sent it to the bottom of the sea.

Ma Liang returned to his village and used his magic paintbrush to do kind deeds and help the poor.

What You Need
Heavy white paper
Pencil
Colorful markers
Scissors
Hole puncher
Brads or fasteners
Straws (minimum of 5, more if you will be
    making more puppets)
Tape
White bedsheet
Table
Bright lamp (desk lamp works well)

What You Do

1. Copy the designs or create your own puppets. Additional puppets you can make: rice bowl, cow, oil lamp, crashing wave, or gold mountain. Draw the puppets on the white paper and color them. Traditional colors used for shadow puppets are brown, black, green, and red.
2. Cut out with scissors.
3. Punch holes where directed. Line up holes with matching numbers and fasten together with brads.
4. Tape straws to the back of the figures. On Ma Liang, tape one straw to the top of his back and another straw below the hand that is holding the paintbrush. For the boat, tape one straw to the back of each sail.
5. Set up the theater by draping a bedsheet over a table and shining the lamp from behind.
6. Perform *The Magic Paintbrush* by climbing inside the table space. The puppets must be held very close to the sheet in order for the colors to show through.

CHINESE SCHOOL

Many Chinese Americans send their children to Chinese school in addition to public school. Chinese school usually centers on teaching the Chinese language, but it also teaches geography, history, calligraphy, and traditional Chinese arts. This is how many Chinese American families pass on the rich language, culture, and traditions of China to the next generation.

53

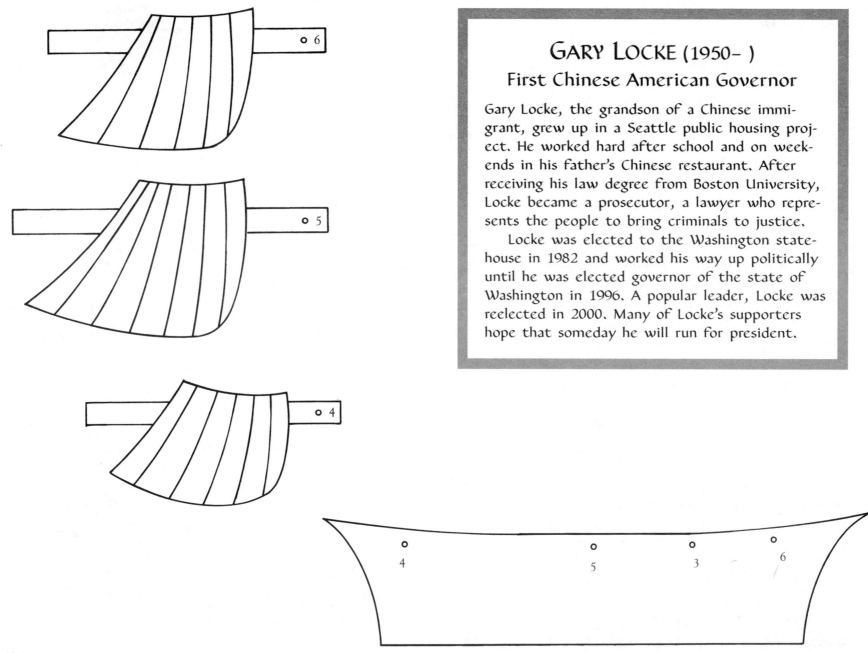

GARY LOCKE (1950–)
First Chinese American Governor

Gary Locke, the grandson of a Chinese immigrant, grew up in a Seattle public housing project. He worked hard after school and on weekends in his father's Chinese restaurant. After receiving his law degree from Boston University, Locke became a prosecutor, a lawyer who represents the people to bring criminals to justice.

Locke was elected to the Washington statehouse in 1982 and worked his way up politically until he was elected governor of the state of Washington in 1996. A popular leader, Locke was reelected in 2000. Many of Locke's supporters hope that someday he will run for president.

Chinese American Weddings

When a Chinese American couple decides to marry, the first thing they do is pick a wedding date that is *auspicious*, which means lucky or likely to be favorable according to their horoscopes. The seventh lunar month is avoided because in old times it was believed to be the ghost's month and was extremely bad luck.

Chinese American weddings are a good example of the combination of two cultures. New- and old-world traditions are practiced side by side, from the Chinese lion dance to the American custom of throwing the bride's bouquet. The bride usually spends part of the day in an American-style white wedding gown and veil and then changes into one or more Chinese wedding dresses over the course of the day: the kwan qua, the traditional red silk wedding suit with phoenixes and dragons embroidered on it, and the cheongsam, a long slim gown with a high collar and slits up the side. The groom wears a tuxedo for the day.

The bride and groom are presented with red envelopes of lucky money as well as a bounty of jewelry, of which the bride wears *every piece* to the wedding banquet. This can mean an armful of gold bracelets, many necklaces, and lots of rings!

The Chinese character called *double happiness* is present on everything from napkins to wedding favors. A multi-course banquet is served with meaningful foods, such as a whole fish to symbolize abundance.

DIM SUM:
A Little Bit of Heart

In Cantonese "dim" means "a little bit" and "sum" means "heart." *Dim sum* is a Chinese brunch with a *lot* of heart. Picture a teahouse filled with people and moving carts filled with little round steamers of food. A little of this and a little of that. The waiter zips by your table with his cart and tells you in Chinese which food is on his cart. You point to what you want and hope that it will be something you like! If you missed something that you wanted on the first cart, don't worry—another cart will be passing soon with different steamer bowls of dim sum.

Kids' Favorite Dim Sum Dishes

Sticky rice and meat wrapped in lotus leaf
Shrimp dumplings
Barbecued pork in a glazed roll
Sesame balls filled with lotus or bean paste
Custard egg tart

Dim Sum for Adventurous Eaters

Chicken feet
Duck feet
Steamed shark's fin dumpling
Cold jellyfish
Beef tripe (cow's stomach)

Design a Double Happiness Signature Cloth

When the guests arrive at the wedding banquet, they sign a red silk cloth instead of a guest book and often include a blessing such as "May you live many years together." The signature cloth is usually embroidered with a dragon and phoenix. The dragon is traditionally associated with the emperor and is the symbol of the groom on his wedding day. The phoenix signifies life-giving forces and symbolizes the bride.

What You Need

½ yard red polyester fabric (the type that has a silky finish)

Pinking shears (available in sewing and craft stores) or scissors and fabric glue

Ruler or yardstick

Pencil

Squeeze bottles of three-dimensional fabric paint in gold, black, and green

Black marker

What You Do

1. Cut out a rectangle of fabric 45 inches by 26 inches, using pinking shears to prevent the edges from fraying. (If you do not have pinking shears, use scissors, tuck the cut edges under about ½ inch all around, and glue to fasten.)

2. With the pencil, lightly draw the dragon, double happiness symbol, and phoenix along the top of the cloth. Copy the picture below or design your own.

3. Squeeze paint over the lines of the designs. Most of the designs should be painted gold. Use the black and green to add some outline and color. Be creative! Let dry for 24 hours.

4. Invite friends and family to sign your signature cloth with the black marker. Ask them to write some words of wisdom and encouragement, too.

Practice Tai Chi

Many Chinese Americans practice the martial art of *tai chi*, which allows the good energy, or qi, to flow freely through your mind and body, releasing tension. Tai chi does not involve fighting like other martial arts. It increases strength and balance with its slow, measured moves. Chinese Americans enjoy practicing tai chi outdoors in the early morning.

Here are some tai chi moves that you can practice.

Push Away the Monkeys

Pretend you are out in the wild, with curious monkeys hopping on and around you. Use tai chi movements to push them away. Begin by standing with your feet shoulder's width apart, with your hands relaxed at your sides. Breathe deeply in and out.

1. Step back with your right foot. Slowly bring your left hand in front with the palm down, as if you were pushing a monkey down. At the same time move your right hand back to brush a monkey behind you with the back of your hand. Your waist should turn slightly to the right as you make this movement.
2. Turn back to the front placing your weight onto your right leg. Now pull your left hand close to your hip and flip your hand over so that the palm is up. Bring your right hand straight up over your head and then in front of you, making a stop sign to the monkeys like a traffic cop.
3. Lift up on your right foot and push your right hand all the way forward.
4. Repeat on the other side.

57

Chinese Restaurants

Chinese restaurants were originally created to feed the many bachelor Chinese workers with foods that reminded them of home, but even in the early gold mining days, non–Chinese Americans enjoyed Chinese food as well. The first Chinese restaurants in San Francisco served traditional Cantonese Chinese food alongside familiar American foods such as steak and eggs. (Cantonese food is eaten in Canton, in the south of China where most of the immigrants came from.) These early restaurants hung triangles of yellow silk outside and attracted hard-working miners who appreciated the delicious, afford-able meals. The miners enjoyed a dish called hang town fry, which is made from eggs, oysters, and bacon, and is probably a variation on the Chinese dish egg foo yung.

This unexpected interest in their native Chinese cuisine prompted Chinese American restaurants to change their menus to cater to American tastes. Soon a new cuisine emerged known as Chinese American. Chinese American food is food that is created in America by Chinese cooks. Dishes such as sweet and sour pork with bright red sauce and fried rice emerged. One of the more interesting dishes created was chop suey, which does not come from China. It is a dish originally made by a Chinese cook in America. Chop suey is pork, onions, celery, bean sprouts, and water chestnuts cooked with soy sauce and ginger. It became a food craze so widespread that it was even served to the American military in World War II.

More recently, the newest Chinese immigrants to America have introduced the spicy cuisines from the Szechuan and Hunan provinces of China. The American public has eagerly embraced these new dishes, such as Szechuan Kung Pao chicken and Hunan orange beef. Immigrants from Beijing in the north have brought Mandarin cooking, dumplings and noodles; and immigrants from Shanghai have brought tangy seafood recipes from the eastern coast of China. Chinese restaurants can now be found in every small town and city in America. Chinese food is one of the most popular cuisines enjoyed not only in the United States but all over the world.

FORTUNE COOKIES

Did you know that fortune cookies were invented in the United States? It is unclear who invented them, but they were first served to the public by the Japanese Tea Garden in Golden Gate Park, San Francisco, California. They were immediately a hit in Chinese restaurants in the United States. Today fortune cookies are made here and exported all over the world, including to China!

Making fortune cookies takes quick reflexes. The cookie comes out of the oven and the worker has only a few seconds to place the fortune inside and twist the hot cookie before it begins to harden.

Although most Americans are familiar with fortune cookies at the end of a meal, a traditional Chinese family in the United States is more likely to have red bean soup for dessert! Red bean soup is made from sweet red bean paste. Many Chinese desserts are made with red bean paste, including red bean paste cakes, red bean paste rice balls, and moon cakes. It is as popular a dessert flavor as chocolate or vanilla are to Americans.

Chase the Dragon's Tail

This is a game from China that is fun to play with a lot of people.

What You Need

8 or more people

What You Do

1. Everyone lines up and places both hands on the shoulders of the player in front of him or her. The first player is the dragon's head and the last person is the dragon's tail.

2. The object of the game is for the head to chase and tag the tail without anyone letting go. The players in the middle are trying to help the dragon's head.

3. If the head tags the tail without anyone letting go he gets one point and stays as the head to try again. If someone does let go, then the head goes to the end of the line and becomes the tail.

4. The game is over when everyone has had a turn to be the dragon's head.

Construct a Chinese Abacus

Most children have played with an abacus, a box with beads that slide along on poles, but few realize that the abacus is more than a toy. Created in China about 3,000 years ago, it can be used to add, subtract, multiply, divide, and calculate square and cube roots. An experienced user can add or subtract on an abacus six times faster than on a calculator!

What You Need

Adult supervision required

Large shoebox, about 13 inches long by 8 inches wide
Ruler
Pencil
Nail
6 bamboo skewers or 6 12-by-⅛-inch wooden dowels
35 round wooden beads, about ½ inch wide with large holes
    (available in craft stores)
Glue
Scissors

What You Do

1. The shoebox should sit flat on your work area with the bottom of the box on the table and the open side facing up to the ceiling. On one of the long sides of the box, measure and draw a line ½ inch in from the open end. Starting from one corner of the same side, measure and draw 5 lines each about 2 inches apart.

2. Repeat step 1 on the other long side.
3. Where each line meets, ask an adult to poke a hole with the nail. There should be 5 holes on each long side of the box.
4. Slide one end of a bamboo skewer into the first hole. Slide 7 beads over the other end of the skewer and then slide that end into the hole directly opposite the first hole. The ends should stick out an inch or so on each side.
5. Repeat step 4 for the remaining holes.
6. Ask an adult to clip off the sharp ends of the skewers.
7. Separate the beads into groups of 2s and 5s. Start by pushing two beads on each skewer away from you until they are stopped by the box, and five beads on each skewer toward you until they hit the box.
8. Glue the remaining skewer or "crossbar" *over* the other skewers so that each skewer is divided in half by the crossbar. You should have groups of 2 beads above the crossbar and groups of 5 beads below the crossbar. Let the glue dry for an hour or two.

1. make holes with nail

2. slide in rods with 7 beads

3. glue in cross rod

Use an Abacus

To understand how an abacus works you need to know three important rules:

1. *If you look at the abacus from right to left, the first set of 7 beads is the ones column, the second set is the 10s column, the third set is the 100s column, the fourth set is the 1,000s column, and the fifth set is the 10,000s column. A traditional Chinese abacus has 13 columns.*

2. *The beads on the top of the abacus, above the crossbar on all the columns, represent units of 5.* Going from right to left, one bead in the ones column equals 5, one bead in the 10s column equals 50, one bead in the 100s column equals 500, one bead in the 1,000s column equals 5,000, and one bead in the 10,000s column equals 50,000.

3. *The beads on the bottom of the abacus, below the crossbar on all the columns, represent units of 1.* Going from right to left, one bead in the ones column equals 1, one bead in the 10s column equals 10, one bead in the 100s column equals 100, one bead in the 1,000s column equals 1,000, and one bead in the 10,000s column equals 10,000.

What You Need
An abacus

What You Do

1. Practice using an abacus by first making the number 0. To make 0 you slide all the beads away from the crossbar. That means that the beads *above the crossbar* in all columns will go to the very top of the box, as far as they can go. The beads *below the crossbar* in all columns will go to the bottom of the box, as far as they can go.

2. Make the number 234 by sliding the beads toward the crossbar as shown. Return to 0.

3. Make the number 4,639 by sliding the beads as shown. Return to 0.

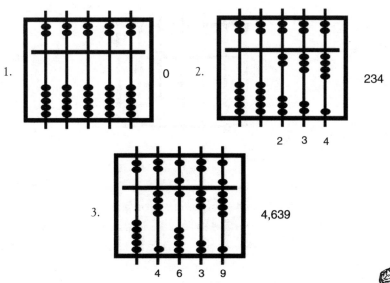

1.　　0

2.　　234
　　2　3　4

3.　　4,639
　　4　6　3　9

61

4. Add the numbers 55 and 34. The beads show that 89 is the answer. Return to 0.

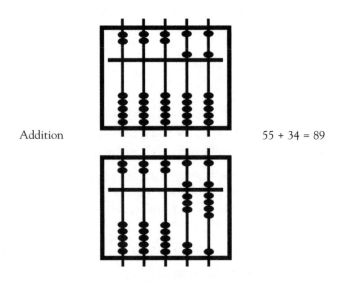

Addition   55 + 34 = 89

5. Subtract the number 15 from 67. First slide the beads to make 67. To subtract, remove beads as shown. The remaining beads should show 52.

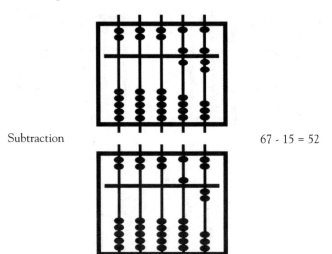

Subtraction   67 - 15 = 52

AN WANG (1920–1990)
Computer Inventor

An Wang was born in Shanghai, China, and grew up to be an excellent engineering student, entering college at the age of 16. After coming to America, Wang became a pioneer in the computer field by inventing the "core memory system," which was used in early computers before the invention of the microchip. He started his own company, Wang Laboratories, which developed and sold the first electronic desk calculator. Wang Laboratories dominated the market for several years with its word processors and computers. An Wang generously gave back to his adopted homeland, donating millions of dollars to charity and the arts.

The Newest Chinese Immigrants

Today's immigrants from China face different obstacles than the first Chinese pioneers. They arrive by airplane in a matter of hours, are able to become U.S. citizens, and are more likely to be female than male! Immigrants from parts of China such as Hong Kong or Taiwan are likely to be college educated and work in professional jobs here. Others from mainland China may not be as well educated, but they work hard to support their families by working in garment factories, manufacturing plants, and restaurants.

Try the Chinese Ribbon Dance

The Ribbon Dance is a 2,000-year-old folk dance that Chinese immigrants have brought to America. This is the type of cultural tradition that is passed down to children through the Chinese schools.

The dancers move and dance with colorful long, thick ribbons attached to sticks. The ribbons symbolize the clouds, and the patterns that the dancer makes with the ribbons are supposed to attract the gods to bring rain and plentiful crops.

What You Need For Each Dancer

2 long, thick ribbons, one color per dancer
    (the ribbon should be as tall as or taller
    than the dancer; the thicker the better,
    but 3 inches is fine)

2 dowels or sticks to attach to the ribbons,
    about 12 inches long

2 strong strings, 12 inches long

For the Performance

Chinese music CD (you can borrow one
    from your library)

CD player

What You Do

1. Tie a ribbon to the end of one dowel. Use the string to secure it. Repeat with the other ribbon and dowel. Repeat for each additional dancer.
2. Turn the Chinese music CD on.
3. Move the ribbons by using the sticks. Dance as you move the ribbons through space to the music. You can make them move up and down or sideways, have them drag behind you as you dance, or dance backward, pulling the ribbons as you go. The ribbons will make interesting patterns before falling.
4. Try moving the ribbons in ways that express emotion such as happiness, sadness, fear, and surprise. Imitate movements from nature such as water moving down a stream or waterfall, or a tree bending in the wind.
5. Bow at the end of your dance.

3
Japanese Americans

In 1853, Japan was a closed country. Foreigners were not allowed to travel there and the Japanese were not allowed to leave. It was a country ruled by warriors known as *shoguns* (shoh-guhns). The shoguns were the chief military commanders in Japan from the 8th to the 12th century. At the end of the 12th century they took control away from the emperor and then reigned for more than 600 years as the hereditary rulers of Japan. That all changed after Commodore Matthew C. Perry of the U.S. Navy stormed into Edo Bay in Japan with four enormous military steamships. The ships held more than 1,000 sailors and marines who were well armed with guns and swords. The Japanese had never seen steamships before and were awed by the black smoke and cannon fire that were set off to demand attention. Perry came with a letter from President Fillmore of the United States, requesting that American ships be allowed to trade with the Japanese.

This brazen ploy by the U.S. was very effective. The Japanese shoguns feared that they would not be powerful enough to take on the U. S. military. By the next year when Perry returned, Japan had agreed to open their borders to the American "barbarians," as they called them. As the country became open, the shoguns lost the tight control they held over the country, and in 1868 the last of the shoguns resigned. The power was then returned to the empire. The new emperor, 15-year-old Mutsuhito, was crowned Emperor Meiji. Under his reign, Japan underwent a 50-year transformation from an agricultural country where most citizens were peasant farmers, merchants, or craftsmen into a modern industrial nation.

With the end of the shogunate, farmers in Japan were allowed to own their own land instead of farming for a landlord. Unfortunately the government demanded a lot of taxes from each farmer, even after bad harvests. The Japanese began to look to America for a chance at a better future.

Plantation Life

At the time, Hawaii was looking for people to work on their sugar and pineapple plantations. Recruiters came to the little towns and villages in Japan to find new workers. They described Hawaii as a tropical haven that would provide an abundance of riches to the farmers who immigrated there. In 1868, before emigration from Japan was legal, 150 Japanese were secretly recruited by the Hawaiian counsel general to become laborers on sugar plantations in Hawaii. When reports came back about harsh working conditions and mistreatment of the laborers, the Japanese government insisted they be sent home.

The next group of 600 immigrants did not leave until 1885. The people in this group were contract laborers, who were chosen from among thousands of volunteers by the Japanese government. The government believed that it was important to choose the best workers to send overseas because they viewed them as representatives of Japan. By 1885, Hawaii was desperately in need of Japanese laborers to work on the sugar plantations, as Chinese laborers had been barred from entering the country under the Chinese Exclusion Act. Japanese laborers saw a chance to improve their lot in life by working for far higher wages in Hawaii than they could ever make in Japan.

Life on the plantations was difficult. Most of the laborers had signed contracts that forced them to work for three years in return for the cost of their ocean voyage, room, board (meals), and health care. The day started at 6 A.M., with men, women, and children as young as 13 years old heading out to the sugarcane fields for a 10-hour workday.

The sugarcane plants grew to be 12 feet high. When it was time for the plant to be harvested, the dead leaves were stripped and the stalks chopped down with a machete (mah-shet-ee), which is a large knife. Finally the sugarcane was tied into bundles and sent to the sugar mills by rail. Sugarcane workers were covered from head to toe to protect them from the sharp leaves of the plants, the blazing sun, and the centipedes and other insects that crawled over them as they worked. Field bosses called *lunas* (loo-nahs) watched the workers from horseback and had the power to deduct pay or whip a worker they thought was not working hard enough.

The last step in the processing of sugarcane took place in the sugar mills. The sugar mills were hot, dangerous places where the workers pressed and boiled the juices of the sugarcane into sugar and molasses.

THE DOORS TO AMERICA FINALLY REOPEN

In 1952, the McCarran-Walter Act was passed. This law allowed all immigrants from Japan to legally become American citizens. Limited immigration also resumed. The Immigration and Nationality Act that was passed in 1965 made the immigration quotas for European and Asian immigrants equal.

Make a Bento Lunch

Bento (behn-toh) is a very old Japanese-style boxed lunch that is still made today. Japanese farmers, hunters, and warriors as far back as the fifth century brought bento lunches of rice out to the fields and forests where they worked. Today's bento lunches usually include rice and different combinations of eggs, meat, fish, and pickled or cooked vegetables. Japanese workers on the sugar plantations were the first to bring the bento lunch to America.

When preparing a bento, consideration should be given to making the food colorful and appealing. Japanese American mothers sometimes cut the food into fun shapes or use cut pieces of food to make happy faces for their children.

What You Need
Adult supervision required
Rice balls (recipe on p. 78)
Container with lid (you can buy a special bento box at an
   Asian store, use a divided Styrofoam container or plastic
   sectioned storage container with lid, or use any box with
   a lid and separate the various foods by placing them in
   muffin cups)
2 thick slices ham
Star-shaped cookie cutter
Cutting board
1 kiwi fruit
Vegetable peeler
Knife
Small can or plastic tub of mandarin oranges
Fork

What You Do
1. Make the rice balls ahead of time and refrigerate. When ready to assemble bento, place the rice balls to one side of the container.
2. Use the cookie cutter and cutting board to cut star shapes out of the ham slices. Arrange in one of the box sections.
3. Peel the kiwi fruit with a vegetable peeler as you would an apple, and then cut into circular slices. Place in a box section.
4. Open the mandarin oranges, drain, and use the fork to place several in the last box section.

Create an Otedama Beanbag Game

Otedama (oh-teh-dah-mah) is a Japanese juggling game that was brought to Hawaii by the first immigrants. It is a game traditionally played by girls. These beanbags were popular because they were inexpensive to make using scraps of cloth and a few azuki (ah-zoo-kee) red beans.

5 beanbags

What You Need
Adult supervision required
Newspaper work surface
Hot glue gun (low melt)
3 or 4 colorful felt sheets
Pen
3-inch circle to trace (such as the bottom of a margarine
       container or the inside of a roll of masking tape)
Scissors
1 bag (16 ounces) dried red kidney beans
Measuring teaspoon

What You Do
1. Lay out the newspaper work surface.
2. Plug in the hot glue gun.
3. Trace 10 circles onto the various pieces of felt. Cut out.
4. Match up 5 pairs of circles. To make the beanbags more colorful use one color for the top and another for the bottom.
5. For one of the pairs of circles, pour 2 heaping teaspoons of beans into the middle of the bottom piece.
6. Squeeze a thick line of glue all around the edges of the bottom circle. Quickly place the top circle on top and press down with your fingers all around the edges. If the glue gets on your fingers, rub them together and it will peel right off.
7. Repeat steps 5–6 with the other 4 sets of circles. Remember to unplug the glue gun when you're done.

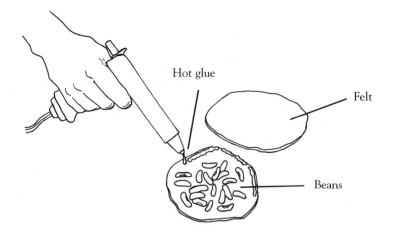

Hot glue

Felt

Beans

Play Otedama

Here's how you play the game:

What You Need

5 otedama (beanbags)

What You Do

1. Place all the beanbags in your left hand.
2. Throw one in the air, and while that bag is in the air, pass another bag to your right hand. Catch the bag in the air with your left hand.
3. Toss the bag up again, and pass a second bag to your right hand. Catch the bag in the air with your left hand.
4. Throw the bag up again, and pass a third bag to your right hand. Catch the bag in the air with your left hand.
5. Toss the bag up a fourth time, and pass a fourth bag to your right hand. Catch the final bag with your right hand.

Japanese on the Mainland

Japanese immigrants also settled in states such as California, Oregon, and Washington. Some came as students who intended to return to Japan, while others were laborers who took jobs as cannery workers, fishermen, railroad workers, servants, miners, gardeners, boardinghouse owners, store and restaurant owners, and farmers. In farming, Japanese Ameri-

HAWAII

When the first Japanese immigrated to Hawaii, it was a kingdom, independent of the United States. In 1898 it was annexed by the United States, and in 1900 it was made into a territory. It became the 50th state in 1959. Hawaii has a wonderful mix of diverse racial and ethnic groups. It is truly an integrated society, in which Japanese, Chinese, Filipino, American Indians, native Hawaiians, Pacific Islanders, African Americans, Caucasians, and others live peacefully side by side.

cans made some of their most amazing contributions to America. They introduced new crops such as strawberries, celery, and rice, and turned abandoned land into lush growing fields. In California by the start of the 20th century, although they owned only 2 percent of the farming lands, Japanese Americans produced 10 percent of California's crops.

Japanese women worked alongside their husbands, putting in long days in the fields or cooking and cleaning for family-owned businesses such as boardinghouses and stores. In addition to working, the women also had to take care of their own home and family. Typically, Japanese women were the first ones up in the morning and the last ones to bed at night.

Racism and Discrimination

Japanese Americans were at first welcomed with open arms by Americans, when laborers were needed to work at difficult, dangerous jobs that Americans didn't want. The Japanese *did* work hard, and after a few years of working and saving they began to buy homes and businesses of their own. As they became more successful, some other American workers started to complain publicly, accusing the Japanese of taking jobs away from them.

In 1906, the city of San Francisco tried to force Japanese American children to go to separate schools from the children of native-born Americans. The federal government stepped in and President Theodore Roosevelt convinced the school board to reverse its decision.

The anti-Japanese crusade continued, carried on by activist groups as well as many newspapers. President Roosevelt was worried about keeping peace at home and with the country of Japan, whose government was concerned at the way their citizens were being treated. The United States and the government of Japan reached a compromise in 1908 that called for Japan to prohibit any further emigration of Japanese laborers. It was called the Gentlemen's Agreement. The agreement allowed three categories of Japanese immigrants: those who had lived in the United States previously and wanted to return, skilled workers, and immediate family members of Japanese already living in the United States. An unintended consequence of the law resulted in thousands of women immigrating to the United States to be reunited with their husbands or meet their husbands for the first time as "picture brides."

Because the Japanese were so successful as farmers, many native-born Californians feared that the Japanese would buy up all the land available. (This was an unfounded worry because, as mentioned earlier, the Japanese owned only a small percentage of the farmland in the state.) In 1913, the California Alien Land Law was passed in order to prevent any *alien* (a person who is not a citizen of a particular country) from owning land, unless that person was eligible to become an American citizen. At the time, all Asian American immigrants with the exception of Filipinos were prevented by law from becoming citizens. The Japanese fought back by buying the land in the names of their American-born children or by leasing the land from white landowners.

All immigration from Japan was shut down following passage of the Immigration Act of 1924. It forbade the immigration of all Asians. The door to America would not open again until 1952.

Picture Brides

Do you think you could choose someone to marry just by looking at his or her picture? That is what thousands of Japanese men and women did at the turn of the 20th century. In the first years of immigration, Japanese men vastly outnumbered Japanese women in America. This first generation of men were busy working hard in order to succeed in their new country. As a result, many of them were 10 or 15 years past the usual age of marriage.

There were several obstacles to finding a suitable wife. First, there were American laws in place prohibiting the marriage of native-born women to Japanese men. Second, few saved enough money to make the trip back to Japan to find a wife. Last, many men avoided returning to Japan because a visit of more than 30 days would make them eligible for Japanese military service.

A practical solution was found in the practice of *picture brides*. When a man decided to marry, he sent a letter home to his family or a matchmaker to find a wife. He sent a picture of himself, with a description of his job and home. Women looking to marry a Japanese man in America sent pictures of themselves and letters outlining their family histories to the family or matchmaker, who decided on a good pairing. The couple themselves had very little say in the decision.

The next step was the recording of the bride's name in the groom's family register, followed by an actual wedding in Japan without the groom present. The bride then made the trip across the Pacific to meet her new husband. Often there was disappointment and tears at the dock. The husband might be years older than the picture had shown. Sometimes men sent pictures of friends that they thought were better looking than themselves. Other disappointments included the job or home of the husband. A ranch turned out to be a shanty with an old horse in the backyard, or the restaurant owner was really a waiter.

Surprisingly, most of these marriages lasted, though some women did return to Japan. It was a great disgrace to the bride's family to have her return, so most women chose to stay and make the best of things.

Generations of Japanese Immigrants

Japanese Americans gave names to each generation who immigrated here from Japan. The first generation that came over in the 1800s was called the *Issei* (ee-say), their American-born children were called the *Nisei* (nee-say), and their children called *Sansei* (sahn-say). The fourth generation are known as the *Yonsei* (yohn-say); fifth, the *Gosei* (goh-say); and sixth, the *Rokusei* (roh-koo-say).

The new generation of Japanese immigrants who came to America after World War II, when immigration restrictions were lifted, are called the *Shin Issei* (sheen ee-say), which means "the new first generation."

Japantowns

If you were thousands of miles from home, living in a foreign land, wouldn't it be comforting to go to a place where you could read the signs in your native language? Speak that language and be understood? Dine on foods from your native land? For new Japanese immigrants, Japantowns offered this and much more.

A Japantown was like a city within a city where the majority of the homes and businesses were owned by Japanese Americans. Located mostly in California and Hawaii, these communities offered a welcome haven to new Japanese immigrants. Here they read Japanese newspapers, frequented Japanese businesses, and socialized with other Japanese immigrants. In these places, too, Japanese immigrants didn't feel like outsiders, because they were among other Japanese immigrants who had similar needs, interests, and desires.

The homes in Japantown were mostly boardinghouses. The neighborhoods were like the towns that the immigrants came from in Japan. They had Japanese bathhouses; sushi, tofu, and noodle shops; Japanese theater; and Japanese newspapers. Japanese immigrants enjoyed sumo wrestling tournaments, baseball games, and Japanese music and dance concerts. Most Japantowns disappeared during World War II because of the forced relocation of Japanese Americans (see p. 95).

Today, Japantowns in San Francisco and San Jose and Little Tokyo in Los Angeles work hard to keep their Japanese American communities intact. At its highest point, 30,000 Japanese Americans lived in Little Tokyo. This community sponsors celebrations such as Nisei Week, tofu festivals, and Japanese American New Year. In San Francisco's Japantown, you can find taiko drumming (see p. 83), mochi pounding (see p. 87), and the Cherry Blossom Festival (see p. 93). Japantown in San Jose is home to the Japanese American Museum of San Jose, a farmers' market, and an annual Obon bazaar (see p. 89).

In these neighborhoods you can buy anything Japanese: electronics, books, magazines, DVDs, CDs, video games, and more. You can also find the very popular Japanese *anime* (ah-nee-may), animation films, and *manga* (mahn-gah), Japanese comic books.

It is hard to visit Japantowns without wanting to follow the tantalizing smells of Japanese food wafting through the air. You can enjoy such delights as *miso* (mee-soh) *soup*, made with soybean paste; *sushi* (soo-shee), fish, usually raw, and vegetables, wrapped in rice and seaweed; *tempura* (tehm-poo-rah), batter-fried meats and vegetables; *ramen* (rah-mehn), wheat noodles; and *gyoza* (gee-oh-zah), pan-fried dumplings.

Japanese Americans and visitors alike enjoy the many sights and sounds of traditional Japanese culture when they visit a Japantown.

GO: A TRADITIONAL JAPANESE GAME

Go is one of the world's treasures, an ancient board game that started in China more than 4,000 years ago! It came to Japan in the sixth century. Go appears to be simple, but it is actually a complex game that involves a lot of strategy, like chess. The first immigrants played Go in Japanese communities for hours. With limited income, and family far from home, they found that Go was a pleasant diversion from loneliness. Young people in Japan have revived the game in recent years after it was featured in a popular Japanese manga comic book.

Paint a Daruma Doll

Japantown is where you would find *daruma* (dah-roo-mah) dolls. They are Japanese good luck charms. When you buy (or make) a daruma, the eyes are blank. You paint in one eye when you make a wish for something. The other eye is painted in only when the wish comes true. Darumas are also used to set goals. When you decide on a goal you paint in one eye, and when you have achieved your goal you paint in the other eye. The tradition of making daruma dolls originated with the legend of the Indian Buddhist priest Bodhidharma, also known as Daruma.

The Legend of Daruma

Daruma is a shortened name for the Indian Buddhist priest Bodhidharma who lived in the sixth century. He sat perfectly still and meditated for nine straight years. When he finally got up, he found that he had lost the use of his arms and legs. The daruma is a Japanese symbol for strength and patience.

What You Need

Empty pudding or gelatin cup, washed and dried
Newspaper
Masking tape
Scissors
Plastic spoon
Glue
Water
3 paper cups
Red water-based paint
Thick paintbrush
White acrylic paint
Black marker

What You Do

1. Stuff the empty pudding cup with newspaper. Tape the opening shut with masking tape.
2. Make a simple papier-mâché mix by cutting up strips of newspaper into 1-by-3-inch strips. With the plastic spoon, mix 2 parts glue to 1 part warm water in a paper cup. Dip the strips one at a time into the mixture and cover the pudding cup on all sides. Let dry overnight.

3. Paint the pudding cup with the red paint. Let dry.

4. Paint a square of white for the face on one side. Let dry.

5. Draw the face and designs with the black marker as shown.

6. Decide on a goal for yourself and fill in one eye of the daruma. When you fulfill your goal, fill in the other eye.

1. Papiér-mâché over the cup

2. Paint

3. Draw face and designs

SCHOOLBOYS

A lot of the early Japanese immigrants at the turn of the 19th century were students who received room and board from American families in exchange for doing domestic work. Their days began at dawn with starting a fire and setting the table for breakfast. They came home from school about four, when preparation for dinner would begin. Duties included such things as peeling potatoes, setting the table, and washing dishes afterward. On Saturday the boys had a full day of chores; Sunday they were off.

The schoolboys sometimes felt as though they had "lost face"—that is, lost their dignity—by taking these jobs. In Japan, household work was never done by men. Another insult was when families gave the boys American names like Bill or Charlie because they didn't want to take the time to learn how to pronounce their Japanese names.

Over time the list of chores that the schoolboys were asked to do would grow so lengthy and tiring that they had little time and energy left for their studies.

Prepare Miso Soup

Miso soup is a flavorful and healthy soup that is commonly found on the Japanese American table. It is made from miso (soybean paste) and tofu, which is also made from soybeans. Tofu is very plain and takes on the taste of whatever it is cooked with. Let's try a very simple miso soup.

5 servings

What You Need

Adult supervision required

1 cup firm tofu, cubed

Knife

Cutting board

2 green onions (also called scallions)

Medium large pan

5 cups water

1 extra-large cube or 2 regular-size cubes fish stock bouillon

Optional: 2 teaspoons wakame seaweed flakes (cut, dried seaweed in a bag)

⅓ cup miso, any type (found in Asian and health food stores)

Stirring spoon

Ladle

5 serving bowls

What You Do

1. Cut the tofu into cubes the size of a sugar cube.
2. Wash and slice the dark green tops of the scallions into thin slices. You can also use a clean pair of scissors instead of a knife to cut these.
3. Fill the pan with the water, cube(s) of fish stock, and optionally the seaweed flakes (the seaweed will expand in the water). Bring to a boil, and then simmer for 10 minutes.
4. Stir. Add the tofu and miso and simmer for a minute or two longer.
5. Ladle into serving bowls and top off with a few scallion slices.

Japanese Clothing

Japanese Americans quickly adapted to American dress to try to avoid the discrimination that the Chinese had faced before them. The Issei were the only generation to wear the traditional kimono (kee-moh-no). The *kimono* is a loose-fitting garment that can be worn by men, women, and children. It wraps around and is secured at the waist with a wide sash known as an obi (oh-bee). Boys wear a shorter kimono with a divided skirt, or loose pants called a hakama (hah-kah-mah).

Early pictures of Japanese immigrants arriving from Japan show them in kimonos, with geta (geh-tah), wooden sandals, and zori (zoh-ree), rubber or straw sandals, with tabi (tah-bee), a special sock that separates the big toe from the rest of the foot. By the turn of the 20th century, most Japanese men arrived wearing Western-style suits and ties.

Japanese women were introduced to American corsets and dresses that felt excruciatingly tight after the comfort of the kimono. They also had to adapt to American high heels that pinched the toes and made walking more of an effort.

Today, both here and in Japan, the kimono is worn only for special occasions and holidays. Japanese immigrants arrive wearing the same type of clothing as Americans.

Japanese Food

Japanese food is similar to Chinese food in that it is usually boiled, fried, or grilled instead of roasted in the oven. Food is chosen for color and appearance as well as taste, and great care is taken to include a balance of both.

Rice is always served at the Japanese table, as are different types of soup. Food is served in several small bowls and trays, and eaten with chopsticks. Soybeans are important in Japanese cooking. They are used to make soy sauce, miso, and tofu. Green tea is served with all meals. Fish and vegetables are plentiful, as are different types of noodles.

Many Japanese dishes have become American favorites as well. Sashimi (sah-shee-mee) and sushi; ramen noodles, an instant form of Japanese noodle; and tempura, deep-fried fish and vegetables, are all popular in the United States.

Generally most Japanese Americans eat the way other Americans do. During holidays and special festivals, they celebrate with more traditional foods.

KRISTI YAMAGUCHI (1971–)

Olympic Figure Skater

Kristi Yamaguchi had to wear casts to correct her deformed feet when she was a little girl. She was born with a condition known as clubfoot (when one or both of your feet is twisted out of position). At five years old, Kristi began taking ice skating lessons to help strengthen her legs. She went on to become the first Japanese American woman to win the gold medal for figure skating, at the 1992 Olympics. After years as a professional figure skater, Kristi remains one of America's favorite athletes.

Craft a Furoshiki

Japanese immigrants arriving in America used a square cloth called a *furoshiki* (foo-roh-shee-kee) to carry small possessions, similar to the way a pocketbook is used today. The original use for a furoshiki in Japan was to carry things back and forth to the bathhouse. Furoshiki usually have dramatic designs that are embroidered or dyed into the cloth.

What You Need
Ruler
Pencil
4 sheets heavyweight tissue paper in a
    stack, any color
Scissors
Stapler
Blank paper
Wrapping paper scraps
Glue

What You Do
1. Measure and cut a 16-by-16-inch square through all 4 sheets of the tissue paper.
2. Staple the stack at the corners.
3. Practice drawing the outlines of some Japanese designs on the blank paper until you discover the ones you like best. Some traditional designs include cranes, Japanese fans, flowers, mountains, and fish.
4. Cut one or more shapes out of your drawings to use as stencils.
5. Lay the stencils over different scraps of wrapping paper. Outline 5 or 6 pieces using the pencil and cut out.
6. Glue onto the tissue paper, and let dry.

Make Rice Balls

Rice balls, or *onigiri* (oh-nee-gee-ree), have been a staple in Japanese American homes from the first generation of Japanese immigrants to today. They are easily portable and can be eaten at breakfast, lunch, or dinner. Rice balls are also fun to make!

12 rice balls

What You Need
Adult supervision required
2 cups water
1 teaspoon salt
Medium-size pan with lid
1 cup Japanese-style short grain white rice (available at Asian and health food stores)
Stirring spoon
Cutting board
Knife
½ cucumber
4 ounces imitation crabmeat
1 box nori (sheets of toasted seaweed, available at Asian and health food stores)
1 deep bowl filled with warm water
1 or 2 plates

What You Do
1. Pour cups of water and salt into the pan and bring to a boil.
2. Add rice, cover, and simmer for 20 minutes or until the liquid is absorbed by the rice. Stir as needed.
3. Cut the cucumber and imitation crabmeat into tiny pieces. Slice the nori into ½-inch strips.
4. The rice needs to be warm, but if it is too hot to touch, wait a few minutes longer.
5. Wet your hands in the water bowl. This will prevent the rice from sticking to your hands. Use the stirring spoon to take a scoop of rice out of the pan. Roll it into a ball like a meatball. Press a hole into the middle and push a small amount of imitation crabmeat and cucumber inside. Fill up the hole with more rice.
6. Shape into a triangle and wrap a strip of seaweed around it. Place on a plate.

Japan Today

Japan is a very modern, technologically advanced country. It is made up of hundreds of small islands that stretch for about 1,875 miles (3,018 km) off the eastern coast of Asia. Because most of Japan is made up of rocky, volcanic land, 98 percent of the population live on the four main islands of Hokkaido (hohk-kye-doh), Honshu (hohn-shoo), Shikoku (shee-koh-koo), and Kyushu (kyoo-shoo).

An average of 861 people live in a single square mile in Japan, compared to an average of 76 people per square mile in the United States. During rush hour in Japanese cities, subway workers called "pushers" push the people onto the train cars in order to allow the doors to close! Stores, restaurants, apartments, and car garages are all stacked vertically in tall buildings to make the most of the space. Because the streets are so crowded, many Japanese use bicycles instead of cars to commute short distances. Wherever you go in Japan—stores, restaurants, trains, offices, schools, hotels, and city streets—they're all bulging with people.

It Started in Japan!

A wealth of technology that we use every day is from Japan. The first video game systems—Nintendo, Sega, and Sony PlayStation—came from Japan, as did the Sony Walkman. The first compact discs (CDs), digital video discs (DVDs) and recorders, VHS recorders and tapes, and CD-ROMs were all Japanese inventions.

Folding fans were invented in Japan more than a thousand years ago. *Bonsai* (bone-sigh), the art of cultivating miniature trees, came from Japan, and so did sumo wrestling. We can thank the Japanese for karaoke machines, futons, and popular automobiles such as Toyota, Honda, Nissan, and Mazda.

Japanese *Noh* (no) is Japan's oldest form of theater. It is distinctive because the actors wear white wooden masks. Japanese anime featuring such characters as Sailor Moon and Astro Boy are shown all over the world. Traditional art from Japan includes *ukiyo-e* (yoo-kee-oh-ay), which means "pictures of a floating world." You have probably seen reproductions of this 17th-century art, which was made through woodblock printing.

KENJINKAI PICNIC

Kenjinkai (kehn-jeen-key) picnics were very popular among the Issei generation in the early years of the 1900s. "Ken" means "prefectural" (the district the immigrants came from in Japan), "jin" refers to people, and "kai" is a social organization. The Issei gathered to share memories, games, and food from their home region. They brought bento lunches and organized games and activities for the kids. There was Japanese music, dancing, and singing. It was enjoyed by all ages.

Say It in Japanese

The first generation of Japanese immigrants, the Issei, spoke mostly Japanese. The Nisei, the second generation, grew up speaking Japanese to their parents and English to each other and everyone else. The generations that followed spoke English and very little, if any, Japanese. Today Japanese is primarily spoken by new Japanese immigrants.

Welcome:	*irasshaimase* (ee-ras-shy-mah-say)
Hello:	*konnichiwa* (kohn-nee-chee-wah)
Good-bye:	*sayonara* (sah-yoh-nah-rah)
Thank you:	*domo arigato gozaimasu* (doh-moh ah-ree-gah-toh goh-zah-ee-mah-su)

Japanese Writing

The Japanese adapted a character-based system of writing from the Chinese more than one thousand years ago. The Japanese characters are called *kanji* (kahn-jee), and like Chinese characters they represent whole words or ideas rather than sounds. Japanese also has two other forms of writing known as *kana* (kah-nah), which are sound-based like the letters in our alphabet. However, unlike the letters in our alphabet, the kana symbols are *syllabaries*, which means they stand for complete syllables rather than individual sounds. The two types of kana are hiragana (hee-rah-gah-nah), which has curved symbols, and katakana (kah-tah-kah-nah), which has angular symbols.

Shintoism

Shintoism (shin-toh-iz-m) is the religion of Japan. The early people of Japan worshipped nature gods and goddesses. Followers of Shintoism believe that all aspects of nature—mountains, trees, animals, and rivers—have a living spirit called kami (kah-mee). There are thousands of Shinto shrines in Japan, which followers visit to pray for good fortune. Followers often have a small altar at home as well, to show reverence and respect for ancestors and recently deceased relatives.

Fold an Origami Dog and Cat

The Japanese art of paper folding, called *origami* (oh-ree-gah-mee), is hundreds of years old. It was originally used to make images of Shinto gods for religious ceremonies. Until the early 1900s, it was an art practiced only by the wealthy, because the cost of paper was so high. Now origami is enjoyed by people all over the world. This origami dog and cat will take you less than a minute to make!

What You Need
2 squares origami paper (or other thin
  paper), 8 inches by 8 inches, any color

What You Do
1. To make the dog: Hold the paper so that it is in a diamond shape and fold in half. Fold the top right corner down about 2 inches, and repeat with the top left corner to make floppy dog ears.
2. To make the cat: Hold the paper so that it is in a diamond shape and fold in half. Fold each of the top two corners halfway down on each side. Next, make a second fold on each side, about ½ inch down from the first fold. Now flip the point of each folded side up to make cat's ears.

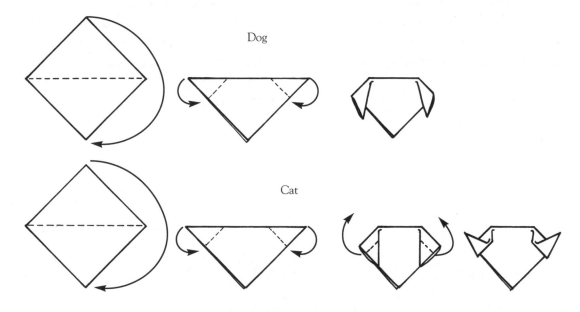
Dog

Cat

Write Haiku

Haiku (hy-koo) is a very popular type of poem that Japanese people have shared with Americans and people all over the world. Haiku poems are short, only three lines long. Traditional Japanese haiku have 17 syllables: 5 in the first line, 7 in the middle line, and 5 in the last line. To write haiku you must be a careful observer. A traditional haiku captures a moment in nature. The writer notices little things like how the late afternoon sun bathes the landscape golden, or how snow falls silently, or how the air feels thick before it rains. Then he or she writes about the moment in a few carefully chosen words. Many haiku poems also leave a clue as to what season it is, such as mentioning pumpkins to indicate fall.

Before writing your haiku, read this traditional one by a famous Japanese haiku poet named Matsuo Basho. It has fewer syllables because it has been translated from Japanese into English.

A Bee
A bee
staggers out
of the peony

What You Need
Paper
Pen

What You Do
1. Go outside and try to clear your mind so you can be open to what you see. It helps to close your eyes and breathe deeply for a few moments before you begin.
2. Make simple observations about a moment in time that you might not ordinarily notice. Some examples of such moments are the sun melting snow off a pine branch, a ladybug making its way across a rock, or a squirrel clutching a nut.
3. Get ready to write your haiku with pen and paper. Think about what you saw, heard, smelled, felt, or tasted. See if you can leave a clue as to what season it is in your poem.
4. Read your haiku to a friend.

Practice Taiko Drumming

Taiko drumming is a 2,000-year-old musical form that was brought to the United States in the 1960s. *Taiko* (ty-koh) means "big drum" in Japanese, but there are also small and medium-size taiko drums. The biggest drums are usually about five feet wide, and the bachi (bah-chee), or drumsticks, look more like baseball bats! Taiko drums are a familiar sound at Japanese American celebrations. There are more than 200 taiko drumming groups that perform in the United States and Canada.

What You Need

Clean, empty round plastic wastebasket, the bigger the better
2 thick wooden drumsticks (available in music stores), wooden dowels, or cooking spoons
Optional: hachimaki (ha-chee-mah-kee) headband (a long strip of white cloth)

What You Do

1. Optional: tie the hachimaki over your forehead like a bandanna.
2. Turn the wastebasket over to create a drum.
3. Clap out a rhythm using pauses, taps in a row, and single taps. Vary the tempo from fast to slow.
4. Repeat the rhythm using the drumsticks on the drum.

Hachimaki

Bachi

Create Gyotaku: Japanese Fish Printing

Fish printing began in Japan when fishermen recorded their catch by making prints or rubbings of the day's bounty. The practice developed over the years into a very beautiful art form that was introduced to the United States by Japanese artists. *Gyotaku* (ghee-yoh-tah-koo) art is displayed in museums throughout the world.

What You Need

1 whole fish, including head and tail

Paper towels

Thick newspaper work surface

Black acrylic paint (or another color of your choice) in a paper cup, thinned with a little water

Thick paintbrush

Manila drawing paper, 18 inches by 12 inches

Black marker

Assortment of colored pencils

What You Do

1. Gently wash the fish and pat it dry with paper towels.
2. Lay the fish on top of the newspaper and paint it on one side. Use other newspapers to practice making fish prints. Put the fish on top of the paper, painted side down. Use your fingertips to press each area of the fish down gently.
3. When you feel ready, use the same technique to press the fish down on a piece of manila paper. Don't worry if every part is not there when you lift the fish. You will be drawing in what is missing afterward. Make 2 or 3 prints on the same page, letting the prints overlap. Let dry.
4. Using the real fish as a model, draw in the outline of the fish, the eyes, the tail, and any other details you see with the black marker.
5. Color the fish in with the colored pencils, right over the black print. It will look like a watercolor painting when you are done!

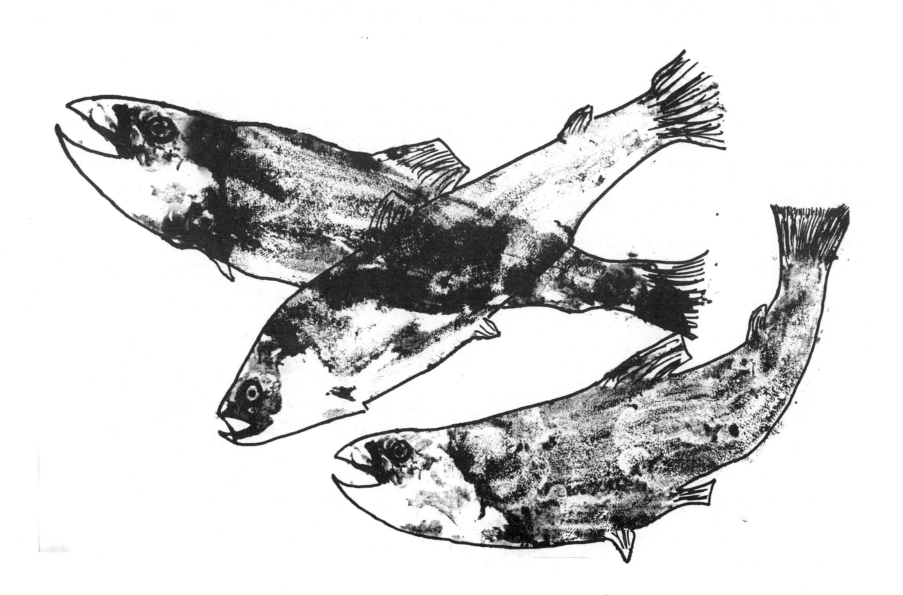

Paint Your Face Like a Kabuki Actor

Kabuki (kah-boo-kee) is a traditional Japanese form of theater that was brought to America with the Issei generation. Plays involve a lot of singing and dancing, dramatic costumes, and face painting. Male as well as female roles are played by men. The men who specialize in female roles are called onnagata (ohn-nah-gah-ta). Kabuki actors have white-painted faces with designs in black, red, blue, and other colors that tell the audience whether the character is good or bad.

What You Need

Newspaper work surface
Mirror
Watercolor paintbrush
Paper cup filled halfway with water
Water-based white, red, and black face
    paint (available in craft stores)

What You Do

1. Lay out the newspaper work surface and place the mirror so you can see yourself.
2. Dip the brush into the water and then the white paint. Paint all the white areas first. These areas are noted with a W in the illustration.
3. Wash the brush in water. Dip the brush in red and paint the red markings. These areas are noted with an R in the illustration.
4. Wash the brush and paint the black designs, as shown in the illustration.
5. Wash the brush in water.

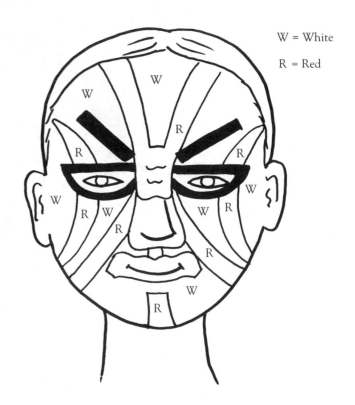

W = White

R = Red

Celebrations

Oshogatsu: Japanese New Year

Japanese Americans celebrate *Oshogatsu* (oh-shoh-gah-tsoo), or New Year's Day, on January 1. They prepare by cleaning the house from top to bottom. They settle old debts and any unfinished business so that they can begin the new year with a clean slate. Many symbolic foods are prepared in advance of the holiday. On New Year's Eve families gather and eat long, unbroken noodles called *soba* (soh-bah). The noodles symbolize longevity, or long life.

Mochitsuki (moh-cheet-soo-kee), pounding rice to make mochi (moh-chee) cakes, is a popular demonstration you might see at a Japanese American New Year's celebration. It involves pounding an enormous wooden mallet into a tub of steamed rice. The mochi is then hand-rolled into balls. This is a tradition that has faded in Japan, as most people use store-bought mochi cakes. Pieces of mochi along with fish and vegetables are used in the New Year's soup called ozoni (oh-zoh-nee).

Other symbolic foods eaten on New Year's are: otoso (oh-toh-soh), which is spiced sake (rice wine, pronounced sah-keh); herring roe (fish eggs) to encourage new life; and stewed black beans for good health. Participants may visit shrines and temples, call on friends and family, and play games. A traditional home may have a *kadomatsu* (kah-doh-maht-soo), a pine and bamboo arrangement, at the front door for good luck in the coming year.

SEIJI OZAWA (1935–)
Conductor

Seiji Ozawa was born in China to Japanese parents. He studied music in Japan and Europe and came to the United States in 1961. In 1969 he became the first East Asian to become conductor of a major symphony orchestra, the San Francisco Symphony. He went on to become the youngest and most long-running musical director of the highly acclaimed Boston Symphony Orchestra, which he led from 1973 to 2002. In 2002 he became the conductor of the Vienna State Opera. Ozawa is known for selecting unusual types of music for the orchestra and for his energetic style of conducting.

Make a Kadomatsu to Place at Your Front Door

The kadomatsu ushers in the new year with its combination of bamboo for strength, pine for long life, and a flowering branch for prosperity. The bamboo remains open for good spirits to enter.

What You Need

Adult supervision required

1 long dried bamboo stalk (available where floral supplies are sold) or fresh bamboo stalk (if they sell them in your area)

Small coping saw or craft saw (for adult to use)

2 pieces 6-inch-long rope

3 or 4 feet rope

Garden clippers

Pine branches, in bunches of 3 (cut outside with clippers)

Optional: flowering plant branches in bunches of 3 (cut outside with scissors or buy from a florist; plum branches are traditional but not easily available outside of Japan)

What You Do

1. Ask an adult to cut the bamboo into three different-size pieces with the saw. The cuts should be made at a slant, with the bamboo buds pointing upward.
2. Tie the 3 bamboo pieces together with the two small pieces of rope, one about 2 inches from the bottom of the bamboo bunch and the other about 6 inches from the bottom. Wind the longer piece of rope around and around from the bottom up about 8–10 inches, covering the small pieces of rope. Tuck the ends of this rope into the tied rope pieces.
3. Tuck in bunches of pine branches. Each bunch should have an odd number. Do the same with the flowering plants if desired.
4. The kadomatsu should be placed outside your front door, with the bamboo touching the floor or ground. It should not be in the house.

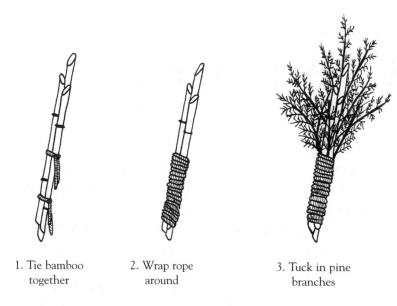

1. Tie bamboo together

2. Wrap rope around

3. Tuck in pine branches

Obon Festival

The *Obon (oh-bohn) Festival*, also called the Bon (bohn) Festival, is a time when Japanese Americans honor their ancestors and remember loved ones who have died. It is observed in July or August of each year and is sometimes called the Feast of Lanterns.

The holiday began with the legend of Mokuren (moh-koo-rehn), a student of Buddha. After Mokuren's mother died, he visited the spirit world and saw that she was starving. Mokuren was told that if he did good deeds for people on earth, such as helping his fellow monks, his mother would be released. When his mother left the land of hungry ghosts, Mokuren danced with joy.

Traditionally families visited the graves of ancestors and lit their ancestors' spirits homes with lanterns. At home, offerings of food, flowers, and incense were given to the spirits. After three days the lanterns were set on a river to send the spirits back to their graves.

Today Obon Festivals are usually held at Buddhist temples. The festivals are fun and lively, culminating in a *Bon Odori* (bohn oh-doh-ree), a Japanese folk dance that shows one's appreciation for family and ancestors. Participants wear light summer kimonos and dance in a circle, accompanied by the sound of taiko drums. At some festivals hundreds of people join in the dances and everyone, Japanese and non-Japanese alike, is encouraged to participate.

Children's Day

Children's Day, *Komodo No Hi* (ko-mo-do no hee), is a day that honors children and encourages participation in traditional Japanese culture. Families gather together for festivals that feature martial arts demonstrations, Japanese theater, Japanese food such as noodles and sushi, and Japanese crafts. It is celebrated every year on the same day as Boys' Day, Tango No Sekku (tahn-go no seck-koo). On that day, special warrior dolls are displayed to inspire strength and courage, and carp streamers fly in honor of the family's children. The carp represent strength because they must swim upstream to lay their eggs. Traditionally, a bamboo pole was placed in the ground and a carp streamer flew for each boy in the family. The largest carp represented the oldest son, and they went down in size for each younger son. In today's Japanese American celebrations, boys as well as girls are often invited to make carp streamers at a community festival.

89

Join in a Bon Odori Dance

There are many types of Bon Odori. The Tanko Bushi (tahn-ko boo-shee), or Coal Miners' Dance, is the most widely known.

What You Need
6 or more people (the more the better!)
Japanese music CD (you can borrow one
    from your library)
CD player

What You Do
1. Gather in a circle and turn so you are facing the back of the person in front of you. As you do the movements of the dance, follow the person in front of you around the circle.
2. Turn the Japanese music CD on.
3. Tap your right heel to the ground, then step down on your right foot. Pretend to shovel coal to the right of you. Repeat.
4. Tap your left heel to the ground, then step down on your left foot. Pretend to shovel coal to the left of you. Repeat.
5. Step forward on your right foot and pretend to throw coal (with cupped hands) over your right shoulder.
6. Step forward on your left foot and pretend to throw coal (with cupped hands) over your left shoulder.
7. Step back on your left foot and pretend to shade the sun from your eyes with your right hand.
8. Step back on your right foot and pretend to shade the sun from your eyes with your left hand.
9. Step forward on your right foot, then left, and pretend to push a cart of coal forward. Repeat.
10. Drop your hands by your side and clap once. Then clap 2 times quickly. End with one slow clap.

Make a Carp Steamer for Children's Day

What You Need

2 strips 24-by-4-inch poster paper or card
    stock
Stapler
12 sheets (approximately) tissue paper in a
    bright color
Scissors
Black water-based paint in paper cup
Paintbrush
Hole puncher
18 inches string or yarn

What You Do

1. Make a holder for the fish's mouth by stapling together the narrow ends of one piece of poster paper to form a circle. Make a holder for the tail with the second piece.
2. Make 2 stacks of tissue paper with 3 pieces in each. Make 2 stacks of paper with 2 pieces in each.
3. Staple the top (short side) of a 3-piece stack of tissue paper inside the holder for the fish mouth, so that it goes about halfway around the edge of the mouth. Scrunch it up between staples like a window curtain. Use the second stack of 3 pieces to go the rest of the way around the mouth.
4. Flip the mouth holder so that it is inside the tissue paper.
5. Take the tail holder and staple the other side of the tissue-paper stacks all around the outside of the tail holder. The tissue paper should reach about halfway down the holder.
6. Lay one stack of 2 pieces on top of the fish body and holder. Staple the short edge of the tissue paper to the tail holder, over the tissue paper that you just stapled. The new staples should be about 1 inch closer to the mouth side than the staples you used in step 5. Finish going around with the second stack of 2 pieces. Now flip the paper over and you have a long tail.

7. The tail should be about half as long as the body. Scrunch together any excess paper at the bottom of the tail and cut.
8. Use the paint and a marker to draw eyes and scales.
9. Punch a hole on either side of the top of the streamer. Tie the string or yarn from one side to the other. Hang inside or outside.

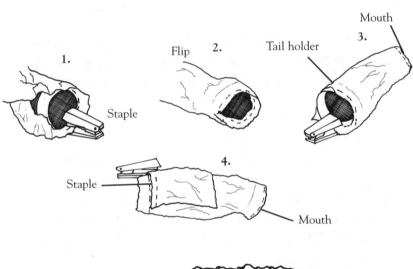

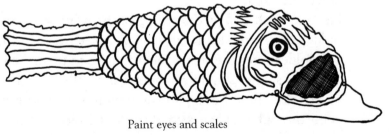

Paint eyes and scales

PRIVATE FIRST CLASS SADAO S. MUNEMORI (1922–1945)

First Japanese American to Win the Medal of Honor

Private Sadao Munemori was born in California and won the Medal of Honor, the highest U.S. military decoration for bravery and valor on the battlefield. He was awarded the medal posthumously, meaning after his death. He died in order to protect the lives of the men he fought with in Italy during World War II. When an unexploded grenade hit his helmet, it rolled toward the other soldiers. He smothered the blast by heroically throwing his body on top of it.

Hina Matsuri: Girls' Day

Girls have their own special holiday called *Hina Matsuri* (hee-nah maht-soo-ree), which is celebrated on March 3 of each year. The holiday celebrates the health and happiness of girls. Early Japanese immigrants took great pleasure in celebrating Girls' Day with their daughters in their new country.

Traditionally, mothers set out beautiful dolls on shelves covered with red cloth. The dolls are created to look like ancient Japanese royalty and are for viewing, not playing. Sometimes the dolls are passed down from mothers to daughters for generations. This holiday from Japan is more than a thousand years old. It was originally celebrated by placing paper dolls in the river to carry bad spirits away after the long winter.

Today if Japanese American families celebrate Hina Matsuri, girls dress in traditional kimonos and invite their friends and neighbors to see the dolls and enjoy traditional foods such as hishi mochi (diamond-shaped rice cakes), clam soup, and shiro-zake (shee-roh-zah-keh), a drink made from rice. More modern celebrations serve American-style cake iced with pink and green frosting. Japanese Americans whose parents and grandparents were born in America may first celebrate Hina Matsuri at a community center or school.

Cherry Blossom Festival: A New Japanese American Holiday

The Cherry Blossom Festival is a uniquely Japanese American celebration. It is a time to remember and appreciate the gift of 3,000 cherry trees made in 1912 to Washington, D.C., from the country of Japan. The festival celebrates Japanese American culture and features traditional Japanese dance, music, and arts. Events for this festival include sake tasting, anime festivals, and kimono exhibits. The highlight of the festival is the National Cherry Blossom Festival Parade, which takes place at the end of the two-week festi-

val. It features marching bands, dancers, taiko drumming, clowns, antique cars, and more.

Nisei Week: A Japanese American Celebration

Nisei Week was started in 1934 by young Nisei who wanted to rejuvenate the businesses of Little Tokyo in Los Angeles, California. The goal was to show that while this second generation of Japanese immigrants were fully American, they had a proud ethnic background to share as well. These first celebrations featured a special dance called ondo, calligraphy, tea ceremony, and *ikebana* (ee-keh-bah-nah), which is Japanese flower arranging. Nisei Week in Little Tokyo today is celebrated in August of each year and brings in more than 500,000 visitors. It includes many of the same attractions as the original Nisei Week, plus events such as karate tournaments, anime festivals, sumo wrestling, baby pageants, and traditional Japanese foods.

PATSY TAKEMOTO MINK (1927–2002)

U.S. Representative from Hawaii

Patsy Mink was the first Asian woman to be elected to the U.S. House of Representatives. She represented the state of Hawaii for 24 years, fighting for legislation to protect poor women, children, and minorities.

Enjoy Chanoyu: The Japanese Tea Ceremony

The Japanese tea ceremony, called *Chanoyu* (chah-no-yoo), is a centuries-old tradition that is preserved by Japanese Americans. Influenced by Zen Buddhism, the tea ceremony is considered an art form and has many ritualized steps. It is usually reserved for special occasions such as weddings and holidays, where participants wear traditional kimonos. Chanoyu is designed to purify your mind and put you in touch with nature. Pieces of artwork and beautiful arrangements of flowers are displayed to show appreciation for beauty created by man as well as nature.

Most people skilled in the tea ceremony take classes to learn the proper ways. We will enjoy a simple Japanese tea ceremony.

5 servings (usually 4 guests plus the host)

What You Need
Adult supervision required
5 mats or pieces of thick paper to sit on
Pictures of scenery
Simple vase of flowers or ikebana
(see p. 100)
Kettle to heat water on stove (use about 5 cups water)
5 teaspoons matcha, a powdered green tea (available in Asian grocery stores) or 5 green tea teabags
Cookies*
Serving plate
5 small plates
5 napkins
5 teacups, any type (Japanese teacups have no handles)
Bowl
Whisk or spoon

*Tea ceremony sweets are usually filled with sweet bean paste and are highly decorative. You can substitute a cookie with a fruit filling.

What You Do

1. Lay out mats or paper to sit on, four side by side for the guests and one facing the guests for the host.
2. Display pictures and flowers.
3. Heat water for the tea.
4. Place cookies on serving plate.
5. Invite guests in. Ask them to remove their shoes and sit comfortably on the mats.
6. Encourage guests to quietly admire the artwork and flowers.
7. Pass out small plates, napkins, and teacups.
8. Offer cookies to guests.
9. Pour hot water into bowl. Place powdered green tea in bowl, and stir with whisk until you see small bubbles.
10. Pour tea into guest's cups.
11. Sip the tea and enjoy quiet conversation.

Japanese American Internment Camps

Can you imagine if you came home from school to find out that your family had a week to sell your house, your car, and most of your possessions? And that you would then be forced to move to a desert camp watched by armed guards and surrounded by barbed wire for months or even years? You would have to say good-bye to all your friends and even your pets. Your parents would have to quit their jobs. "Why?" is the question you would ask. "What did we do wrong?" And the answer would be because you or one of your parents, grandparents, or great-grandparents was born in Japan.

On December 7, 1941, the country of Japan bombed the U.S. Naval Base at Pearl Harbor in the state of Hawaii. It was a devastating attack, one that caused the United States to enter World War II. The attack destroyed 183 planes, sunk 14 ships, and killed 2,403 people.

Japanese Americans were just as shocked as the rest of the country. Many were second- and third-generation Japanese Americans who spoke English and had never even been to Japan. They went to American schools, flew American flags, worked in American businesses, and raised their families with American ideals. Sadly, many Americans began to treat Japanese Americans differently after the bombing of Pearl Harbor. They grew suspicious, afraid these Americans might side with Japan and sabotage (destroy or cause problems with) defenses from inside the United States.

THE ALL-JAPANESE AMERICAN 442ND REGIMENTAL COMBAT TEAM AND 100TH BATTALION

In January 1943, the American government decided to allow Japanese Americans to fight in the army against the Japanese in World War II. Thousands of Nisei men volunteered, far more than the 442nd Regimental Combat Team had room for. This included Hawaiians and men incarcerated at internment camps on the mainland. Altogether, 4,500 Japanese American troops in the unit headed for battle in Italy, eager to prove their loyalty to America.

In June 1944, they were joined by the 100th Battalion, an all-Nisei group as well, who had already been fighting in North Africa and Italy. Both units had suffered heavy casualties and had to be constantly replaced by new Japanese American troops. Over the course of the war, about 14,000 men served in the 442nd Regimental Combat Team and 100th Battalion; over a two-year period they earned more than 18,000 medals for bravery, hard work, and courage, becoming one of the most decorated units in military history.

America was also at war with Germany and Italy during World War II, but Italian Americans and German Americans were not discriminated against in the same way. Japanese Americans looked like the enemy Americans were seeing on newsreels and reading about in newspapers. Italian and German Americans, with their European-Caucasian features, blended in with the general population.

What followed was a very dark time in American history. Discrimination and fears about Japanese Americans rose to such a level that the U.S. government decided to round up persons of Japanese ancestry from the Pacific Coast (the coast closest to Japan) and relocate them to camps in the desert areas of California, Arizona, Wyoming, Idaho, Utah, and Arkansas. Signs were posted in public areas all over the West Coast informing all citizens of Japanese ancestry to voluntarily register for a time and date of evacuation. Men, women, and children, whether they were U.S. citizens or not, had to register. It was a disgraceful violation of civil rights. After registering, families went by train to assembly centers for processing and then finally to long-term *internment camps*.

Japanese Americans were suddenly forced to sell all their possessions and leave their homes to relocate for the duration of the war. They were allowed to bring only what they could carry. Many people took advantage of the Japanese Americans and paid only a small amount of money for their household goods, furniture, cars, and personal treasures, knowing that the Japanese had to sell them in a hurry.

Life in the Camps

The camps were in barren, desert locations where temperatures reached 100 degrees during the day and (sometimes) dropped to near freezing at night. This was a big shock to the Japanese Americans, many of whom were used to the mild temperatures of California. The camps also suffered terrible dust storms, which would blow through the camps and cover everything with a fine layer of sand. The camps were hastily built, and living quarters were drafty and stark, with wooden cots and straw-filled mattresses.

JAPANESE BASEBALL LEAGUES

In the early 1900s, Japanese American men organized their own baseball leagues, because American baseball leagues at the time were separated by race. Many had learned the game in Japan, where it was introduced by Americans in the 1870s. The first team, the Excelsiors, was formed in Hawaii in 1899. These teams drew large crowds of Japanese American fans. Despite being interned during World War II, Japanese American teams continued to play, within the confines of the relocation camps.

FRED KOREMATSU (1919–2005)
Activist

The son of Japanese immigrants, Fred Korematsu was a 23-year-old man with a strong sense of right and wrong. When he received orders during World War II to evacuate to an assembly center (the processing center where internment began), he ignored the order and continued to live freely outside the camps. After two months he was arrested and convicted of violating the order. He was sent to Tanforan (an assembly center in California) and eventually to an internment camp in Utah. He fought back by bringing a lawsuit against the United States to fight his own internment. Korematsu lost his case several times, yet continued to appeal these rulings right up to the Supreme Court. While he eventually lost his case, his lawsuit and those of other Japanese Americans contributed to the eventual closing of the camps.

In 1984, the court overturned Korematsu's original conviction, and in 1999 President Clinton awarded him the Presidential Medal of Freedom, America's highest civilian honor.

YOSHIKO UCHIDA (1921-1992)

Children's Book Author

Yoshiko Uchida was born in California and sent to an internment camp with her family during World War II. There, in the Topaz Relocation Camp in Topaz, Utah, she worked as a teacher. She refused to let the internment camp experience color her feelings about being a Japanese American. Instead she went back to Japan to study traditional culture and returned to write 28 children's books about Japanese and Japanese American culture.

FREEDOM

The feelings of the freed Japanese Americans can be best described in their own words. Helen Murao was a 17-year-old teenager leaving the relocation camp at Minidoka, Idaho:

> I felt wonderful the day I left camp. We took a bus to the railroad siding and then stopped someplace to transfer, and I went in and bought a Coke, a nickel Coke. It wasn't the Coke, but what it represented—that I was free to buy it, that feeling was so intense. You can get maudlin, sentimental about freedom; but if you've been deprived of it, it's very significant.

—From *And Justice for All: An Oral History of the Japanese American Detention Camps* by John Tateishi

Because the Japanese Americans were good, law-abiding citizens and not criminals, they soon transformed the camps into livable, thriving communities. The camps had parks, libraries, gardens, community government, schools, churches, Boy Scout troops, baseball fields, fire departments, and beauty parlors. Young couples were married, babies were born, students graduated from high school, and some people died. Years went by. It might seem that some of these internment camps were transforming into small towns just like elsewhere in America. But small towns in America don't restrict freedom with barbed wire and lookout towers.

Closing the Camps

A young woman named Mitsuye Endo, a loyal Japanese American, challenged the right of the U.S. government to hold her in an internment camp against her will when she had committed no crime. After two and a half years of legal fights, the Supreme Court ruled in favor of Endo that the government did not have the right to detain citizens indefinitely. As a result, the government allowed all Japanese Americans to return to their homes. It was the end of the internment camps.

Reparations

Japanese Americans wanted to make sure that what happened to them would never happen to anyone else in

SENATOR DANIEL K. INOUYE

(1924–): U.S. Senator from Hawaii

Daniel Inouye, a Japanese American from Hawaii, lost his arm while fighting with the 442nd Regimental Combat Team in World War II. He went on to become the first Japanese American to be elected to the U.S. Congress (representing Hawaii), where he served for two terms. Inouye then ran for the U.S. Senate and won; he began his eighth term in 2004. He is most well known for serving on the Senate Watergate Committee, which investigated the wrongdoings of then-president Richard Nixon and his associates in 1972.

JAPANESE AMERICAN WARTIME INTERPRETERS

The U.S. military had an advantage over the Japanese in that many U.S. citizens (Japanese Americans) were able to speak, understand, and write in Japanese, while very few citizens of Japan could speak English. A group of Japanese Americans took special training at the Army's Military Intelligence Service Language School. These graduates provided valuable information to the military, because they were able to read and translate secret information that had been captured from the Japanese. They were also able to question Japanese prisoners of war and translate the answers for the American military.

America again. In 1981, a special commission reported that Japanese Americans had been unfairly targeted and that their relocation had never been necessary. The commission recommended that every survivor of the internment camps be paid $20,000 as reparation (a way to make up for an injury to someone).

Starting in 1990, the checks were sent out with an apology from President George H. W. Bush. It is hoped that the lessons learned from the internment camps will help bring an end to prejudice and discrimination in America.

Build a Japanese Rock Garden

Gardens were popular in internment camps. Many Japanese Americans had been farmers or professional gardeners before internment, and they transformed the desert landscape into calm havens of plants, rock, and earth. You can see the remains of some of these rock gardens nearly 50 years later.

We will make a miniature dry landscape garden. In this garden the sand represents water, and the rocks symbolize mountains and islands. The Japanese garden is a serene place for quiet contemplation.

What You Need

Shallow cardboard box, like the kind that
    holds a case of bottled water
Clean sand (available at toy stores that sell
    sandbox sand) or clean kitty litter
Rocks, various sizes
Wide-toothed comb

What You Do

1. Pour the sand into the box.
2. Place large rocks on one end to look like a mountain range. Arrange one or two flat rocks in the sand to represent islands.
3. "Rake" the sand with a wide-toothed comb to make it look like moving water.
4. Stand back and imagine how this garden might make you feel if *you* were in a place where you were not free to leave. Would it make you feel calm? At peace? Do you think being able to control a small portion of your world might lift your spirits?

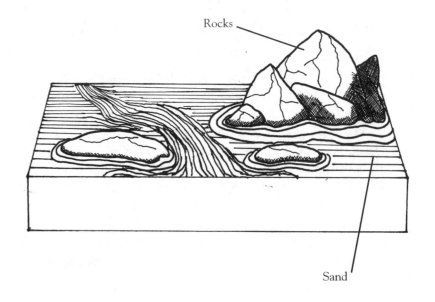

Rocks

Sand

Create Ikebana: A Traditional Japanese Cut Flower Arrangement

Ikebana is a uniquely Japanese art. It began about 1,300 years ago as an offering of worship by Buddhist monks. Japanese Americans created beautiful ikebana arrangements in the relocation camps. Such arrangements are spiritual as well as beautiful—they reminded the Japanese Americans of their connection to the natural world outside the walls of the camps.

An ikebana arrangement uses space and line as part of the composition, making branches and leaves as important as blossoms. The deliberate use of space allows you to see and appreciate a single flower. The bending lines of the branches and leaves give movement or flow to the arrangement. Any type of flower or branch can be used to make ikebana. In the desert relocation camps, people used willow, cattails, and sagebrush.

Let's try making the form of ikebana known as nageire. "Nageire" (nah-geh-ee-reh) means "tossed in flowers." Traditional nageire designs use cut-plant material to hold the branches in place. In this activity we'll use marbles or washed pebbles instead of cut-plant material.

What You Need
Adult supervision required
A tall, thin vase or a tall, thin empty jar
    such as an olive jar
Bag of marbles or washed pebbles
Garden clippers (to cut branches and
    flower stems)
2 branches (any kind)
3 cut flowers with long stems
Water

What You Do
1. Fill the vase about halfway with marbles.
2. Cut the branches so that branch A is a little more than twice as tall as the jar, and branch B is between A and the jar in height.
3. Place branch A into the marbles so that it leans slightly to the left of the center. Cut off any leaves that fall below the rim of the jar.
4. Place branch B into the marbles so that it leans almost straight out to the left. Again, remove any leaves that fall below the rim of the jar.

5. Cut and place the flowers so that they will show in the front and to the right, just above the rim of the jar. Cut off any leaves that fall below the rim.

6. Fill the jar to about an inch from the top with water.

Branch A

Branch B

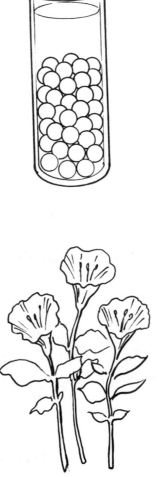

Play Jan, Ken, Pon: The Original Rock, Paper, Scissors Game

Jan, Ken, Pon (jahn, kehn, pohn)—which translates to "Rock, Paper, Scissors"—is a popular game that was brought to Hawaii and the United States with the first immigrants from Japan. Children all over the world play it, often to decide who goes first in another game.

What You Need
2 people

What You Do
1. Two players stand face to face with their hands behind their backs.
2. Together players say, "Jan-ken-pon." Immediately after saying "pon," each player displays one of three hand signals:

    Jan (rock): A clenched fist
    Ken (paper): An open hand
    Pon (scissors): Hold index finger and middle finger straight out, just like a pair of scissors

3. Here's how you determine who's the winner:

Jan (rock) beats pon (scissors) because the rock can make the scissors dull.

Pon (scissors) beats ken (paper) because scissors can cut paper.

Ken (paper) beats jan (rock) because paper can cover the rock.

4. The player who wins is awarded one point.
5. Continue playing until one player scores 10 points.

Jan = Rock   Ken = Paper   Pon = Scissors

Make a Milk-Cap Game

The milk-cap game, sometimes called POG (POG is a trademarked name for a game made by the World POG Federation), originally came from a game called *menko* (mehn-koh) from Japan. Menko is played with decorated pieces of clay, wood, or lead. The first Japanese immigrants brought the game to Hawaii, where they soon replaced the traditional game pieces with the waxed cardboard inserts used to seal milk bottles. In the 1970s the Haleakala Dairy in Hawaii printed "POG" on their milk cap insert to promote a new drink of Passion fruit, Orange, and Guava, which started the POG craze. The game fizzled out after a few years but became popular again in the early 1990s when a Hawaiian schoolteacher introduced the game to her students.

What You Need

1 9-by-12-inch foam sheet, any color
1½-inch circle to trace (such as a small jar lid)
Pen
Scissors
Quarter

What You Do

1. Place the circle on the foam and use the pen to trace it onto the foam. Make about 10 circles for each player.
2. Cut out the circles with the scissors to make your caps.
3. Decorate your caps with Japanese designs such as flowers, kimonos, cranes, fish, and tea cups.
4. Each player takes an equal number of caps, usually between 2 and 10, and adds them, facedown, to one stack.
5. Using a quarter as a "slammer," the first player throws it at the stack. Any caps that land face up then belong to that player.
6. Stack up the remaining caps and let the next player throw their slammer, also collecting caps that land face up. Take turns going around in a circle. Continue to play until every player has had a chance to go first (to potentially gain the most number of caps).
7. The player with the most caps at the end of these rounds wins.

4
Korean Americans

The first wave of immigrants from Korea began to arrive in America in the early 1900s. Korea had been a closed country for 250 years, because their leaders had an *isolationist* policy, meaning that they did not want to have international relationships. The government did not allow any countries other than China to trade with them, because they were afraid that foreigners would bring new ideas and religions that would change Korean culture. As a result, Korea was not able to benefit from many of the technologies and other innovations that the rest of the world had shared.

Foreign invaders such as China, Japan, and Russia saw weakness and began to fight for control of Korea. Finally the Japanese won that fight and invaded Korea in 1904. By 1910, the Japanese had taken complete control of the Korean government. The Japanese tried to wipe out many aspects of Korean culture. They forced citizens to speak Japanese instead of Korean, change their Korean names to Japanese names, and convert to the Japanese native religion of Shinto. They also forbade them to wear traditional Korean clothes. Koreans felt as if they were strangers in their own country.

Koreans also faced famine, along with drought, or lack of rain. Crops withered and died. People had no food to eat or money to spend. Times were hard, and Koreans began to look to America as a way out.

Christian missionaries from the United States had been a powerful influence among the Koreans for many years. More than half of the Koreans who immigrated were Christians. The missionaries had told the Koreans about opportunities to work and live in a free America. The Hawaiian sugar plantations encouraged Koreans to come to work there, promising them 15 dollars a month to work for 60 hours a week, plus free housing and

HARRY KIM (Kim Hyung-soon)

Created the "Fuzzless Peach" Known as the Sun Grand Nectarine

Kim Hyung-soon came to California in 1913, and in 1921 he and a man named Kim Ho formed a partnership they called the Kim Brothers Company. As owners of their own orchards and nurseries, the "Kim Brothers" became an immigrant success story. They went on to make history when Kim Hyung-soon and an employee crossed peaches and plums to come up with a new type of fruit, the Sun Grand nectarine.

medical care. To people who were living in poverty, this seemed like a wonderful opportunity. On January 13, 1903, the SS *Gaelic* arrived in Honolulu, Hawaii, with the first group of Korean immigrants.

As we saw in the last chapter, plantation life was difficult. In addition, the owners of the plantations took advantage of the hostilities between the Koreans and the Japanese and hired groups of each to work together. This was a way to ensure that workers would not unite to go on strike against the owners of the plantations for better wages and working conditions.

In 1905, in order to prevent any more Korean workers from competing for jobs with Japanese immigrants in Hawaii, the Japanese put a sudden stop to Korean emmigration. The only ones allowed to leave were the wives of men already in the United States.

Koreans Move to the Mainland

Koreans, like the Chinese and Japanese before them, faced discrimination and racism in the United States. A series of laws were passed out of fear that Asians would take jobs away from native Americans, including a 1907 law that forbade Koreans and Japanese to immigrate from Hawaii to the mainland, the 1913 Alien Land Law in California (see p. 70), and the Immigration Act of 1924, which shut down immigration from nearly every part of the world to the United States.

Of the few thousand Korean immigrants who reached the mainland of the United States, most of them were men. Despite the discriminatory laws, they were resourceful in establishing themselves in the United States. Some became railroad workers, farmworkers, restaurant workers, fishermen, and domestic workers. Some saved money and purchased farms and businesses, formed cooperative groups through which they combined their savings to lease and own land, and in California avoided the Alien Land Law Act by putting land deeds in the names of their American-born children.

Koreans became barbershop and laundry owners; hotel owners; and restaurant, grocery store, and tobacco shop owners. They found that self-employment eliminated many of the problems of discrimination, such as not being hired, being treated differently than other employees by bosses and coworkers, and not receiving raises and promotions that they had earned.

Dr. Philip Jaisohn (1864–1951)

Korean Pioneer

Philip Jaisohn arrived in the United States in 1885, and became the first Korean to become an American citizen. He also became the first Korean American medical doctor. In 1896 he returned to Korea for two years to help with political reform, and published the first Korean-language newspaper there. Jaisohn helped his adopted country, as well, by becoming an advisor to the U.S. Military Governor of Korea, General John Hodge, after World War II.

The Drive to Educate

Koreans felt that the best hope to achieve a free Korea was through the education of their children. Young Korean Americans were taught that they had an obligation to do well in school so that they might one day take back their homeland. Girls were encouraged as well as boys, and they entered public and private schools. Today Korean American children are still expected to do well in school. A bad report card is seen as a reflection on the family as well as the child.

Say It in Korean

In Korea, there is only one language: Korean! There are several dialects, but they are easily understandable by all Koreans.

Welcome:	*oso oseyo* (oh-soh oh-saeh-yoh)
Hello:	*annyongha-simnikka* (ahn-nyong-hah sim-nik-gah)
Good-bye:	*annyeonghi gaseyo* (ahn-nyong-hee gah-saeh-yoh)
Thank you:	*gamsa hamnida* (gahm-sah hahm-nee-dah)

MICHELLE WIE (1989–)

Korean American Golfer

Michelle Wie was born in Honolulu, Hawaii, and began playing golf with her father when she was four years old. Michelle has won most of the amateur events that she has played in, accompanied by her dad, B. J. Wie, who also served as her caddy. In June 2003, at age 13, Michelle became the youngest golfer to win the Women's Amateur Public Links. Now 6 feet tall, Michelle has been a professional golfer since October 2005.

KOREAN WOMEN IMMIGRANTS

Some Korean men brought their wives and children with them when they immigrated. Others sent for their families after establishing themselves in America. Like the Japanese, Korean men relied on picture brides (see p. 70) as a way to marry without needing to incur the expense of traveling to Korea or the uncertainty of going back to a Japanese-controlled country.

The Korean Independence Movement

In some ways, Koreans straddled two cultures more than immigrants from other countries. Immigrants usually broke into two groups: sojourners, who immigrated to America to work and save enough money to return to their native country, and settlers, who came to stay and make America their new home. For Koreans, however, it was different. They did not feel as if they had a home to go back to. Many became involved in the Korean independence movement and devoted themselves to supporting a Japanese overthrow. On the other hand, they felt obligated to maintain Korean culture here in America, because it was in danger of being destroyed at home.

Make a Korean Flag

The Korean flag became a powerful symbol to Korean Americans. It represented pride in their Korean past and the need to fight current oppression in their homeland, where the flag had been banned in 1910 and replaced with the Japanese flag. Korean American families were proud to fly the American and Korean flags alongside each other in their adopted country. The flags represented their past and their future.

The black markings on the flag represent heaven, earth, fire, and water. The red-and-blue yin-yang symbol represents the balance of opposites, or harmony, and the white represents peace and purity.

What You Need

4-inch circle to trace (such as the plastic
　　cover from a cream cheese tub)
1 sheet 9-by-12-inch red craft foam
Pencil
Scissors
1 sheet 9-by-12-inch white craft foam
1 sheet 9-by-12-inch blue craft foam
Glue
Ruler
1 sheet 9-by-12-inch black craft foam

What You Do

1. With the pencil, trace the circle shape onto the red foam. Cut out.
2. Draw the yin-yang symbol with pencil in the center of the circle-shaped red piece. Cut out the bottom half and set aside. Center the top piece in the middle of the white foam.
3. Use the red piece you set aside to trace a piece of blue foam. Cut the blue foam out, turn it upside down to fit snugly with the red piece, and place on the center of the white foam to form the yin-yang symbol. Glue both pieces down.
4. With the pencil, draw the black bars onto the black foam. Each bar should be about 2½ inches long (in total, including the spaces in the middle of some of them) and ½ inch wide.
5. Cut out and glue down as shown.

Join in Tuho: Arrow Throwing

Tuho (too-hoe) is a traditional game from Korea in which participants take turns throwing arrows into a narrow pot. This was originally an exercise to help warriors hone their skills. Today Korean Americans may learn tuho from their elders or through a cultural center.

What You Need

2 or more players
Masking tape or chalk
Several thin wooden dowels to use as
    arrows, 2 or 3 feet long
Small heavy, narrow wastebasket

What You Do

1. Set the game up by putting masking tape on the floor, or drawing a chalk line if you are outside. This is where you will stand when it's your turn to play. Place the basket 5–10 feet away.
2. Split the total number of players into 2 teams.
3. Determine who goes first by having a representative from each team take turns throwing arrows into the basket. The first team to get an arrow into the basket goes first.
4. One person at a time from each team takes turns throwing arrows into the basket. The team with the most arrows in the basket at the end wins.

Have Fun with Jegi-chagi: Tassel Kicking

I f you have ever played hacky-sack, you will know how to play the traditional Korean game of *jegi-chagi* (jay-ghee chah-ghee). In ancient times the game was designed to help develop skills for the martial arts. Today it is played by Korean Americans because it is fun!

The original game was played with an ancient coin that had a hole in the middle and rice paper. Modern jegi-chagis are colorful, lightweight shuttlecocks similar to what you use to play badminton.

What You Need
1 package metallic shred (looks like tinsel
    or bike tassels, and is sold in stores that
    sell gift-wrapping supplies)
1-inch metal key chain circle

What You Do
1. Tie one or a few pieces of metallic shred at a time onto the key chain. You can tie them at the end or in the middle of the tinsel pieces; it doesn't matter. Keep adding tinsel until you have gone all around the key

chain and can no longer see the metal. Make it very full. It will be like a fluffy ball by the end.
2. To play jegi-chagi, keep one foot on the ground and kick the jegi into the air with the inside of your ankle. See how many times you can kick it back up before it falls to the ground.

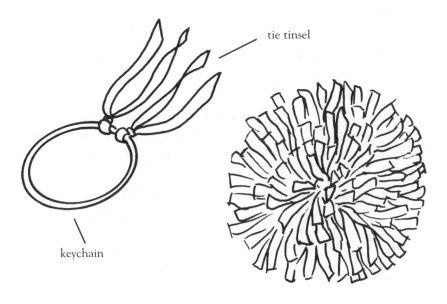

tie tinsel

keychain

Korean Clothing

The traditional clothing of Korea is called the *hanbok* (hahn-bohk). The woman's hanbok has a short jacket called a choguri (choe-gue-ree), which hangs over a wraparound skirt called a chima (chee-mah). The jacket ties into a bow in the front, with two long ribbons that gracefully flow down the front of the skirt.

SARAH CHANG (1980–)
Korean American Violinist

Violinist Sarah Chang was born in Philadelphia to Korean parents, and declared a child prodigy by the time she was in first grade. A *child prodigy* is a young person with extraordinary talents. Sarah began taking violin lessons at age four, and made her debut with the New York Philharmonic Orchestra at only eight years old! Her first album was recorded when she was only nine. Today Sarah is considered to be one of the world's most gifted violinists. She plays with orchestras in the United States, Europe, and Asia, and records music as well. In 1999, she won the highly respected Avery Fisher Prize for her work as a musician.

The man's hanbok has baggy drawstring pants called paji (pah-jee) that tie at the ankles. The jacket falls below the waist and is secured with a tie. Traditional hanbok is all white, but the hanbok for special occasions is very colorful, in solids as well as patterns.

At the turn of the 20th century, Korean boys and girls wore their hair in braids. When a woman got married she would then change her hairstyle by wrapping it into a low bun, secured with a pin. Men in Korea wore braids that they twisted into a knot at the top of their heads—they shaved a space at the top of their heads to allow a place for the braids, and then the braids were twisted into a coil about four inches long. Next a tight-fitting gauze skullcap was placed over the topknot to keep it from moving, and the Korean man's hat, or kat (kaht), designed to hold the topknot, was placed on top. During the Japanese occupation, Koreans were forced to cut their hair.

The first generation of Korean immigrants quickly adapted to American styles of clothing. The only time a hanbok is worn in America now is for holidays and special ceremonies.

Korean Food

Koreans eat with chopsticks, so their food is chopped before cooking. Food prepared in the Korean style is very spicy and flavorful. Koreans use a lot of scallions, red pepper, garlic, and ginger in their cooking. Chicken, fish, tofu, and vegetables are the staple foods, cooked by stir-frying, simmering, or barbecuing. *Pulgogi* (pool-goh-gee) is the most

well-liked Korean dish in America. It is made from barbecued strips of beef.

Traditional Korean American meals always include
kimchi (kim-chee), pickled vegetables (usually cabbage or
radishes) seasoned with hot pepper flakes, garlic, and other
spices. Rice is served at every meal, too, and usually soup
as well.

Food is placed in the middle of the table and everyone
reaches to take a portion. It is considered more polite to
reach than to bother someone to pass it to you.

Kimchi

Kimchi became popular in Korea because it was a way to
preserve vegetables before there was reliable electricity and
refrigeration. Women would gather the harvest of vegetables
in the late fall and make large batches of kimchi. Vegetables
such as cabbages, radishes, and green onions were soaked in
salted water and then combined with spices such as red pepper, garlic, and ginger root. The result was stored in big,
brown earthenware pots in the ground, with just the cover
sticking out. Placing the pots in the ground kept them cool
and protected the vegetables from rain, snow, and heat. The
clay pots allow air to circulate, keeping the kimchi fresh for
a long period of time.

Today kimchi can be bought in Asian grocery stores,
natural food stores, and supermarkets with ethnic food sections. It is a side dish that is served at every meal, even
breakfast!

HERBERT CHOY (1916–2004)
Appointed to the U.S. Court of Appeals

Senior Circuit Judge Herbert Choy was born in Makaweli, Hawaii, to poor sugar plantation workers from Korea. He worked his way through law school at Harvard to eventually become the first Korean American attorney to practice in the United States. In 1971, Judge Herbert Choy became the first Asian American federal judge, and he was the first Asian American judge to represent Hawaii on the U.S. Ninth Circuit Court of Appeals.

Korean Americans and World War II

World War II was a difficult time to be a Korean American.
When the Japanese attacked Pearl Harbor in December
1941 and the United States declared war on Japan (see p.
95), Americans became suspicious about the loyalties not
only of Japanese Americans, but also of Korean Americans,
because technically their homeland was under Japanese
occupation and therefore they were considered Japanese
subjects. Korean Americans who worked in defense plants
were forced to wear badges that classified them as Japanese.

After protests, workers were allowed to add "I am Korean" to the badges.

In spite of the long-standing hostilities between their native countries, many Korean Americans had lived and worked alongside Japanese Americans long enough to realize that they were no more a threat to America than Korean Americans.

Korean Americans were hearty supporters of the United States war effort. They bought U.S. War Bonds by the thousands, signed up for the armed services, and offered their skills in reading and writing Japanese to American military intelligence. A total of 109 Korean Americans joined the California National Guard. They formed an all-Korean unit known as the *Tiger Brigade*. (The tiger is the national symbol of Korea.)

Korea was finally liberated from Japanese occupation by the United States and the Soviet Union at the end of the war, but it now had another problem. The United States wanted Korea to be democratic, and the Soviet Union wanted it to be a Communist country. The solution was to temporarily split the country into North and South Korea, with the North supported by Communist nations and the South by the United States. In 1948, the United Nations planned elections so that the citizens of both North and South Korea could elect a leader together. North Korea refused to participate, so elections were held only in South Korea, where Rhee Syngman was elected president.

The Korean War

In 1950 the Communist leader of North Korea, Kim Il-Sung, invaded South Korea, and the country went to war against itself, much like the North and South had in the American Civil War. The United States sent troops with the United Nations to support South Korea, and the Communist People's Republic of China provided defense for North Korea. In 1953, a ceasefire was called and Korea was permanently divided into two countries. The Democratic People's Republic of Korea (North Korea) was a Communist country, tightly controlled by a one-party system, and the

MARGARET CHO (1968–)
Korean American Comedian

Margaret Cho grew up in San Francisco, the daughter of Korean parents. She developed a comedy routine based on her personal experiences growing up as an Asian American woman in the United States. In 1994 she won the American Comedy Award for Best Comedian. She was the first Asian American to have her own television show, *All-American Girl*.

CHAN HO PARK (1973–)

First Korean American Major League Baseball Player

In 1994, Chan Ho Park became the first Korean American to play Major League Baseball when he became a pitcher for the Los Angeles Dodgers. Born in Kong Ju City, South Korea, Park became the first South Korean to reach 100 career wins in the majors on June 4, 2005, while playing for the Texas Rangers. He was traded in 2005 to the San Diego Padres.

Republic of Korea (South Korea) was a democratic republic with elected officials, similar to the United States. The division persists to this day.

During the Korean War, Korean Americans were not subjected to the same type of national discrimination that they and the Japanese had faced during World War II, because the Americans were on the same side as the (South) Koreans. In addition, the United States was never directly attacked by Korea as it had been by the Japanese in World War II.

Small Business Owners

Korean Americans today are more likely than any other ethnic group to be self employed or to work for a family-owned business. Korean professionals with degrees in such areas as medicine, law, and business often have difficulty with the English language and getting the licenses required for some professions in the United States, and so they turn to self-employment. They buy businesses in affordable neighborhoods, which are sometimes poor and run-down, and establish greengroceries (fruit and vegetable stores), grocery stores, dry cleaning shops, and gas stations. Businesses such as these can be run without complete knowledge of English, but the danger in running businesses in poor urban neighborhoods are significant, including an increased chance of robbery or crime-related death.

The Los Angeles Riots of 1992

On April 29, 1992, four police officers in the city of Los Angeles were found not guilty in a case in which they were accused of beating a black motorist named Rodney King. Although the beating was captured on videotape, the officers were not convicted. This set off a wave of riots in the poor, mostly black and Latino communities of South Central Los Angeles, where residents felt that justice had not been served. Many of the businesses in these neighborhoods were owned by Koreans.

After three days of rioting including looting (stealing), arson (intentionally setting fires), and murder, more than 3,000 businesses were ruined, hundreds were injured, and at least 58 people were killed. Out of the more than 3,000 damaged businesses, more than 2,000 were Korean owned.

Some believe that Korean businesses were targeted because of racial tension between Koreans and their black and Latino neighbors. The neighborhood people felt as if the Koreans should be friendlier and hire people from the community. Koreans generally employ only family members and are culturally more reserved and less sociable with their customers than other Americans. These cultural differences may have contributed to why Korean businesses were singled out.

Role of Christianity

The Christian church plays a big part in Korean American life. Church is a place to relax and socialize with other Korean Americans. Churches sponsor sporting events, dinners, Sunday school for kids, and special events. The church service itself starts about noon on Sunday and may be followed by a dinner of Korean food. The people then break up into groups for different activities such as Bible study in Korean, or Korean arts and crafts for the kids. Church for traditional Korean American families may last up to five hours or more.

War Brides

Thousands of Korean *war brides* (wives of U.S. servicemen) came to the United States after the Korean War ended, under the War Bride Act that was passed in 1945, and later

under the McCarran-Walter Immigration Act of 1952, which allowed Asians to immigrate in small numbers and become American citizens. These acts allowed American servicemen, who had been stationed all over the world during World War II and the Korean War, to bring their foreign-born wives home to America. Prior to this, even the foreign wives of American servicemen were banned from entering the country under the Immigration Act of 1924.

EUGENE CHUNG (1969–)

First Asian American Chosen in the First Round of the National Football League Draft

Born in Virginia, Eugene Chung made history in 1992, when he was chosen by the New England Patriots to play for them in the first round of the NFL draft. He was drafted from Virginia Tech to be an offensive lineman. He went on to play for the Jacksonville Jaguars, the Indianapolis Colts, and the Kansas City Chiefs. Chung retired from football in 1999.

The Great Wave of Korean Immigration

The passing of the Immigration Act of 1965 (see p. 20) led to an enormous increase in Korean immigration. Many war brides helped their parents and siblings immigrate to America, which led to a type of chain immigration, each group settling in before helping the next group over. Other Koreans immigrated because of the need for medical professionals in the United States in the 1960s. Thousands of Korean students immigrated to the United States to attend college and many have stayed.

A great portion of the last wave of immigrants settled on the West Coast, especially in the Los Angeles area of California, but there are Koreans living in large cities and small towns all across America.

Korean Adoptees

The Korean War left thousands of babies behind. Some had parents who had died and others were the abandoned children of Korean mothers and U.S. servicemen. When Harry and Bertha Holt, an Oregon couple with six children of their own, heard about how Korean babies were being abandoned after the Korean War, they wanted to do something to help. Bertha Holt went before Congress and lobbied for what became known as the Holt Bill, which allowed Americans to adopt international children. In 1955 they adopted eight Korean orphans and flew them to their home in Oregon. Soon afterward, the Holts established an international adoption center, Holt International Children's Services.

An amazing wave of transracial adoption between the United States and Korea followed. American families from Maine to California began opening their homes to Korean orphans. Eventually between 150,000 and 200,000 Korean children were adopted in the United States, Europe, and other parts of the world. Holt International Children's Services is still in operation today.

TOL: A UNIQUE BIRTHDAY CELEBRATION

Korean babies are considered to be one year old at birth. This is the traditional Korean way to calculate age. One year later, their birthday is celebrated in a fun tradition known as *tol* (tole). The tol celebration is one that many American parents enjoy giving their adopted Korean babies. Friends and family come bearing gifts for the child's future such as jewelry and money. Traditional foods served include fruit to symbolize the prosperity of the child's children and grandchildren in the future, and rice cakes, to symbolize the child's pure spirit.

The baby is dressed in traditional clothes and put in front of a table with an assortment of symbolic objects on it, such as rice or money to represent wealth, a pen or book for scholarly pursuits, yarn or thread for long life, and an arrow for a career in the military. Korean tradition says that whatever the baby picks up first predicts his or her future.

Set Up a Tol: A Fortune-Telling Birthday Party

On your next birthday, have a tol-style celebration. In advance, set up a table with symbols of things you might like to see in your future. Some choices include a toy airplane to represent future travel or a ball to symbolize success in sports. You can also include career symbols: a pen for a future writer, a tie for a businessman, or a first aid kit for a doctor.

What You Need

3 or more people
Symbolic items (see suggestions above)
Traditional Korean tol foods, such as rice
    cakes and fruit
Blindfold

What You Do

1. Set the table with rice cakes, fruit, and symbolic items.
2. Sit at the table and ask someone to tie a blindfold over your eyes.
3. Another person should mix up the symbolic items.
4. Choose two items without looking. Take off the blindfold and see what you chose. Do these objects symbolize things that you would like to pursue?
5. Invite other guests to pick symbolic items.
6. Enjoy the treats and this shared celebration with friends!

Korean Schools, Cultural Centers, and Camps

With each generation, Korean Americans become more Americanized and less connected to Korean culture and tradition. Attending Korean schools, cultural centers, and camps is an important way for children to learn about their Korean heritage. These programs offer classes, workshops, and overnight camps to expose children to Korean language, arts and crafts, martial arts, games, music, and more.

Such programs are especially important to the American families of Korean adoptees. Customs and traditions that a person grows up with usually reflect the background of his or her family. For families who are not familiar with the cultural traditions of their adopted child's birthplace, this can be an enriching experience.

Most of the children have no memory of having been in Korea. In culture camps they enjoy the opportunity to meet other Korean American adoptees and share their experiences of growing up Korean in a non-Korean family.

Koreatowns: Korean American Communities

Unlike the earlier Chinatowns and Japantowns, Koreatowns did not really emerge until after the largest wave of immigration to the United States in the 1960s and 1970s. Until then, Koreans did not live in great enough concentrations in specific cities for such a community to evolve.

SAMMY LEE (1920–)

First Korean American Olympic Medalist

Dr. Sammy Lee grew up in Fresno, California, the son of Korean parents. Dr. Lee set early goals for himself: to be a top diver and a doctor. Dr. Lee achieved both. In 1948 he won the Summer Olympics championship for platform (high) diving, and he returned four years later to win it again.

Dr. Lee continues to be a role model for young athletes, acting as an Olympic advisor and coach. In 1984 he carried the Olympic Torch; he was inducted into the Olympic Hall of Fame in 1990.

A Koreatown is usually a small area—a strip of businesses or a few streets—where Korean Americans can find Korean restaurants, Korean grocery stores and greengroceries, karaoke bars, and gift shops that feature Korean and other Asian goods. Today you can find Koreatowns in Chicago; Los Angeles; Manhattan; Annandale, Virginia; San Diego; Atlanta; Dallas; Oakland; and Bergen County, New Jersey.

Try a Front Kick in Taekwondo

Taekwondo (tie-kwahn-doe) is Korea's martial art. It uses the whole body but in particular the hands and feet. The skills involved in mastering taekwondo take many years. Through the different forms, one is expected to develop character, as well as physical and mental discipline.

The art of taekwondo is thought to have evolved from religious ceremonies that were performed when the nation was made up of tribal states. The Korean Taekwondo Association was founded in 1961. Taekwondo became an official Olympic sport in the 2000 Australian games.

The front kick or ap chagi (ahp chah-ghee) is one of the first kicks learned in taekwondo.

What You Need

Comfortable clothes

An open area

What You Do

1. Warm up by running in place for 5 minutes.
2. Stand with your feet shoulder-width apart.
3. Pull your arms close to your body, bend your elbows, make your hands into fists, and hold them in front of you.
4. Step forward on one leg and bend your front knee. Keep your back leg straight.
5. Bring your back leg forward and lift it high, so that the top half of your leg will be straight in front of you, and the half below the knee hangs down.
6. Quickly kick your leg straight out to the front. Pretend you are hitting something with the ball of your foot. Pull your toes back so that they are pointing upward. This is to prevent your foot from being hurt in a real competition.
7. Snap your leg back to the hanging position.

Create a Colorful Pojagi: Korean Wrapping Cloth

S omething you might find in a Korean American home is a pojagi wrap. Pojagi wraps are used to wrap presents, carry things, and store things. *Pojagi* (poe-jah-ghee), or *po* (poe) for short, is a traditional patchwork craft that is useful as well as artistic. Scraps of fabric that might have gone to waste are sewn into beautiful reusable cloth wraps.

There are special types of pojagis for different occasions. Some are very formal, such as wedding or religious pojagis, and others have uses as ordinary as being a holder for socks. Traditionally when a Korean daughter was married the family would shower her with homemade pojagis to start her new life.

In our pojagi we will glue the scraps instead of sewing them.

What You Need
1 solid-colored bandanna (without the black ink patterns bandannas sometimes have, available in craft stores)

3 bright colors fabric, ½ yard each
Ruler
Pen
Pinking shears (available in sewing and craft stores)
Tube of fabric glue (available in sewing and craft stores)
Paper towels
Wide ribbon or seam binding (available in sewing and craft stores)
Sewing needle and thread

What You Do
1. Lay the bandanna out flat. This will be the backing that you glue squares of material to.
2. Using the pen and ruler, draw several 3-by-3-inch squares on the back side of the colorful fabric. Make about 20 for each color.
3. Cut out each square, using pinking shears to prevent fabric from unraveling after it's cut.

4. Spread glue around the edges of each square on the back side of the fabric. Do not put any glue in the center of the square.

5. Place the square, glue side down, on the bandanna and press around the edges with your fingers. Use a paper towel to blot away any excess glue. The squares can overlap slightly. Alternate the colors of the squares, so that no two squares of the same color are next to each other.

6. Let dry for several hours or overnight.

7. Use the thread and needle to sew a ribbon or piece of seam binding in the middle of two sides of the bandanna as shown.

You can use your pojaji to wrap a special present. Place the present in the middle of the pojaji, (on the plain side) with the ties to the left and right of the present. Wrap the top of the pojaji down over the present and then pull the bottom of the pojaji up and over to overlap. Pull the left and right sides over the top and tie.

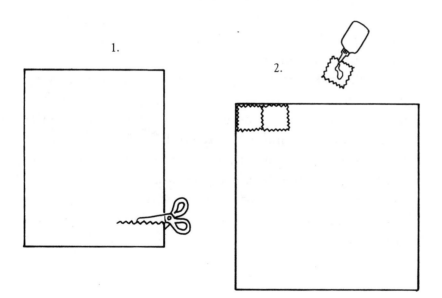

1.

2.

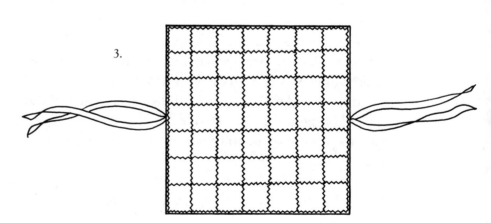

3.

LEONARD CHANG (?–)

Korean American Novelist

Born in New York, Leonard Chang writes novels about the racial conflicts of life in America. He has a successful series of books featuring a Korean American detective. He has won several writing awards.

Seol: Lunar New Year

In a traditional Korean American family, *Seol*, or Korean New Year, is celebrated on the first new moon of the year, which is either at the end of January or at the beginning of February. Many Korean American families celebrate the American New Year on January 1 as well.

In the days leading up to Seol, Koreans clean out the old and bring in the new. Houses are cleaned, debts are paid, food is prepared, and traditional clothes are made ready to wear.

Participants begin New Year's Day by paying respect to their elders and ancestors. In a traditional Korean family this includes offerings of food and incense and ceremonial bowing in honor of relatives who have died. Children also bow to parents and grandparents, as well as older brothers and sisters. In return they receive money, which the children tuck into a good luck purse called a *jumoni* (juu-moe-nee) (see p. 126).

The first thing eaten on New Year's Day is *ttok-kuk* (toke-kuke), a rice cake soup (see recipe on p. 125). Traditionally in Korea, people did not celebrate their individual birthdays but observed them together on New Year's Day. They would say that after eating ttok-kuk soup on that day, you are one year older. Other New Year's foods include a pancake called pindaettok (peen-day-toke), made from mung beans, dumplings, rice, and a special noodle dish made with meat and vegetables.

Traditional Korean games played on New Year's Day include kite-flying, which is supposed to release bad luck before the new year begins, and the board game *yut* (yoot), which involves tossing sticks (see p. 127). In old Korea, there was a see-saw game that only girls played. It allowed girls to pop into the air and see the world beyond their gated homes—once a year! Nowadays the game is played by boys and girls in Korea, and sometimes played in the United States.

Prepare Ttok-kuk Soup

Ttok-kuk soup is a velvety, thick soup made with chewy rice cakes. Years ago it was only served on Korean New Year, but now it is enjoyed year round.

What You Need

Adult supervision required

4 cups frozen rice cake sticks (available in
    Asian food stores)
Knife
Cutting board
Large bowl
4 stalks green onion
2 teaspoons chopped garlic
½ pound skirt steak
Large pan
2 tablespoons vegetable oil
Salt
Pepper
Optional: garlic powder
Optional: onion powder
Stirring spoon
4 cups beef broth
2 cups water
½ teaspoon sesame oil (available in most grocery
    stories in the ethnic foods section)

What You Do

1. Thaw the rice cake sticks in the refrigerator for a day.
2. If the rice cake sticks did not come presliced, cut them into nickel-size slices. Place in a bowl and cover with cold water. Leave for 30 minutes to allow rice cake to soften.
3. Cut green onions into small pieces and set aside with the garlic.
4. Slice the steak into small bite-size strips.
5. Pour oil into the pan and fry the steak on medium heat. Sprinkle with salt and pepper, and optionally garlic powder and onion powder. Stir until cooked through, about 5–7 minutes.
6. Remove steak from pan.
7. Pour the beef broth and water into the pan. Add the chopped garlic and half the green onions and bring to a boil.
8. Add the rice cakes and steak. Simmer for 10 minutes, or until rice cakes are chewy.
9. Add sesame oil and serve. Sprinkle a few green onions over each bowl.

Make a Jumoni: Good Luck Bag

On New Year's Day, children bow to their elders and receive money that they tuck into a jumoni.

What You Need
8-inch round plate
1 piece 9-by-12-inch red felt
Pen
Scissors
Hole puncher
Ruler
1 round shoelace, 22 inches long

What You Do
1. Lay the plate upside down in the middle of the felt, and trace it with the pen.
2. Cut the circle out with scissors.
3. Punch holes 1 inch down from the edges and about 2 inches apart, all around the circle of felt as shown. This will make a hole in the felt, but the piece will not fall out like they do with paper.
4. Thread the shoelace from outside to inside, inside to outside, back and forth until you have it through all the holes and the lace ends are outside.
5. Pull the end of the laces together as a drawstring to squeeze the pocketbook together.
6. Tie.

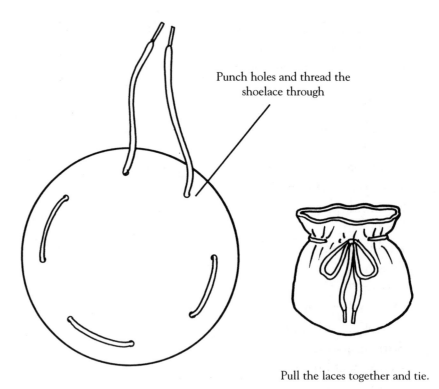

Punch holes and thread the shoelace through

Pull the laces together and tie.

Enjoy Yut: A Game Played with Sticks

Yut is a popular game played by Korean Americans. Young children as well as grandparents join in the fun. The traditional yut game is played with a stick that is round on one side and flat on the other. We will make our game with craft sticks and foam.

What You Need
4 craft sticks (popsicle sticks)
1 sheet brown foam
Pencil
Scissors
Glue
1 piece posterboard
Thick black marker

What You Do
1. Place a craft stick on the foam and trace around it with the pencil to make 8 shapes.
2. Cut out the foam shapes.
3. Glue 2 foam shapes to the same side of each craft stick to make yut sticks.
4. Draw the game board on the posterboard with marker as shown. Do not draw the arrows.

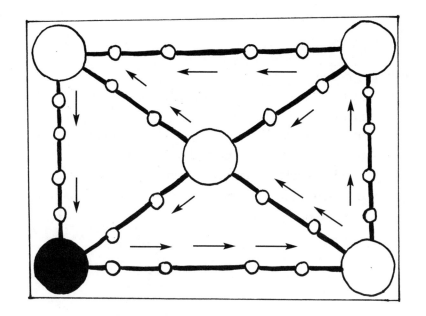

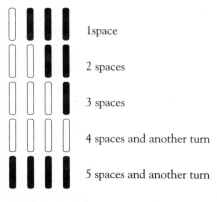

1 space

2 spaces

3 spaces

4 spaces and another turn

5 spaces and another turn

127

Play Yut

What You Need
2 players or 2 teams
Blanket
Game board
8 place markers, 4 for each player or team
(objects to use as markers include:
nickels and pennies, 2 colors of poker
chips, red and black checkers)
4 yut sticks

What You Do
1. Lay the blanket on the floor. Lay the game board next to it.
2. Put all your markers on the game board next to the home space, the one that is blackened in.
3. Hold the sticks in your hand with the foam side up. Toss them high into the air so that they will land on the blanket.
4. To score: The craft stick side is called the flat side, and the foam side is called the round side. Each combination has a Korean term for it:
    1 flat side up = *do* (pig): 1 space
    2 flat sides up = *gae* (dog): 2 spaces
    3 flat sides up = *geol* (sheep): 3 spaces
    4 flat sides up = *yut* (ox): 4 spaces and another turn
    4 round sides up = *mo* (horse): 5 spaces and another turn
5. Count your points and move one of your markers that many spaces around the game board. You can move the same marker every time or start another marker. All of your markers must make it around the board (follow the arrows) to win. If you land on your opponent's space, he must go back to the beginning. If you land on your own space, then the 2 markers may move together. If you land on one of the two corner circles on the right side of the board, you can take a shortcut through the middle.
6. The first team to get all their markers around the board wins.

Construct a Korean Kite

Kites are traditionally flown on Seol as part of the New Year's festivities. Korean kites have a hole in the middle that makes them easier to fly. The hole makes the kite aerodynamic, which means it allows the air to flow over it quickly.

Sometimes kite flyers engage each other in kite-flying fights, as they have done for hundreds of years. They sharpen the strings on their kites with powdered glass, and the object of the game is to cut the strings on the other players' kites. The last one flying is the winner!

What You Need

1 piece 12-by-18-inch manila paper (rice paper is
    traditionally used, but it may be difficult to find in craft
    and stationary stores)
Bowl or round object to trace for center circle
Pencil
Scissors
Red, yellow, black, and green markers or crayons
10 straws
Clear packing tape
Kite string

What You Do

1. Fold the paper into quarters.
2. Open and trace your circle over the middle of the paper as shown.
3. Cut out the circle.
4. Color the kite in traditional Korean colors as shown.
5. Tape down the middle straw that goes over the circle in line 1.
6. Tape down the middle straw that goes over the circle in line 2.
7. Repeat for lines 3 and 4.
8. Because each straw is not long enough to reach the end of the kite, you need to cut and tape extra straws and straw pieces to fill in the lines as shown in the diagram. Do it by eye, it's not necessary to measure.
9. Tie kite string to the 2 bottom corners of the kite. Secure with a strip of tape.
10. Fly it!

see diagram on next page

129

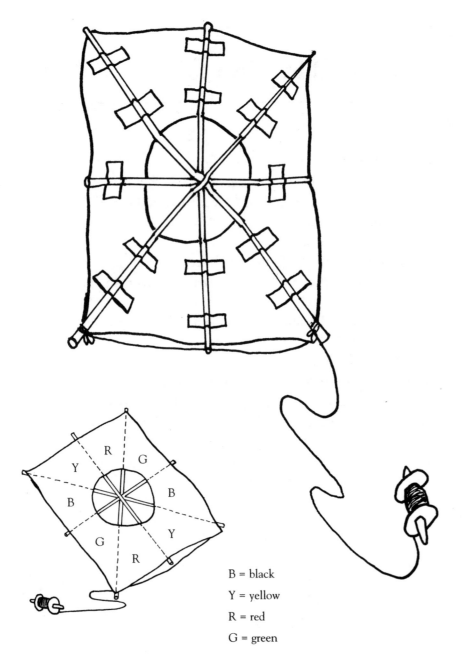

B = black
Y = yellow
R = red
G = green

Korea Today

The Korean peninsula is a mountainous region that borders China and Russia to the north and is surrounded by water to the south. Korea's history goes back 5,000 years. There is very little intermarriage among other ethnic groups, so the people are almost 100 percent Korean.

North Korea (The Democratic People's Republic of Korea)

North Korea is a restrictive Communist country, with one "leader for life," Kim Jong-Il. North Korea spends most of its resources on building an enormous military. Thousands of people have died of famine in North Korea, and everything from telephones to television to the Internet is controlled by the government. There is concern in the U.S. government and other countries of the world that North Korea may be making nuclear weapons. In the summer of 2006, North Korea test-fired several types of long and short-range missiles.

North Koreans have made an effort to try to preserve traditional folk arts, crafts, music, and theater.

South Korea (The Republic of Korea)

South Korea is a democratic republic, with free elections. It is a true success story, having built itself into one of the world's strongest economies after the Korean War. South Korea manufactures steel, automobiles, ships, computers, and more. They are one of the world's top rice-growing nations, despite the fact that only 30 percent of the land is fertile enough to farm.

In 1988, Seoul, South Korea, hosted the Summer Olympic Games, and in recent years the country has become a popular tourist destination as well.

It Started in Korea

Celadon ceramics are a treasure from Korea. Korean potters created this unique creamy green glazed pottery more than 750 years ago. Preserved pieces such as teapots, bowls, and figures of animals have been found in royal tombs and are displayed in museums to allow us to enjoy this ancient art today. Koreans also invented the first self-chiming water clock, which dates back to the 1400s.

Koreans have folk dances that are hundreds of years old. They were revived and encouraged after the end of the Japanese occupation, during which Korean dance had been forbidden. These folk dances include the farmers' dance, various mask dances, and the fan dance.

There are 60 traditional Korean instruments. The most representative of Korean music is the gayageum. With 12 strings, it is played like a sideways harp on the floor.

Americans are familiar with products made by two very successful Korean companies: Samsung, which makes everything from telephones to dishwashers to computers, and Hyundai, the automobile manufacturer.

HANGUL

Hangul (hahn-gool) is a scientific alphabet that was created in Korea under King Sejong in the year 1446. King Sejong was a wise and intelligent leader who commissioned a group of scholars to come up with an easy-to-learn alphabet for the Korean language. The consonants were designed to resemble the position of the lips, tongue, or mouth when pronouncing them. It is divided into syllables that suit the Korean language perfectly. Before that, Koreans used Chinese characters, which did not quite fit with the Korean language and took years to learn. Until hangul was created, most Koreans had no way to communicate other than through talking.

Hangul is unique because it is based on human sounds. It has 10 vowels and 14 consonants. Korean words are written in blocks, with each block representing a syllable made up of letters.

5
Filipino Americans

Did you know that Filipinos may have been the first Asians to settle in America? These first Filipino immigrants were called *Manilamen*, after the city of Manila in the Philippines. In the 1700s, the Spanish forced Filipinos to serve as slaves aboard Spanish ships called galleons. These ships were used for trade between the Philippines and another Spanish colony, Mexico. By 1763, desperate Filipino sailors began to jump ship and make their way north, where they settled, undetected, into the marshlands of the Louisiana Territory.

The Manilamen survived by building houses on stilts in the wet land and fishing for food. They set up self-governing, peaceful communities. These Filipino fishermen introduced the process of shrimp drying to Louisiana in the early 1800s.

A History Intertwined: The Philippines and the United States

The Philippines is a series of more than 7,107 islands that stretch between Taiwan and Indonesia in the Pacific Ocean. The majority of the Filipino population live on just 11 of the thousands of islands. Many islands are completely uninhabited. The weather is tropical—warm and humid.

Thousands of years ago, during the Ice Age, the islands were connected to Asia by land bridges. The first inhabitants of the Philippines, the *Ati*, traveled there over the land bridges seeking food. Then the ice caps melted and the land became surrounded by water.

Over the years of its history, many different ethnic groups have explored or settled in the Philippines.

They include Indonesians, Chinese, Arabs from the Middle East, Spanish, Portuguese, and Americans. More than 70 different languages are spoken in the Philippines, including Spanish and English. The primary language is called *Filipino*. Any person from the Philippines can be called *Filipino* as well, and Filipino women are sometimes called *Filipinas*.

Spanish explorers colonized the Philippines in 1565, and ruled the people with an iron fist for more than 300 years. The colony was named after the Spanish king, Philip II. In 1898, when the United States was at war with Spain, Filipinos joined in the fight and together they drove the Spanish out of the Philippines. The Filipinos wanted an independent country, but the United States resisted and fought the Filipino independence seekers for control. After a bitter battle, the United States took over the Philippines as a territory of the United States.

The Americans had a profound influence on the Philippines. They brought needed medicine and vaccines, built roads and railroads, and established schools. American teachers taught the schoolchildren the English language and American history, and encouraged students to travel to the United States for better opportunities.

Because the early Filipino immigrants were citizens of an American territory, instead of a foreign country, they were labeled "American nationals" and allowed to immigrate freely. Being nationals instead of aliens gave Filipinos freedom from immigration restrictions that had been placed on other Asian groups, but they were not American citizens and could not vote.

PHILIP VERA CRUZ (1904–1994)
Led the 1965 Filipino Farmworker's Strike

For more than 30 years, Philip Vera Cruz, a native of the Philippines, worked in manual-labor positions on farms, in canneries, and in restaurants. In the 1950s, Cruz began to organize small groups of farmworkers in California to protest low wages, poor working conditions, and discrimination. In September 1965, Cruz and other Filipino labor leaders led a successful strike against grape growers in Delano, California. He joined forces with the famous Mexican labor leader Cesar Chavez and formed the powerful United Farm Workers Union.

During World War II, the Philippines was occupied by Japan. It wasn't until 1946 that Filipinos finally won their independence.

Filipinos Leave for Hawaiian Sugar Plantations

The Filipinos, like the Chinese, Japanese, and Koreans before them, were lured to work on Hawaii's sugar plantations by the promises of wealth. Recruiters came to the

Philippines and showed movies of Hawaii as a land of golden opportunity. Filipinos joined the other Asian groups in the long hours and hard work on the plantations.

Pensionados

Pensionados were Filipino immigrants who came to the United States through an American sponsorship (meaning the government paid their expenses) to be educated. The American government in the Philippines wanted to prepare future Filipinos to take over their own government. They believed that an American education would be the best foundation for these future leaders. The first group of 100 pensionados arrived in 1903, mostly sons and daughters of wealthy Filipinos. Most of the pensionados graduated from American colleges and brought their skills and education back to the Philippines, but some stayed to follow better prospects in the United States.

After the pensionado program ended, thousands of Filipino students continued to immigrate to the United States to attend college and work. This route proved to be much more difficult. They worked all day to save enough money to be able to attend school at night. They usually took jobs that involved manual labor; they worked as bellboys, janitors, busboys, and the like. Many gave up school altogether and stayed to work in low-level jobs.

Migrant Farmworkers

Between 1906 and 1934, a large number of Filipinos immigrated to the United States to pick crops in the West. Many

WATSONVILLE ATTACKS

A terrible incident happened in December 1929 in Watsonville, California. The police arrested a Filipino man because he was seen with a young white woman. The woman's mother explained to the police that the couple were together with her blessing, and that they were planning to get married. The police released the man. Soon afterward the newspaper published a picture of the couple. It unleashed a fury from white citizens, newspaper writers, and community leaders who didn't want the races to mix.

The verbal attacks soon gave way to physical violence. A group of 400 white men attacked a Filipino dance club. Similar incidents of beatings and fights continued for four days, and eventually one man was murdered. Afterward, the attacks were blamed on the Filipinos.

This type of concern about the "mixing of the races" led to more racial confrontations, especially when jobs became scarce during the 1930s. Native-born Americans began to blame Filipinos for taking over "American" jobs. This hysteria led to a call for politicians to change the laws, in order to stop the flow of Filipinos into the country.

arrived after the Immigration Act of 1924 forbade people from other Asian nations to immigrate. American employers needed Filipino workers to fill openings left by the Chinese, Japanese, and Koreans.

Farmwork was backbreaking labor; workers had to bend over and pick asparagus, lettuce, and tomato crops for long hours at low wages. They lived in shacks and were treated poorly.

Alaskeros

Filipinos first immigrated to Alaska in the 1850s, as workers on whaling ships. Later other Filipinos worked in Alaskan gold mines or were involved in laying underwater cable from Seattle, Washington, to Juneau, Alaska.

In 1909, Alaskan salmon canneries recruited hundreds of Filipinos to work in their plants. The workers called themselves *Alaskeros*. Many were students who came for the spring and summer season and went back to school in the fall; others were migrant farmworkers. The cannery work was hard and the hours were long. The jobs ranged from setting up boxes for shipping, to hosing down the fish, to cutting and sorting them, to filling the cans.

World War II and the Fighting Filipinos

World War II brought a change in American attitudes toward the Filipinos. Instead of seeing them as foreigners who were here to work, they began to see them as noble partners in the American-Filipino fight against the Japanese.

TYDINGS-MCDUFFIE INDEPENDENCE ACT OF 1934:
A Law to Keep the Filipinos Out

Responding to concerns by native-born Americans, Congress passed this law to eliminate the free immigration status of Filipino Americans. The law called for a 10-year preparation period for Filipinos to set up an independent government based on the American model. If the Philippines became a separate country instead of a territory of the United States, then Filipinos would be aliens (see p. 70) and not American nationals.

Because previous laws prevented most aliens from immigrating to America, it essentially put an end to Filipino immigration. The act also prohibited Filipino immigrants from bringing their wives and families to the United States. As a small compensation, the government offered to pay the costs involved in returning to the Philippines, but few Filipino Americans did.

In December 1941, only seven hours after the Japanese bombed the United States Naval Base at Pearl Harbor (see p. 95), Japan invaded the Philippines. Stories reached the United States about Filipinos and Americans fighting side by side in heroic battles. Many Filipino men living in the United States immediately lined up to enlist in the U.S. military, eager to both prove their allegiance to their adopted home and to fight for their homeland. They were shocked to be told that they couldn't serve because they were not American citizens. President Franklin Roosevelt reacted quickly, changing the law to allow Filipinos to fight for the United States and the Philippines.

In 1942, more than 7,000 Filipinos signed up for the First Filipino Infantry Regiment and the Second Filipino Infantry Regiment. (Segregation laws prohibited Filipinos from serving in the same units as Caucasian Americans.) Filipino soldiers were able to fight behind enemy lines, because they could easily blend in with the locals. They destroyed Japanese communications and worked to sabotage Japanese war plans.

All Filipino soldiers, as members of the U.S. Armed Forces, were allowed to become American citizens. On February 20, 1943, 1,200 proud Filipino soldiers became American citizens at Camp Beale in northern California.

When the war was over, laws were changed to allow all Filipino immigrants to become citizens.

Little Manila: Stockton, California

The largest ethnic community of Filipinos to live in one area outside of the Philippines was Little Manila in Stockton, California. From the 1920s to the 1970s it was a busy,

ARMY SGT. JOSE CALUGAS (1907–1999): Awarded the Medal of Honor in World War II

On January 16, 1942, a battle was raging in the Bataan province of the Philippines. A gun battery, which is a place where several large guns are set up for defense, was being bombarded with enemy Japanese explosives. The blasting and shelling went on until all the crew members were killed or wounded and the gun battery was put out of commission. Without orders, Sgt. Calugas left his own battery, and put himself in grave danger by running 1,000 yards across a "shell swept" area to the gun battery. Together, he and a volunteer squad fixed the gun and put it back into service. For his efforts Sgt. Jose Calugas was awarded the Medal of Honor.

thriving center of Filipino culture. It was a comforting place for Filipino immigrants, who were mostly bachelors, to shop, dine out, and seek entertainment. Grocery stores sold familiar foods such as sardines, noodles, coconut milk, dried fish, and salted duck eggs. Restaurants served up home-style meals of fish, rice, and tea. There were pool halls, gambling houses, dance halls, barbershops, tailor shops, dry cleaning shops, and clothing shops.

Unlike the Chinese and Japanese who lived and worked in Chinatown or Japantown, many of the Filipinos who visited Little Manila were only passing through. Their jobs as farmworkers, cannery workers, and service people required frequent travel. As a result only a few of the businesses other than restaurants and dry cleaning shops were Filipino owned.

In the 1970s many factors contributed to the demise of Little Manila. Filipinos who had earned enough money moved into the suburbs, freeways were built, and old buildings were torn down to make room for urban development. A group called the Little Manila Foundation, founded in 2001, is working hard to preserve what is left of the historic Little Manila area of Stockton and educate the public about the history of the Filipino American community.

VICTORIA MANALO DRAVES
(1924–): Olympic Diver

Victoria Manalo Draves was born in San Francisco to an English mother and a Filipino father. She was so talented in diving, the coach of the Fairmont Hotel Swimming and Diving Club, Phil Patterson, established a new swimming club with Victoria as the only member, because the Fairmont would not allow Filipino Americans to join. She was asked to use her mother's maiden name, Taylor instead of Manalo, but that didn't last long. In her first interview she declared her name to be Victoria Manalo.

Victoria married her swim coach, Lyle Draves, in July 1946, and went on to compete at the London Olympic games of 1948. She was the first woman to win Olympic gold medals for diving in both the 10-meter platform and the 3-meter springboard events. She was inducted into the Swimming Hall of Fame in 1969.

Filipino Shell Crafts: Make a Picture Frame

One of the most abundant natural resources of the Philippine islands comes straight from the sea—shells! Some of the most beautiful shells of the world are found on the beaches of these islands, such as the lovely opalescent capiz, silvery gray abalone, cone-shaped troca, tiger, cowry, and tibia shells. They are natural treasures that are sold all over the world.

Filipino shell crafts have always been a way for poor people to create beautiful jewelry and adornments for their homes. Today, Filipino shell crafts are enjoyed by rich and poor alike. Shell wind chimes, chandeliers, placemats, candleholders, jewelry, picture frames, and jewelry boxes are found in Filipino and Filipino American homes.

What You Need
Thick newspaper work surface
Assorted medium-size shells (available in craft stores)
1 4-by-6-inch picture frame with flat 1-inch border (another size frame is fine, but it should have at least a 1-inch border)
Tacky craft glue

What You Do
1. Lay out the newspaper work surface.
2. Arrange the shells around the picture frame border. Here are some suggestions:
   - Since some frames can be used to display a horizontal or vertical photograph, know which kind of photograph you want to frame first before arranging the shells.
   - Place one-of-a-kind shells in the center of the top and bottom of the frame.
   - Place similar shells across from each other.
   - Place similar shells on each corner of the frame.
3. Once you're happy with the arrangement of the shells, glue them down. Let dry overnight.
4. Insert a favorite photograph and display.

Interesting fact: Many shells for sale in the United States are imported from the Philippines.

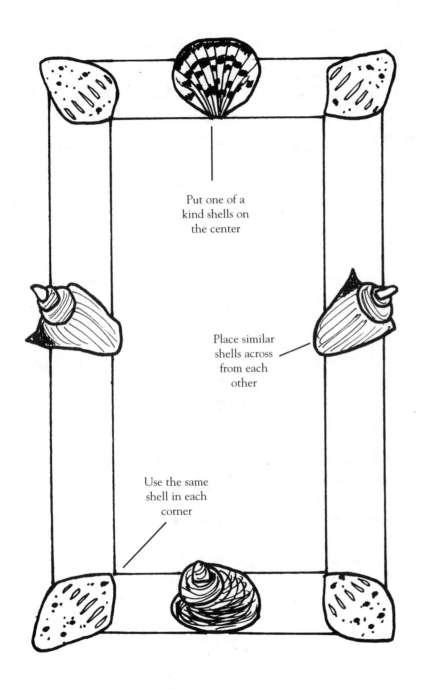

Put one of a
kind shells on
the center

Place similar
shells across
from each
other

Use the same
shell in each
corner

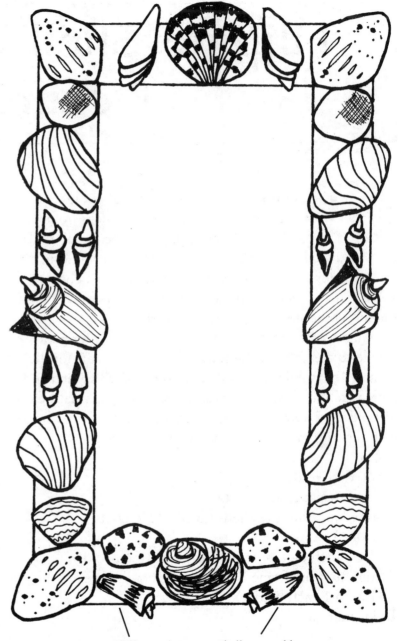

Fill in with as many shells as you like

Say It in Filipino

Filipino is the official language of the Philippines. It is sometimes referred to as Tagalog, which is the dialect the language is based on, or Pilipino, an older version of Filipino. Most Filipinos speak both English and Filipino, which is helpful for new immigrants to the United States.

Welcome, hello: *mabuhay* (ma-boo-high)
Good-bye: *paalam* (pa-ah-lam)
Thank you: *salamat* (sah-lah-mat)

Filipino Food

Filipino food is an interesting mix of East and West. More than any other aspect of Filipino culture, it reflects the influence that foreign cultures have brought to the islands. The original native or Malay food (the Malay were the first people of the Philippines) is prepared using homegrown products such as rice, coconuts, and fresh fish. When the early Chinese came to the islands they brought noodles with them, which led to Filipino noodle-based dishes, the most famous being a dish called pancit. The Chinese also brought dumplings and egg rolls, which gave rise to the Filipino dish known as lumpia. The Spanish brought tomatoes, garlic, and onions, and rich desserts such as flan. The Americans brought the first canned foods to the islands, as well as hamburgers, hot dogs, spaghetti, and pizza. Filipinos adopted the American method of using utensils to eat. Generally they eat with a fork and spoon, although eating with hands is still common. Filipino Americans use forks, knives, and spoons in the same way that other Americans do.

A Filipino dish balances sweet, sour, bitter, and salty. Many different dishes are laid out at the same time to choose from. All meals are served with rice. Desserts are enriched with the tropical fruits of the islands: coconut, pineapple, and banana.

Well-loved Filipino foods include kare-kare, a casserole made with ox-tail; pork, chicken, and seafood adobo, a marinated meat and vegetable dish; champorado, a chocolate rice porridge that is eaten for breakfast; and bibingka, a coconut and rice dessert.

Filipino Americans choose from Filipino and American cuisine at home. Often Filipino dishes take a long time to cook and are reserved for special holidays and celebrations.

Prepare Halo-Halo: A Fruity, Icy Filipino Treat

Halo-halo means "mix-mix," and that's just what this dessert is. You can choose from many different ingredients that are added in layers. Some of the ingredients to choose from include bananas, cantaloupe, melon, coconut, papaya, different types of sweetened beans, and gelatin or tapioca. Next the dessert is covered with shaved ice, evaporated milk, and vanilla ice cream. You stir and eat with a spoon. It's like a fancy snow cone.

1 serving

What You Need
Adult supervision required
Cutting board
Knife
½ cup diced cantaloupe
½ cup diced honeydew melon
½ cup diced mango
Blender
½ cup shaved (crushed) ice
Tall wide glass

2 tablespoons flaked coconut
½ cup evaporated milk
1 scoop vanilla ice cream
Long spoon

What You Do
1. Chop up cantaloupe, melon, and mango.
2. Chop up ice in the blender, a few cubes at a time. You need to add at least 1 cup of water to the blender to help the ice chop evenly. When done, drain the water out.
3. Spoon into the glass in layers: cantaloupe, melon, mango, coconut, ice, evaporated milk.
4. Mix-mix it up!
5. Add scoop of vanilla ice cream on top.
6. Enjoy with a long spoon.

Filipino Respect

Filipino culture has rules that people follow to show one another respect. The way you address someone is important to Filipinos, and Filipino Americans as well. Here are some traditional respectful references:

Nanay/Inay (na-nigh or ee-nigh): Mother
Tatay/Itay (ta-tigh or ee-tigh): Father
Tita (tee-ta): Aunt*
Tito (tee-to): Uncle*
Lolo (lo-lo): Grandfather
Lola (lo-la): Grandmother
Kuya (koo-ee-ya): Older brother
Ate (ah-tay): Older sister
Mano (ma-no): A sign of respect; you greet your older relatives such as grandparents by putting the back of their hand on your forehead
Ho or *po* (ho or po): Is used to show respect when talking to someone who is older

*Tita and Tito are also respectful names for adults, such as friends of your parents.

CARLOS BULOSAN
(1911–1956): Filipino Writer

Carlos Bulosan immigrated to the United States from the Philippines in 1930, at 17 years old. His introduction to the United States was harsh: he worked in an Alaskan cannery, as a migrant farmworker in California, and as a dishwasher and houseboy.

Bulosan was hospitalized for more than two years after having lesions removed from his lung. He used that time to read great American literature, which inspired him to be a writer. *America Is in the Heart*, published in 1946, is the most well known of the several books he wrote. It brought to light the struggles and injustices the Filipino immigrants suffered in America.

Join in Tumbang Preso:
Kick the Can Game

Tumbang Preso is a Filipino version of the game kick the can, but it includes someone protecting the can from being kicked. Games such as this are being taught to second- and third-generation Filipino Americans through Filipino American festivals and celebrations to preserve the Filipino heritage.

What You Need

3 or more players
2 slippers per player (Filipino slippers are
   what we know as flip-flops)
Empty can

What You Do

1. Place the can in an open area.
2. Players should stand a few feet away, with slippers in hand.
3. The person who is "it" must always make sure the can is upright. When the can is knocked over the players are safe.

4. When the can is upright, the player who is "it" can tag the other players. If another player is tagged by the player who is "it," then he becomes the new player who is "it."
5. Players try to knock the can down with their slippers. If they miss, they must run to pick up their slippers without being tagged.
6. After the can is knocked over, the players must retrieve their slippers before the player who is "it" has a chance to put the can upright again.
7. A player can kick the can over with his foot, but he risks being tagged by the player who is "it."

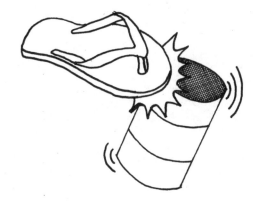

Try Sungka: A Cowrie Shell Game

Sungka is a very old Filipino game, similar to mancala, which many Filipino Americans enjoy playing.

What You Need

2 egg cartons
Scissors
2 plastic cups or bowls

What You Do

1. Cut the top off both egg cartons and discard.
2. Cut a 4-cup segment off the end of one egg carton.
3. Cut a notch in the center of the end piece of the other egg carton.
4. Press the last 2 cups of the uncut egg carton into 2 cups of the 4-part segment to stack them. They should fit snugly without need for tape or stapling. Now you should have a game board of 14 cups.
5. Place a small plastic cup or bowl at either end of the board.

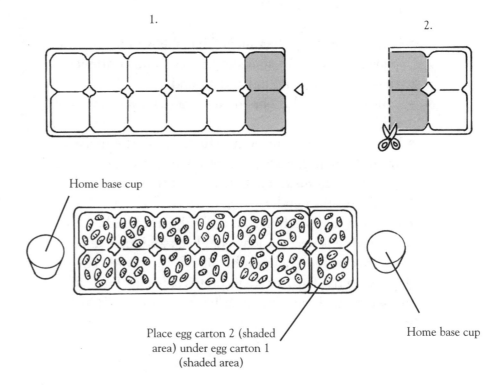

1.

2.

Home base cup

Place egg carton 2 (shaded area) under egg carton 1 (shaded area)

Home base cup

Play Sungka

Put 7 shells into each hole.

1. The first player chooses a cup on his own side and takes the shells out of it. He then deposits the shells one at a time counterclockwise into the small cups and into his own home base cup, which is the larger container to the right. (He does not put one in his opponent's home base cup.)

2. If the last shell:
   - Lands in any cup that already has shells in it, the player takes all the shells in that cup and continues to deposit them around and around.
   - Lands in one of his opponent's empty cups, his turn ends.
   - Lands in his own empty cup, he takes all the shells from the adjoining cup on his opponent's side and puts them in his home base cup. (If there are no shells, his turn ends).
   - Lands in his own home base cup, his turn ends.

5. No counting is needed. Play goes back and forth until one player has no shells on his side of the board. The player who has leftover shells on his side puts them in his own home base. Whoever has the most shells in home base wins.

LEA SALONGA (1971–)
Tony Award–Winning Actress

Lea was born in the Philippines and started her theatrical career in *The King and I* at age seven. She is a talented singer and actress who performs in the United States, the Philippines, London, and Singapore as the lead in plays such as *Les Misérables, West Side Story, Flower Drum Song, Into the Woods, Proof, Annie,* and more. She is also the singing voice of Mulan in *Mulan* and Princess Jasmine in *Aladdin,* two Disney films.

Her latest venture is a singing tour of the United States.

Put Together a Balikbayan Box

A *balikbayan box* is an ordinary cardboard box, but it has great meaning to Filipino Americans. "Balik-bayan" means "to return home." Filipino Americans use the balikbayan box to share the wealth of living in the United States with their (usually) less-well-off relatives in the Philippines. It is also a way to show love and appreciation, especially when it is not possible to go home. The boxes cost a flat rate to ship, no matter how heavy, which allows Filipinos to cram them full of gifts.

Favorite items found in balikbayan boxes include: disposable razors, candy, jeans and other clothes, canned food, computers, soap, American T-shirts, instant coffee, coffee creamer, popcorn, corned beef, toothpaste, hot chocolate mix, chocolate cake mix, and Spam. Many are American products Filipinos became familiar with when the country was a U.S. territory.

Thousands of balikbayan boxes are delivered from the United States to the Philippines each year, especially at Christmas.

You can put together a balikbayan box for the needy in your area. Contact a local charity such as a homeless shelter or food pantry, ask what the needs are for the community they serve, and fill a box with some of the suggested items, which may include such things as peanut butter, tuna fish, jars of spaghetti sauce, canned vegetables or fruit, beans, and soup. This is a good project for a group, too, so that more boxes can be created and more people can be assisted.

What You Need
Thick 2-by-3-foot cardboard box
Newspaper
Packing tape
Marker

What You Do
1. Fill the box with the suggested items, placing heavier things on the bottom, lighter things on top. Fill spaces with crumpled-up newspaper.
2. Tape the top closed.
3. If mailing: neatly print address on the top of the box, and take to the post office to mail.
4. If delivering locally: ask an adult to drive you to the charity to deliver the box.

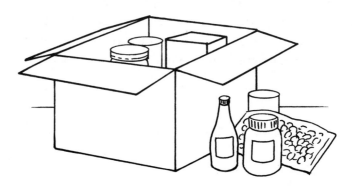

Religion

Most Filipino Americans (80–85 percent) are members of the Roman Catholic Church, a Christian religion. There are also Muslim Filipinos and Filipinos of other Christian denominations. In the Philippines, some islanders follow a native religion called *animism*, which is a nature-based form of worship.

Filipino Catholics weave religion into their daily lives, decorating their homes with religious paintings and symbols, saying the rosary (a string of beads that count prayers), and enjoying Christian feasts and celebrations including Pasko (the Filipino Christmas season), Easter, christenings (baptism into the church), confirmation ceremonies (choosing as an adult to be a member of the church), and weddings.

Celebrations

Filipinos love to celebrate! They are very social and everyone is invited to parties and gatherings, from family to friends to neighbors to people who deliver the newspaper or cut your hair. When family or friends visit from the Philippines it's customary for the Filipino American family to give up their rooms and beds for their guests. The favor is always returned by the other family. Filipinos are very hospitable and place a high value on interpersonal relationships. They believe that getting along in a community of people is more important than satisfying the needs of the individual.

Pasko: The Filipino Celebration of Christmas

In the Philippines, the Christmas season is known as *Pasko*. It starts on December 16 with an early-morning church service, called Misa de Gallo or "mass of the rooster" because it begins before dawn when the rooster calls. Filipinos attend Misa de Gallo services on each of the nine mornings before Christmas.

The Christmas season is a feast for the senses. There are wonderful lantern festivals, Christmas trees are bought or made out of palm branches, tables are heaped high with traditional foods, and visiting goes on for weeks. The celebration doesn't end until the Feast of the Three Kings, in January. The night before the feast, children leave their shoes by the bed, and when they wake they find presents that the Three Kings left in their shoes.

Filipino Americans have continued many of their Pasko traditions in the United States. Some communities have lantern competitions featuring the parol, the beautiful Filipino star lantern. Filipino American celebrations often include lechon, the traditional whole roasted pig; puto bumbong, rice, coconut, and sugar wrapped in bamboo; and the sweet rice dessert bibingka.

Make a Parol: A Star Lantern

The *parol* is the symbol for the Filipino Christmas season. Parols are made of bamboo and paper with a light inside. Some can be up to 100 feet high! Families hang smaller parols at home.

What You Need

10 precut dowels, 3/16 inch by 12 inches
20 small, thin rubber bands, natural color
Scissors
1 yellow kitchen sponge, new
Glue
30 inches ribbon
Optional: 6 feet tinsel garland (available in
    craft stores) or glitter
Tissue paper

What You Do

1. Lay 5 dowels down into a star shape as shown. It doesn't matter which dowel goes above or below the other.
2. Tie the 5 points of the star together using one rubber band for each point.
3. Cut 5 rubber bands. Use them to tie the dowels together at the 5 intersecting points in the middle of the star.
4. Make a second identical star.
5. Cut 5 strips of sponge about 2½ inches by ½ inch each.
6. Take a sponge strip and soak it on all sides with glue. Squeeze the end of one side inside the top tip (the triangular space) of one star under the rubber band. Leave about a 1½-inch space, and attach the other end inside the top tip (the triangular space) of the other star under the rubber band. The sponge will look like a bridge between the two. Squeeze the sponge tightly into both spaces. Repeat with the other five star tips, so that you have a two-sided star frame. Let dry completely.
7. When the star frame is dry, lay it on top of two pieces of tissue paper. Trace around it, adding about 2 inches all around. Cut out the shape through both pieces of tissue paper.
8. Apply glue all around the outside of the star frame. Place in the middle of the two pieces of tissue paper like a sandwich.

9. Press the pieces of tissue paper all around the outside of the star frame. You can use additional strips of tissue paper to cover any holes. The cover will be textured, not smooth, so don't worry about making it perfect. The glue can be used inside and outside the tissue paper. It will dry clear. Let the star dry overnight.

10. Gently poke a hole on each side of the star at the top, right below the sponge. Thread the ribbon through the holes and tie.

11. Optional: Glue tinsel garland or glitter to both sides as shown.

12. Hang in a window so that the light shows through it.

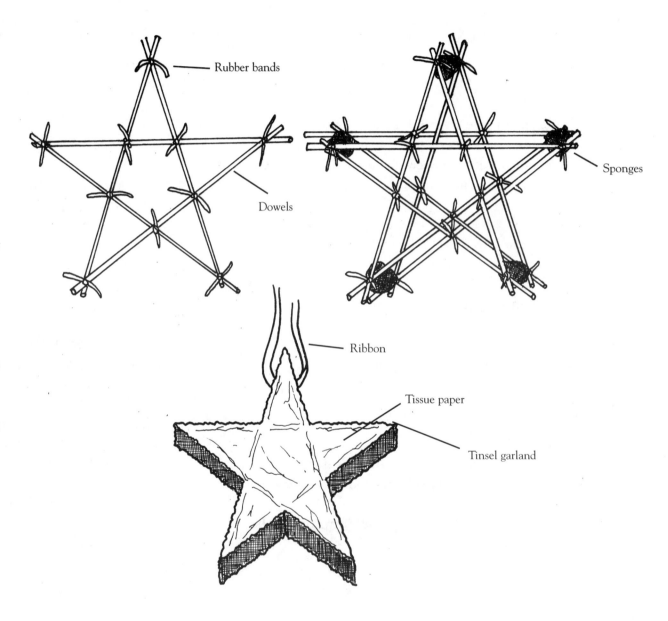

150

Cook Up Bibingka: A Sweet Rice Dessert

Bibingka (bi-bing-kah) is the traditional Christmas treat of the Philippines. The native way of cooking bibingka is on banana leaves. This recipe is cooked on foil.

6–8 servings

What You Need
Adult supervision required
8-by-8-inch baking pan
Aluminum foil
2 tablespoons butter
2⅓ cups coconut milk (available in cans in the grocery store)
Cooking spoon
Large frying pan
2 cups water
2 cups short grain white rice (may be called glutinous rice, sticky rice, or sushi rice)
1 teaspoon salt
1⅓ cups brown sugar

What You Do
1. Line the baking pan with foil.
2. Grease the foil with the butter.
3. Pour 2 cups of the coconut milk into the frying pan and set ⅓ of a cup aside for the topping. Add the water and bring to a boil. Mix in the rice and salt and cook over medium heat, stirring, until the rice is tender and almost dry, about 20 minutes.
4. Add 1 cup of brown sugar to the rice, leaving ⅓ cup aside for the topping. Lower the heat and cook for another 5 minutes. Remove the frying pan from the heat.
5. Mix the remaining coconut milk and brown sugar together in a small bowl.
6. Pour the rice mixture into the baking pan and spread until even.
7. Pour the brown sugar mixture over the top and spread with a spoon.
8. Broil in the oven for 5 minutes or until the top is brown.
9. Cut into square slices and serve warm.

Practice the Pandango Sa Ilaw

Rizal Day: Philippine Independence Day

Rizal Day, or Philippine Independence Day, is celebrated on June 12 every year by Filipinos all over the world. In America the celebration may take place through a church, home, or an organization of Filipinos.

José Rizal was a medical doctor and writer of the late 19th century who wrote about the need for Filipinos to rise up against the Spanish. In 1896, he was shot to death by the Spanish government after being found guilty of starting an insurrection (a revolt against the government). The truth was that Rizal was calling for reform of the Spanish government, not an overthrow of it. After his death, the name "Rizal" became a rallying call for the Filipino fight for independence.

On Rizal Day, there is always an abundance of food, and native dances such as the tinikling or the pandango sa ilaw may be performed.

Pandango sa ilaw is a dance with oil lamps. It's a colorful, lively dance that is interesting to watch because of the flickering lights. Originally dancers balanced lit oil lamps on their heads and the backs of both hands while dancing! Modern dancers use battery-powered candles inside clear cups.

What You Need For Each Dancer
3 clear plastic cups
Tape
3 battery-operated tea lights (available in
   craft stores)

For the Performance
Filipino music or island music CD (you
   can borrow one from your library)
CD player

What You Do
1. Place a circle of tape at the bottom of each cup.
2. Turn on one of the 3 tea lights and place inside one of the cups. Press the light down over the tape. Repeat for the remaining lights and cups.
3. Turn on the music.
4. Ask someone to help you place the cups on your head and the back of your hands. (If it is too difficult, hold the cups inside your hands.)
5. Try balancing these lit cups on your head and hands while walking. Move your right hand up while moving your left hand down. Then move your left hand up and your right hand down. Continue to walk or dance to the music!

Clear plastic cup

Battery-operated
tea light

The Tinikling

The *tinikling* (ti-ni-kling) is a traditional Filipino dance that is seen at many Filipino American celebrations. It is performed in bare feet. The dancers must move rapidly inside and outside of bamboo sticks that are tapped together at floor level. The dance is supposed to imitate the tinikling bird, which moves gracefully among tree branches and long grass in nature.

Filipino Clothing

The first immigrants from the Philippines who arrived in Hawaii wore clothing made of beautiful, silky sheer fabric called *pina*. Pina is made from the fiber of the pineapple plant. The formal woman's dress is known as the *Maria Clara dress*, and includes a full skirt and butterfly sleeves. It is worn with a scarf called a panuelo over the shoulders. The terno is a form-fitting dress that is also worn by Filipinas.

The *barong tagalog* (ba-rong ta-ga-log) is still the national dress for men in the Philippines. It is a long-sleeved buttoned shirt made of pina or cotton, with intricate embroidery, which is worn over trousers. It is not tucked in nor covered by a suit coat.

The Philippines Today

The Philippines are an archipelago (chain or cluster of islands, often volcanic) in Southeast Asia, in the Pacific Ocean. They have a democratic form of government. The

---

BYRON ACOHIDO (1955–)

Winner of the 1997 Pulitzer Prize for Beat Reporting

Byron Acohido, a reporter for *USA Today*, was born in Hawaii in 1955. In 1997, while working as the aerospace reporter for the *Seattle Times*, he was awarded the Pulitzer Prize for a series of articles he had written about defects in Boeing's 737 aircraft. He exposed how the defects were responsible for several airplane crashes, causing hundreds of deaths. His articles led to technological changes in the tail section of the 737 design.

Philippines is a developing country (a poor country that is remaining stable economically or growing) with a great variety of plant and animal life. Many of the country's workers are farm laborers. The climate in the Philippines is tropical, meaning it is almost always hot and humid, with as much as 100 inches of rain per year! Thousands of tourists visit the Philippines each year to enjoy the many beaches and wildlife.

It Started in the Philippines!

The Philippines are known for their wonderful native crafts. Beautiful, vibrant traditional textiles, pottery, basketry, native shells and shell crafts, wood sculpture, and metalwork are all made in the Philippines. South Sea pearls from the Philippines make exquisite jewelry.

Inventions such as the videophone, which allows you to see as well as hear the person you are calling, came from an inventor in the Philippines named Gregorio Zara. Pedro Flores of the Philippines immigrated to America and became the first manufacturer of the yo-yo in 1929. Flores, an entrepreneur, got the idea from a centuries-old toy from the Philippines called *bandalores*. He was the first to find investors and a manufacturer to produce the toy on a large scale. The yo-yo was eventually sold to the Duncan Company in 1930.

Lively Filipino folk dances have been brought to the United States by dance troupes such as the famous Bayanihan Dance Company. Musical instruments such as the kulintang, a Muslim instrument made up of a set of gongs, and bamboo flutes, pipes, and drums are traditionally Filipino, too.

Americans buy technology equipment, coconut products, clothing, sugar, and copper from the Philippines.

Immigration after 1965

Immigration from the Philippines took a giant leap after 1965, as it did from most other Asian nations, because of the changes in the immigration laws. Thousands of Filipinos left their homeland for better work opportunities in America. Others sought freedom from political problems in the Philippines, such as the repressive political regime under Ferdinand Marcos in the 1970s and 1980s.

PANCHO VILLA (Francisco Guilledo) (1901–1925): Flyweight Champion

A dynamo at only 5 foot 1 inch tall, Pancho Villa is thought to be the greatest Asian boxer of all time. Born in the Philippines, he came to the United States at 20 years of age. He had only 5 losses out of 108 career fights. Although he had just had a wisdom tooth removed, he continued to participate in a fight. He died of blood poisoning 10 days later, caused by the fight. He is in the Ring Boxing Hall of Fame and the International Boxing Hall of Fame.

Because immigration laws favor filling jobs in areas in which there is an American labor shortage, hundreds of Filipino doctors and nurses have immigrated to the United States. Some consider nurses to be the Philippines' greatest export.

The new immigrants are likely to be college educated and to speak English. Although they can still face isolated incidents of racism and discrimination, Filipinos have assimilated with relative ease into American life. They are now the second-largest Asian group after the Chinese in the United States.

Create Your Own Jeepney

When Filipino American children visit the Philippines with their families, one of their favorite trips is a ride in a *jeepney*. After World War II, the U.S. Army left hundreds of jeeps behind in the Philippines, or sold them to Filipinos. Enterprising Filipinos remodeled them into new vehicles to be used as taxis. They painted over the Army olive green with bright colors, extended the back to carry more customers, and to attract even more attention added loud horns, flashing lights, and vivid hood ornaments.

Since most of the original U.S. Army jeeps are gone, Filipinos now create their own jeepneys from scratch, using parts from different cars. The owner chooses a name for the jeepney and paints it above the windshield in colorful, bold letters. No two jeepneys are ever quite the same.

The jeepney is an interesting mix of Filipino and American cultures, just like Filipino Americans!

What You Need

Empty tissue box
1-cup carton or other smaller box
Masking tape
Glue
Scissors

Scraps of colorful paper, felt, foam, foil, wrapping paper, pipe cleaners, cardboard, old magazines, any kind of small metal pieces such as washers and buttons, and other odds and ends
Markers

What You Do

1. Tape down the top of the milk carton so that it lays flat. Now tape the carton to the front of the tissue box to make the front of the jeep.

2. Let your imagination go wild! Draw rainbows, peace signs, or stripes; hang flags; make fancy bumpers, horns, or hood racks. The foil is good for making windows and metal parts; roll it over pipe cleaners to make bars. Cut out pictures of people in old magazines to put in the windows.

3. Trace circles out of cardboard, black foam, or felt to make the wheels. Decorate and glue on at the end.

4. Pick a name for your jeepney and print it above the windshield in large letters.

6
Asian Indian Americans

From 1858 to 1947, India was ruled as a colony of England, just as America was in its early years. When the British took over, they changed laws regarding farming, and many small farmers were cheated out of their land by high taxes and debt. In the last decades of the 1800s, the British also began to export large amounts of rice, wheat, and other Indian grains to feed people in England. This led to a deadly shortage of food in India that caused widespread starvation. To make matters even worse, the bubonic plague (a deadly disease that spreads rapidly) killed thousands of Asian Indians in 1907. Families began to look to the rest of the world for a way to survive.

Fathers sent their sons, nephews, and grandsons to look for work in America, as well as in other places such as Canada, Australia, the West Indies, and England. The idea was that men from a village would leave as a group, accumulate enough money to send home to support their families, and eventually return to India. Almost no Asian Indian women came to America with the first wave of immigrants.

Asian Indian immigrants came mostly from the Punjab region of India. Most of them were *Sikhs* (se-ikh), meaning they belonged to the Sikh religion (see p. 162). Sikhs look very distinctive, even today. Men, and sometimes women, wear large turbans on their heads to cover their hair at all times. Their religion prevents the men from ever shaving or cutting their hair, so they have long beards as well.

Many of the early immigrants to America worked in the lumberyards and forests of Washington. There, Asian Indians worked on crews to cut and process lumber. Vancouver, in the province of British Columbia, Canada, was often the first stop for most Asian Indians before traveling on to America, because Western Canada, as well as Washington and Oregon, were looking for workers to build a railroad. Asian Indians laid hundreds of miles of railroad track for the Western Pacific Railroad in California between 1908 and 1910. When railroad jobs became scarce, Asian Indians became migrant farmworkers. Workers moved with the seasons, picking fruit, asparagus, rice, and cotton, as well as pruning and preparing the fields for planting. Asian Indians were favored by farm owners because of their willingness to work hard.

Work groups were organized with Asian Indian leaders. These labor groups worked, ate, and lived together. They were housed in crowded tents or bunkhouses. Several men slept in one room, and they were responsible for cooking their own meals.

After years of working as farm laborers, many Asian Indian workers successfully pooled their money together and bought their own land to farm.

Racism and Discrimination

Asian Indians experienced a terrible attack in Bellingham, Washington, in 1907. White workers, who feared that the Asian Indians were taking over their mill jobs, handed out flyers imploring native-born Americans to "push the Hindus out of the country." Between 400 and 500 white men brutally beat and chased more than 700 Asian Indians with bats and clubs until they fled over the Canadian border, about 20 miles away. Similar attacks were repeated in other American cities.

MANOJ "NIGHT" SHYAMALAN (1970–): Movie Director and Screenwriter

Best known for the movie *The Sixth Sense*, Shyamalan was born in India and raised in Philadelphia, Pennsylvania. He began making films as a child, and attended the school of filmmaking at New York University. Shyamalan has written and directed several successful films. *The Sixth Sense* was nominated for six Academy Awards in 1999. Other popular, suspenseful films he's directed include *Unbreakable, Signs, The Village,* and *Lady in the Water.*

Responding to pressure from groups wanting to limit Asian Indian immigration, Congress passed the Asiatic Barred Zone law in 1917, which prevented citizens from India, Afghanistan, Southeast Asia, and the East Indies from immigrating to the United States. This applied even to the wives and children of the men who were already here.

Many court cases were brought to argue whether or not Asian Indians were Caucasian or Asian, because if they were Asian than there were laws that prevented them from becoming American citizens. It took several years, but in 1923 the U.S. Supreme Court decided that although Asian

Indians were Caucasian they were not white and therefore could not become American citizens. The Supreme Court made a ridiculous distinction between being "white" and being "Caucasian." They said that being "Caucasian" was simply a physical distinction, but being "white" meant being the descendents of Europeans. It was a very biased and unfair law. It led Asian Indians who were already citizens to lose their citizenship. In addition, because they were now considered aliens, they lost the right to own land in California under the Alien Land Act (see p. 70). People who had worked hard their whole lives in America lost everything. Hundreds of Asian Indians returned to India after the court ruling.

There were some ways around the laws, however. Asian Indians who had American-born children could hold land in their children's names. Many Asian Indian men married Mexican American women who could retain ownership of the land, too.

In 1946, the U.S. Congress passed a bill that permitted Asian Indians to become American citizens. In addition, they set a quota by which 100 people could immigrate from India per year. America was finally aware that the ideals of justice and equality that this country had been fighting for in World War II had to be practiced here as well.

The Immigration Act of 1965 (see p. 20) dramatically increased immigration from India when it raised the quotas to 20,000 per country. In 1940, there were only 2,400 Asian Indians living in the United States. Now there are more than 1.5 million.

DEEPAK CHOPRA (1947–)
Asian Indian Doctor and Bestselling Author

Born in New Delhi, India, Deepak Chopra attended medical school there before training in the United States. Chopra writes spiritual books about the body/mind connection in health and medicine. He introduced ayurvedic medicine (see p. 173) to the United States.

Chopra's books encourage positive thinking, yoga, meditation, deep breathing, and wholesome eating in order to maintain good health.

Asian Indian Men and Mexican American Women

As Asian Indian men looked for women to marry and start families with, they realized that they were prevented by law in many states from marrying "white" women. The laws did not extend, however, to Mexican women, whom the Asian Indian men met while working in the fields.

There were many Asian Indian/Mexican marriages at the beginning of the 20th century. The households practiced a mix of Asian Indian and Mexican traditions.

Generally the children spoke Spanish and English, were given Mexican names, and practiced the Catholic religion of their mothers.

Many of the children of these mixed families had single Asian Indian uncles, because there were so many married men who were never able to reunite with their wives, or who never married at all. They took pleasure in being a part of these new families, and doted on the children as they would have done in India.

Asian Indian Immigration Today

Asian Indians today are the fastest-growing Asian group in America. Industries such as high technology, medicine, business, teaching, and nursing are in need of highly skilled, English-speaking workers. Unlike the first generation of immigrants, today's Asian Indian immigrants are usually highly educated professionals who are attracted to the excellent job opportunities in these fields. A physician can make 15 times the Indian salary working in the United States. Asian Indians are also small hotel and motel owners, convenience store and gas station owners, and owners of restaurants and stores that sell Asian Indian goods and services. Many new immigrants send money back to their families in India, just as the first generation of immigrants did.

Because most Asian Indians speak excellent English, it gives them an advantage over other immigrant groups. Asian Indians as an ethnic group have the highest household income of any group in America, including both immigrants and the native born. The new immigrants are

RAVI SHANKAR (1920–)
Sitar Performer

Born in India, Shankar first belonged to a world-traveling dance troupe before turning to music. He studied the sitar for seven years under the Indian classical music master, Allaudin Khan. As a performer he used his international experiences in his music. He paired up with the American violinist Yehudi Menuhin in concerts and recordings, one of which won a Grammy Award. His daughter Anoushka is also a well-known sitar player. Another daughter, Norah Jones, is a Grammy-winning singer and jazz pianist.

male and female alike, making bachelor communities a thing of the past.

Religion

India is the birthplace of four religions of the world: Hinduism, Buddhism, Sikhism, and Jainism. The large majority of Asian Indians, 80 percent, practice Hinduism. The Muslim religion is practiced by 14 percent of Asian Indians, making India one of the largest Muslim communities in the world. Asian Indians may also be Christian or Zoroastrian.

The earliest immigrants to America were largely Sikh, but now Asian Indian immigrants come from all faiths.

Hinduism

Hinduism originated in India in about 1500 B.C.E. The religion of Hinduism has no one founder. Most Hindus believe that there are many gods and goddesses that are manifestations of one supreme being. The three main Hindu gods are Brahma, the creator of the universe; Vishnu, the preserver of the universe and of goodness; and Shiva, the destroyer of evil. Life is a series of births and rebirths called reincarnation. After you die, you go into another body. It could be the body of an animal or a human. Hindus consider the cow sacred and refrain from eating beef.

Your new life is good or bad depending on your previous life. If you led a good life, your actions, or karma, will be rewarded and you will live a better life in your new body. Eventually the soul is released from the cycle of rebirths when a person's good karma has reached a state of salvation called moksha (mo-kshaa).

Part of Hinduism involved a *caste system* (a hereditary leveling of social groups based on wealth, rank, or occupation) based on the belief that people are born into certain unchangeable levels of society, each with its own responsibilities, or dharma (dar-mah). The original caste system had four sects:

- Brahmins: The highest caste were intellectuals such as teachers, philosophers, and priests who were respected for their knowledge.

SUBRAHMANYAN CHANDRASEKHAR

(1910–1995): Shared the 1983 Nobel Prize for Physics

Born in India, Subrahmanyan Chandrasekhar came to the United States in 1936. As a scientist he made groundbreaking discoveries about space. In 1983, he was the cowinner of the Nobel Prize for Physics for his contributions to the understanding of how black holes are created in space. (The *Nobel Prize* is an international award that is given yearly for achievements in physics, chemistry, physiology or medicine, literature, and peace.)

- Kshatriyas (ksha-at-ree-yahs): This caste included the warriors and rulers whose responsibilities included defense of the country and administration of the government.
- Vaisyas (vysh-yaas): This was the business class of merchants, traders, and farmers.
- Shudras (shoo-drahs): The lowest class was made up of those that performed menial labor. Traditionally their mixing with other classes was not permissible. Today, these codes are not upheld. Shudras are not untouchables (see next page).

- Untouchables: People known as "untouchables" were not part of the original caste system, but considered to be below it. Untouchables performed duties that the Shudras would not do such as burying the dead and cleaning toilets. According to the caste system, the untouchables would spiritually "pollute" the upper classes if they were allowed to mix, so they were not even allowed to be touched by the groups above.

The famous leader Mahatma Gandhi, who led the people of India to independence from Great Britain, renamed the untouchables "Harijan," children of God, and the new Indian constitution outlawed the caste system in 1949. To discourage discrimination based on caste, today's Indian government offers affirmative action programs (educational or occupational assistance) for the "untouchables," now referred to as "Dalits."

Sikhism

Sikhism was founded in India in the 1500s by the leader Guru Nanak. "Sikh" is a Punjabi word meaning "disciple." Sikhs believe in one God. They believe in reincarnation but reject the Hindu caste system. They are not allowed to drink or smoke. Men must not cut their hair or beards. They wear their hair wound into a large turban. Sikhs worship in a gurdwara (gurd-wah-rah) or temple. The women wear a turban or chuni (head scarf) at the temple. There are no priests, but a granthi can offer guidance through his knowledge of Sikh scriptures. The holy book of the Sikhs is the Guru Granth Sahib.

NARINDER KAPANY (1927–)
Developed Fiber Optics

Born in India, Narinder Kapany went to college in his birth country and graduate school in England. He came to the United States in 1955. In 1954, his findings on fiber optics were unveiled in the scientific journal *Nature*. Fiber optics are very thin, hairlike strands of glass or plastic that have the ability to transmit information as beams of light. Because light travels faster than electricity, information moves faster through fiber optic cables (fiber optic strands bundled together) than through ordinary electrical wires. In the United States, Kapany has been a college professor, writer, and founder of two fiber optic companies, as well as a nonprofit organization called the Sikh Foundation.

Jainism

Jainism was founded in India between 500 and 600 B.C.E. by the Hindu priest Nataputta Vardhamana. Jains are completely peaceful. They are not allowed to participate in war or kill anything, including animals. Jains must even be careful to sweep before walking so that they do not walk on ants or small insects. To be a Jain means to give up all worldly pleasures. Jains worship Vardhamana, who became known as

162

the Mahavira, or "great one," because he had reached a state of human perfection in his selflessness.

Little Indias: Asian Indian American Communities

If you would like to get a feel for what India is like, take a trip to a Little India in America. The large numbers of Asian Indian immigrants in recent years has led to several small Asian Indian communities sprouting within larger cities. These areas range from a few stores in a row to city blocks of Asian Indian businesses. It is a welcome gathering spot for Asian Indians immigrants to recapture the sights and sounds of their homeland. There are Little Indias in many U.S. cities, including Los Angeles; New York; Edison and Jersey City, New Jersey; and Chicago.

Walking down the streets of a Little India, you can smell the spicy Asian Indian food cooking, see people dressed in colorful saris and turbans, hear Asian Indian music blaring from storefronts, see signs in Hindi, and shop in Asian Indian grocery stores that are packed to the ceiling with bags of rice, lentils, chutneys, spices, and Asian Indian vegetables. After a while you can stop for a *samosa* (sah-moh-sa), a flaky pastry filled with a tasty vegetable or vegetable-and-meat stuffing; a plate of chicken *tandoori* (tehn-dur-i), spring chicken marinated with herbs and spices; or a refreshing yogurt dessert you can drink called *lassi* (lah-see).

Indian gift shops sell statues of Hindu gods, beautiful textiles, videos of popular Asian Indian movies, and CDs of Asian Indian music. There are beauty parlors that offer henna tattoos, herbal facials, and an unusual eyebrow-plucking technique known as "threading." Jewelry stores sell stunning 22-carat gold jewelry as well as nose-piercing services.

For Asian Indians as well as Americans from other ethnic groups, Little Indias offer an interesting glimpse into the color and richness of Asian Indian culture right here in America.

Asian Indian Clothing

When most people think of Asian Indian clothing, they think of the beautiful, colorful *saris* (sah-rees) that swing gracefully as a woman moves. A sari is a simple piece of fabric about 45 inches wide and 13 to 26 feet long, depending on where in India it is made. Saris are made in many different fabrics, colors, and designs. The sari is tucked into the top of a woman's half slip and pleated into a series of folds that are

---

DALIP SINGH SAUND (1899–1973)

First Asian Indian to Be Elected to the U.S. Congress

Born in India, Dalip Singh Saund came to the United States in 1920 to study at the University of California at Berkeley. Inspired by the writings of Abraham Lincoln, in 1956 Saund became the first Asian elected to the U.S. Congress, where he represented the 29th district of California. He served three terms. While campaigning for a fourth, he had a stroke that ended his political career.

also tucked in. Then the sari is draped around her body using no buttons, zippers, or fasteners. A short blouse in matching material, called a choli (cho-lee), is worn under the sari. The way the sari is wrapped, as well as the material and design, can tell you what state in India the woman comes from.

Saris are made from all types of fabrics, but the finest silk saris are always used for weddings. Wedding saris are traditionally red and adorned with gold thread and jewels. Asian Indian American women generally wear the sari for special occasions such as weddings, holidays, and religious ceremonies.

Asian Indian women also wear the salwar kameez (sehlwar kah-meez), or Punjabi outfit, which is a knee-length tunic worn over matching trousers, with a long scarf that is worn over the head. Another variation of Asian Indian women's clothing is a blouse and ankle-length skirt outfit called the ghagra choli (ghaa-g-raa cho-lee). When leaving the home, Muslim women wear a burqa (bur-kah), an overcoat with a cape and veil.

The *bindi* (bin-dee) is a circle of red powder worn on the foreheads of Hindu women and girls. It is considered an auspicious symbol, and it is applied when getting dressed up or when participating in religious ceremonies. It is also worn by both Hindu women and men on the forehead to honor the seat of intellect.

The first immigrants from India were mostly Sikh men from Punjab. They dressed in American work clothes but were easily distinguishable by their tall turbans and long beards. Today's turbans are made in hundreds of colors and designs that show the region a man comes from in India.

Shawls are worn by men and women and can be made of many different types of materials including silk, cotton, and wool. An article of clothing called the *dhoti* (dhoh-tee) is worn by men in India, but rarely worn except for special occasions by Asian Indian men in the United States. It is a piece of cloth that is wrapped around the bottom half of the body. Men and women wear the *kurta*, a traditional long shirt with four or more buttons in the front and no collar.

VINOD DHAM (1950–)
Worked to Create the Pentium Processor for Computers

Vinod Dham was born in India and received his degree in electrical engineering in Delhi. He came to the United States in 1975 to attend graduate school at the University of Cincinnati.

Dham was invited to work for Intel Corporation in the Silicon Valley of California. (Silicon Valley is a nickname for the area in California where many high-technology companies are located.) In 1993, Dham led a team of computer scientists in developing a tiny microprocessor that is used in computers all over the world. It is called the Pentium chip. Today's Pentium chips are smaller than a postage stamp and contain millions of transistors. This allows computers to become smaller and smaller.

Wrap a Sari

Experience what it might be like to wear the lovely Asian Indian sari.

What You Need
Short-sleeve or sleeveless jersey
Shorts with an elastic waist
Lightweight piece of fabric, approximately
    3 feet by 12 feet
Optional: safety pins

What You Do
1. Put on the jersey and shorts.
2. Start with one end of the fabric. Tuck the material into the left front waistband of your shorts and wrap around your waist to the left, behind your back, and around to the front again, where you tucked the material into your shorts.
3. Now make several pleats with the material (that is in your hand) like a curtain, squeezing it between your hands. Make about 5–7 pleats, each about 3–4 inches long. You can attach the pleats together with safety pins if desired. Check to make sure the length at the bottom is the same all around, then tuck the pleats in across your front.
4. Wrap the fabric around your waist to the left, behind your back one more time until you get to your right front hip.
5. Flip the end piece diagonally across your left shoulder so that it dangles all the way down your back.

Pleats

Say It in Hindi

The government of India recognizes 15 languages. Hindi and English are the official languages of India.

Welcome/hello/good-bye:	*namaste* (nuh-muhs-tay) (also a greeting that honors the personand divinity within each person)
Yes:	*haan* (hahn)
No:	*nahin* (na-hee)
Please:	*kripaya* (krip-yah)
Thank-you:	*dhanyavad* (dhan-yah-vaadh)

KALPANA CHAWLA

(1961–2003): First Asian Indian Woman to Fly in Space

Born in Karnal, India, Kalpana Chawla became the first Asian Indian–born woman to fly in space. Her first trip was aboard the shuttle *Columbia*, in which she orbited the earth in 1997. Chawla received a degree in engineering from Punjab Engineering School in 1982 and went on to achieve master's and doctoral degrees in aerospace engineering in the United States. She became an American citizen in 1990.

On February 1, 2003, while completing a 16-day scientific mission aboard the *Columbia* shuttle, Chawla and her fellow crew members died when the shuttle exploded upon reentry to earth. The explosion of the *Columbia* led to many changes in NASA's shuttle program.

Make Ghungroos: Asian Indian Dancing Bells

Asian Indian classical dance is very popular among Asian Indian Americans, and can be seen at recitals and festivals all across America. It is a meaningful way for second- and third-generation Asian Indians to connect with a traditional Asian Indian art form. Classical Indian dance is more than 2,000 years old.

The dances are very precise and graceful. Dancers have to carefully follow a defined series of hand and foot movements. Performers wear elaborate, colorful costumes bedecked with gold necklaces, bangles, a headset, dangling earrings, a waist belt, and anklets of jingling bells known as *ghungroos*.

What You Need

2 pieces elastic bead cord, each 15 inches
    long (available in craft stores)
40 small bells or 20 medium-size bells
Scissors
Asian Indian dance music CD (you can
    borrow one from your library)
CD player

What You Do

1. Slide the bells onto the cord one by one. Use about 20 if the bells are small and 10 if the bells are larger.
2. Remove your shoes and socks.
3. Tie the bell cord around your ankle so it is loose enough to slip your foot out, but tight enough to stay on while you are moving.
4. Snip off any loose ends with the scissors.
5. Repeat to make a second anklet.
6. Put on some Asian Indian music and dance!

Try Yoga

Yoga is one of India's greatest gifts to America. Yoga is a Hindu practice that is designed to train the body as well as the mind to reach the highest level of spirituality or stillness within oneself. Hindus say that in ancient times, sages (people with great wisdom) and seers (people who could tell the future) practiced yoga and that their knowledge was imparted from teacher to student. Americans of all faiths practice yoga in order to reduce stress and strengthen the body.

What You Need

Comfortable but not baggy clothes
Bare feet
A mat or soft surface

What You Do

1. Meditative pose: Sit quietly with your legs crossed and your hands resting on your knees. Do not arch your back. Pinch your index fingers and thumbs together. Close your eyes. Try to clear your mind of all stray thoughts. Inhale through your nose, deeply and slowly. Exhale (blow out) through your mouth. Try saying the sound "om" very slowly. This will help you to stay calm and focused.

2. Cat pose: Get down on your hands and knees. Arch your back slowly while lowering your head, gently, but stretching as far as you can. Then bring your head back up and relax your back.

3. Mountain pose: Stand with your feet together and your toes facing forward. Let your arms hang by your sides, palms inward. Pretend that you are a puppet whose head is being pulled up by a string. This will keep your spine in the correct position.

4. Tree pose: This pose will help you to achieve good balance. Start with the mountain pose, above. Pull your left foot up and place the bottom of your foot on the inner thigh of your right leg, as high as you can reach. Place your hands together, as if in prayer, and lift them up over your head, as a tree would reach for the sun. Repeat with the other leg.

Meditative pose

Cat pose

Mountain pose

Tree pose

Asian Indian Food

Asian Indian American families cook a variety of delicious Asian Indian dishes as well as American food at home. Visiting and socializing with friends and family is an important aspect of Asian Indian culture. Visits from family from America to India and from India to America can last for months!

Spices such as pepper, saffron, cinnamon, cumin, coriander, turmeric, and dried chili peppers are very important in preparing Asian Indian food. They are often freshly ground before the meal. Traditional Asian Indian food includes flat breads such as tandoori roti, an unleavened whole wheat bread baked in a tandoor (tehn-dur), or oven; chapati (cheh-pah-ti), a flat unleavened bread cooked on a griddle; and naan (nahn), a leavened North Indian bread. Spicy foods such as dhal (dall) lentil soup, and dishes made with yogurt such as cucumber raita (rah-ee-tah) keep the balance between hot and cool food. Rice is also commonly served. Wonderful vegetarian dishes are made with vegetables such as okra, sweet potatoes, mustard greens, spinach, and potatoes.

Some Asian Indians are vegetarians, and others such as Muslims do not eat pork. Strict Hindus never eat any meat, and will avoid eating on plates or using utensils that have been used to prepare meat. Many also avoid eating in restaurants where meat is served. Strict Hindus also do not drink alcohol.

Those Hindus who do eat meat never eat beef, as the cow is sacred. Pork is also not eaten. Non-vegetarian Asian Indians usually eat chicken, goat's meat, mutton (sheep), or lamb. Traditionally an Asian Indian meal is served on a large metal tray, with each dish in a small bowl. Asian Indian Americans use forks and knives, but in India eating with your right hand is considered polite. Asian Indians usually drink water or tea with meals.

Milk-based desserts such as puddings and fudge are the most popular. Indian desserts and sweets are usually made for special holidays and given as presents.

SABEER BHATIA (1969–)
Created Hotmail

Sabeer Bhatia was born in Bangalore, India. He was awarded a full scholarship to attend the California Institute of Technology, and then got his master's degree at Stanford. Bhatia came up with a simple idea, but one that no one had thought of before. In 1995, along with colleague Jack Smith, he created a free form of e-mail that could be used on any computer. He called it Hotmail. One year later the company was sold to Microsoft for $400 million. Now, Hotmail is the largest free e-mail provider in the world.

Make Banana Lassi: A Yogurt Drink

Lassi is a popular drink served by street vendors and in restaurants in India. It is easy and fun to make in the United States, too!

2 servings

What You Need

Adult supervision required

½ cup ice

½ cup cold water

Blender

2 ripe bananas

8 ounces plain yogurt

1 tablespoon sugar

2 tall glasses

2 straws

What You Do

1. Combine the ice and water in the blender. Mix until the ice is crushed.

2. Add the bananas, yogurt, and sugar. Blend until the mixture is bubbly.

3. Pour into 2 tall glasses, add straws, and enjoy!

Play Snakes and Ladders

You've probably heard of the game Chutes and Ladders, but did you know that it came from an Asian Indian game called Snakes and Ladders? This is a very old game, from the 13th century, that Hindu teachers used to teach their students religious values. The ladders lead you to heaven or nirvana as the rewards for good deeds, and the snakes pull you down to be reborn as the punishment for bad behavior.

What You Need

2 or more people
Small poster board
Ruler
Thin black marker
1 die (one of a pair of dice)
2 (or more) different-colored buttons

What You Do

1. Copy the game board below onto the poster board by measuring out 1-inch blocks with a ruler and marker. Draw the words and pictures. Make sure the snakes and ladders start and end at the correct blocks.
2. Each player rolls the die. The highest number goes first.
3. The object of the game is to reach "nirvana." On your turn, roll the die and move that number of spaces across the game board, using a button as a marker and following the numbers on the board in order. The ladders representing good characteristics or deeds give you a shortcut, and the snakes representing bad traits or actions bring you back down.

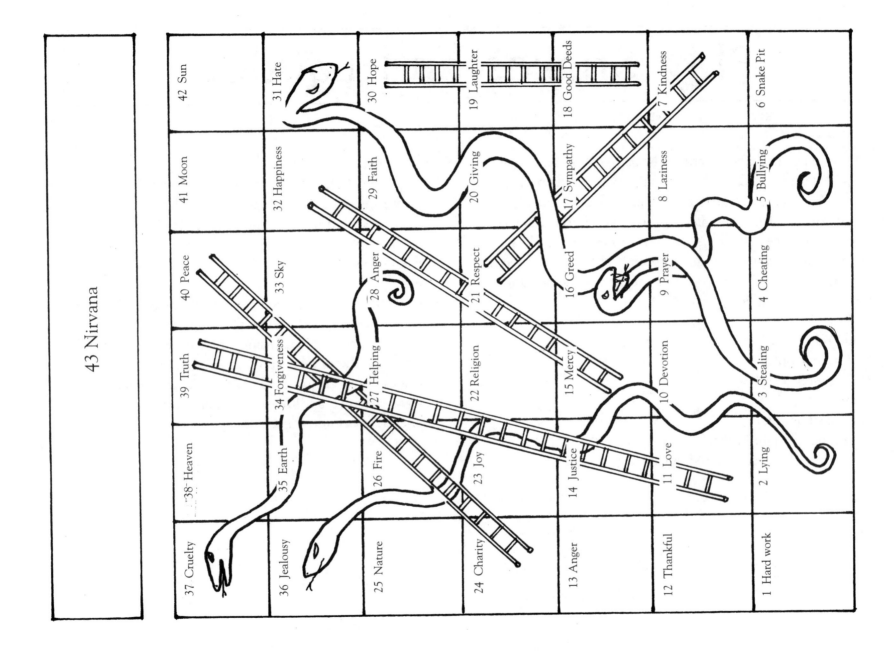

43 Nirvana

42 Sun | 41 Moon | 40 Peace | | 39 Truth | 38 Heaven | 37 Cruelty

31 Hate | 32 Happiness | 33 Sky | 34 Forgiveness | 35 Earth | 36 Jealousy

30 Hope | 29 Faith | 28 Anger | 27 Helping | 26 Fire | 25 Nature

19 Laughter | 20 Giving | 21 Respect | 22 Religion | 23 Joy | 24 Charity

18 Good Deeds | 17 Sympathy | 16 Greed | 15 Mercy | 14 Justice | 13 Anger

7 Kindness | 8 Laziness | 9 Prayer | 10 Devotion | 11 Love | 12 Thankful

6 Snake Pit | 5 Bullying | 4 Cheating | 3 Stealing | 2 Lying | 1 Hard work

India Today

More than a billion people live in India. It is the second most populated country in the world after China and the seventh-largest country in total area. One of the oldest civilizations has thrived there for more than 5,000 years!

India itself is considered a *subcontinent*. A subcontinent is a large landmass that is separate in some way, through either geography or a political division. The geography that separates India are the Himalayan mountains that stretch along the top and the seas: the Bay of Bengal in the east, the Arabian Sea in the west, and the Indian Ocean in the south. Although still a developing country, India is the world's largest democracy.

Most of the people in India are poor farmers who live in small villages. Many people also live in the big cities of India, where there is great wealth as well as extreme poverty. Indian cities have advanced centers of technology and science that coexist with people begging on the streets for food. The cities are alive with the sounds of street vendors selling food and wares, rickshaws (wagons pulled by people on foot or bicycles), auto rickshaws (three-wheeled version of a big scooter with passenger seating capacity), and buses crowded with people sitting everywhere, including on the roof.

It Started in India!

India's contributions to the world are significant and go back thousands of years. Some people believe that the most important Asian Indian contribution to the world was the

AMAR BOSE (1929–)
Inventor of a Symphony-Like Speaker System

The son of an Asian Indian immigrant, Amar Bose grew up in Philadelphia, where he fixed model trains and transistors for money as a teenager. He received a degree in electrical engineering from the Massachusetts Institute of Technology (MIT). Bose invented small speakers that could be used at home but that duplicated the great sound that you hear in concert halls. The Bose Corporation is a world leader in sound technology, including car stereos and waveguide radios. Bose also developed a sound cancellation system that is used in the space program to protect astronauts' hearing. His sound systems are found in the space shuttle, the Sistine Chapel, and Olympic stadiums.

invention of the zero in mathematics. And believe it or not, traditional Indian doctors were practicing plastic surgery in India more than 2,500 years ago to fix noses, ears, and lips.

Asian Indian *ayurvedic (ah-yur-vay-dik) medicine* is an ancient practice that treats the mind and body as one. Healers try to find imbalances in the body's energy. Practitioners of ayurvedic medicine believe that the body is made up of doshas (doe-shahs): vata (vah-tah), wind; pitta (pih-tah),

173

fire; and kapha (kah-fah), phlegm. Imbalances are corrected with yoga, meditation, and herbal medicine.

Did you know that Mumbai (formerly known as Bombay), India, produces more movies each year than Hollywood? The Indian film industry, nicknamed Bollywood (a pun combining the words Bombay and Hollywood) makes more than a thousand colorful song-and-dance movies a year that are wildly popular in India as well as other parts of the world.

Have you ever played the board game pachisi? This Asian Indian game has been played since the 16th century. When the emperor Akbar ruled India in the 1500s, he played a life-size version of this game called chaupar. He had marble laid into the ground for a game board, tossed cowrie shells to determine the number of spaces to be moved, and had servants walk around to mark the spaces. Pachisi is the national game of India.

Indian agriculture has made a number of significant contributions to the world as well. Native people in India cultivated the first sugarcane plant into sugar. Now India is the world's largest producer of sugar and tea. The first crops of cotton were also grown in India. India's cotton, flowing white muslin, printed calicos, and silk were highly sought-after fabrics by traders and are still valued today. The great explorers of the world traveled to India in the 1600 and 1700s in search of Indian spices, especially pepper. Indigo, the plant that was used to dye (color) blue jeans for years, came from India.

A traditional instrument from India is the *sitar* (sih-tar), a long stringed instrument that is similar to a guitar.

JHUMPA LAHIRI (1967–)
Pulitzer Prize–Winning Author

The daughter of Indian immigrants, Lahiri was born in London and brought up in Rhode Island. Her first book, a collection of short stories about Asian Indian Americans called *Interpreter of Maladies*, was translated into 29 languages, became a bestseller, and won the 2000 Pulitzer Prize for fiction. Her work examines the complexities of being both Indian and American in the United States.

Both instruments have strings and frets (ridges that go across the board where the player puts his fingers). A guitar usually has six strings; the sitar has two levels of strings: six or seven strings on top that you play, and 13 resonating strings below that resound from the plucking of the top strings. The sitar has a droning sound to it, as opposed to the guitar, which is more harmonic. Americans became familiar with traditional Indian music through musicians such as Ravi Shankar, who influenced music composed by George Harrison of the Beatles.

A good amount of the computer software and electronics that we use every day is engineered and manufactured in India.

Diwali: The Festival of Lights

Diwali (dee-wah-lee) is the Asian Indian holiday that celebrates the victory of light over darkness and goodness over evil. Literally, "Diwali" means "burning lamps in a row." Asian Indians of all religions enjoy the celebration of Diwali.

The holiday began as a Hindu celebration to honor the goddess of prosperity, Lakshmi. Once a year when Lakshmi comes to earth to observe, she is welcomed with oil lamps made of earthenware pots to light her way. These lamps, called *diyas* (dee-yas), glow around homes, courtyards, shops, temples, and rooftops, and even on rafts that float down rivers and streams. There are firecrackers everywhere to scare off evil spirits and contribute to the festive atmosphere.

Diwali is celebrated in October or November of each year, depending on the Hindu lunar calendar. In India as well as in America, Diwali is seen as a time of hope and renewal. In some parts of India, it symbolizes the beginning of the New Year.

Asian Indian Americans clean their homes and wear new clothes on Diwali. The tradition of drawing *rangoli* (rang-o-lee), or powdered rice flour designs, on the floor or front step may be done. Hindus attend temple and offer poojas (poo-jahs), prayers of thankfulness. In the weeks before the holiday, Asian Indian Americans may attend a Diwali Mela, a type of fair where you can buy things to prepare for the holiday such as Asian Indian food, arts and crafts, Diwali gifts, sweets, and diyas. Community Diwali events may include "Ram leelas," the classic tale of the *Ramayana* played out on stage; classic Asian Indian dancing; and dancing from Indian movies.

On Diwali, families visit grandparents, aunts and uncles, cousins, and friends, and exchange plates of sweets, symbolizing wealth and prosperity for the coming year. Business people will often open new accounts on this auspicious day. Diwali gifts are also a part of the holiday, usually the favorite part for kids. Gifts of gold are especially auspicious.

Make a Diya for Diwali

Diyas are filled with oil and lit to celebrate Diwali. They are traditionally displayed in a row or group.

What You Need
Adult supervision required

3 small clay saucers (flowerpot bottoms, found in nurseries and florist shops, work well)

Gold paint pen

3 tea lights (small, flat candles inside an aluminum base)

Bag of gold glass gems (sold with crafts or florist supplies)

Large, flat round platter

What You Do
1. Use the gold paint pen to draw designs along the edges of the saucers.
2. Place a tea light in the middle of each saucer.
3. Surround the tea lights with gold glass gems as shown to look like oil.
4. Arrange the diyas on the platter.
5. Ask an adult to light the diyas. Dim the lights in the room and imagine how festive it must be to celebrate Diwali in India with thousands of lights!

Create a Chalk Rangoli: An Asian Indian Welcome

Rangoli designs are created on the ground or the front steps to welcome guests for Diwali. Traditional rangoli is made by pouring colored rice powder or sand by hand. Flowers and seeds are sometimes added to give the design depth.

We will make our rangoli with chalk.

What You Need

Paper and pen

Front steps or driveway (can also be done on poster board)

Sidewalk chalk

Optional: flowers (marigolds, chrysanthemums, roses)

What You Do

1. Draw several designs on paper before making your rangoli in chalk. Rangoli designs are usually geometric shapes and are symmetrical, meaning the same on both sides. Popular designs include: 6-point stars, flowers, flower petals, diamonds, hexagons, circles, teardrops, squares, animals, and leaves.

2. When you decide on a design, copy it in chalk onto the front steps or driveway. Draw the outline first, and then color in the middle. Traditional rangoli designs were about 2 feet by 2 feet, but they can be any size.

3. Optional: Sprinkle flower petals inside some parts of the design to make it three-dimensional.

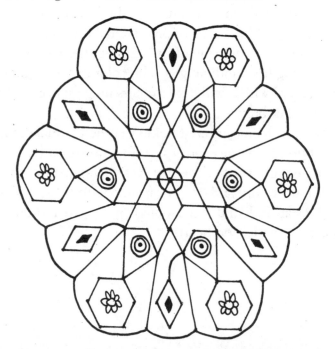

Do Mehndi: Asian Indian Hand Painting

Y ou've heard of tattoos and temporary tattoos, but have you ever heard of hand painting? It's a long-lasting temporary tattoo for your hands! *Mehndi* (meh-hen-thee) hand painting is a uniquely Asian Indian form of body decoration. The paint is made from the crushed leaves of the henna plant—"mehndi" is the Hindu word for "henna." Hand painting is for special occasions, especially for weddings. Traditionally, the groom's name is hidden in the elaborate design of the bride's mehndi. Family members trained in the art or professional artists apply the henna paint over the palm of the hand, either with stencils or by drawing freehand designs. The color of the mehndi paint is green, which will dry to colors ranging from light orange to dark brown.

American teenagers are finding that henna makes for long-wearing temporary tattoos. Henna tattoo parlors are springing up all over the country. Real henna paint takes several hours to dry and can last from one to three weeks. Typical Asian Indian designs include paisley, tear drops, leaves, dots, swirls, and hearts.

Create your own hand painting by copying the designs below, or invent your own. Try hiding your name in the design!

What You Need
Paper and pen to sketch out a design
Washable markers

What You Do
1. Draw out a design on the paper. Use the examples for inspiration. Don't make it too complicated because you may want to redraw this pattern with both your right and left hands.
2. Draw the design on the palm of your hand using washable markers. Use the hand that you *don't* write with first. This will be more difficult.
3. Now draw the same design or a different design on the palm of the other hand.

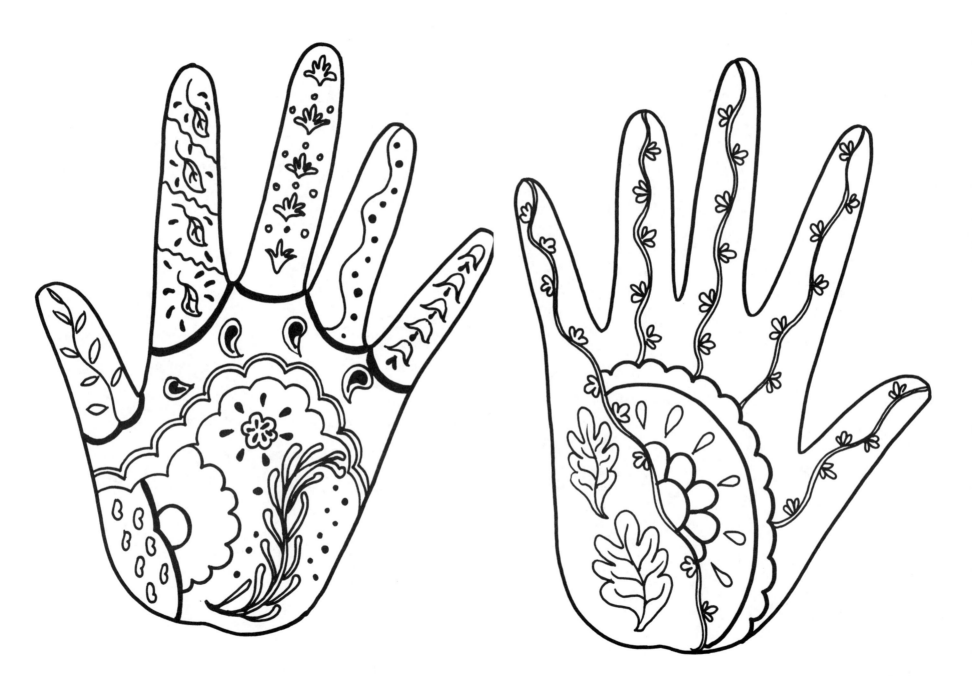

7
Southeast Asian Americans

Many Southeast Asians left for America not because they wanted to, but because they had to. They were fleeing for their lives. The correct term is not immigrant but *refugee*, because they were seeking refuge, or shelter from harm. Many of the refugees left barefoot, with just the clothes on their backs. They ran for helicopters and boats, with people screaming, children crying, and crowds pushing and cramming to be first. Families were split apart, lost in the confusion of leaving.

These refugees were from Vietnam, Cambodia, and Laos, part of what is called Southeast Asia. Southeast Asia also includes the countries of Singapore, East Timor, Burma (renamed Myanmar), Thailand, Indonesia, Malaysia, the Philippines, and Brunei.

Vietnam, Cambodia, and Laos were ruled as colonies by the French from 1861 to 1945. The region at that time was known as French Indochina. During World War II, French Indochina was taken over by the Japanese. A new leader emerged to fight for independence from the Japanese as well as the French. His name was Ho Chi Minh. In 1945, he declared Vietnam an independent country.

Ho Chi Minh was a Communist (see p. 22), and at that time the United States and many other countries of the free world were in great fear of Communism. In a Communist country, all property is shared, and the government owns all businesses. The governments of Communist countries tell their citizens where to live, where to work, when and if they can leave the country, what can be taught in schools, and even what they can read. The United States believed that if one country in Southeast Asia fell to Communism, then the rest of Southeast Asia (and maybe other parts of the world) would too. This was called the *domino theory*. The idea was that countries would fall to Communism like a row of dominoes.

The first Indochina War began in 1947 when the French tried to recolonize Vietnam after World War II. The United States took France's side and for years supplied money and military advisors to help keep the Communists out. The war ended in 1954, when the French withdrew their forces and conceded defeat. The area was split into North and South Vietnam, with Ho Chi Minh the Communist leader of the North, and Ngo Dinh Diem the democratic leader of South Vietnam.

The Vietnam War

America continued the fight against the Communists in Vietnam, sending more and more money, military advisors, and finally American troops to the new South Vietnamese government to help them fight the North Vietnamese, as well as the Viet Cong. The Viet Cong were communists who were hidden among the civilians in South Vietnam and fought the Americans and South Vietnamese in surprise attacks. This was called the Second Indochina War or the Vietnam War. American troops were actively engaged in combat from about 1965 to 1973, but the war did not end

SERGEANT TRAN QUOC BINH
(1978–2004): First Vietnamese American to Die in Iraq War

In 1986, Tran Quoc Binh secretly escaped from Vietnam with his family, carrying one sister on his shoulders and holding the hand of another sister. They left for Thailand, then the Philippines, finally seeking asylum in Mission Viejo, California.

Binh joined the U.S. Army in 2001, and in 2004 joined the California Army National Guard. He was sent to Baghdad, Iraq, to fight in Operation Iraqi Freedom in 2004. He died on November 7, 2004, from wounds he received from an explosive device.

for the Vietnamese until 1975. This war devastated the country. More than 1.5 million Vietnamese and 58,000 Americans died.

The Vietnam War also involved the neighboring countries of Laos and Cambodia. The North Vietnamese transported troops and supplies through a series of trails that wound through the jungles of these countries. It was called the Ho Chi Minh Trail. The United States tried to destroy this route by dropping bombs on military targets in Cambodia and Laos in a secret war conducted by the Central Intelligence Agency (CIA), an agency of the U.S. federal government that spies on other countries to help keep the United States safe.

Two groups were fighting for control of Laos after it gained independence from the French, the Royal Lao (la-how) and the Communist Pathet Lao (pa-tet la-how). The United States sent weapons and supplies to the Royal Lao, as well as to the Mien (mee-ehn) and Hmong (mung) people who lived in the mountains of Laos. They were directed by their village leaders to try to disrupt the movement of supplies on the Ho Chi Minh Trail and elsewhere throughout the country.

Communists Take Over Vietnam, Cambodia, and Laos

By the end of 1973, after suffering years of heavy losses, the United States withdrew from the war. This left the South Vietnamese to continue the fight alone. In April 1975, South Vietnam fell to the Communists. The new Communist government in South Vietnam set up "reeducation camps" for people who had been on America's side. These camps were little more than prisons and forced labor camps. Food was scarce and life became unbearable.

The United States pulled out of Laos at the same time they left Vietnam. Soon after the fall of South Vietnam, Laos fell to the Pathet Lao Communists. This left many Laotians, particularly the Hmong, Lao, and Mien, in grave danger. The Pathet Lao sought them out to punish them for

cooperating with the United States. Many were sent to forced labor camps or executed.

At the same time that South Vietnam fell, Cambodia was taken over by a ruthless Communist group called the Khmer Rouge. They were led by the dictator Pol Pot. During the next four years, 1975–1979, two million Cambodians died under his brutal regime. The Khmer Rouge hunted down and executed everyone associated with the former U.S.–backed government. Pol Pot's vision of an "agrarian utopia," or farm-based society, led his regime to destroy anything deemed "intellectual." He killed all the doctors,

---

VIET D. DINH (1968–)

Assistant Attorney General of the United States

Viet D. Dinh was born in Saigon, Vietnam, and came to the United States as a refugee in 1978. Dinh served as assistant attorney general of the United States under President George W. Bush from 2000 to 2004. His most notable contribution was the creation of the USA PATRIOT Act, designed to be a powerful set of laws in the fight against terrorism. Today Viet D. Dinh is a professor at Georgetown University's Law School. The PATRIOT Act remains controversial.

lawyers, teachers, and professional people, abolished religion, and sent everyone living in the cities to work in the fields. So many people died from the deadly forced labor camps, executions, and mass starvation that places in Cambodia became known as the "Killing Fields."

Fleeing Southeast Asia

Most of the first wave of refugees were Vietnamese military personnel and their families, businesspeople, doctors, teachers, and anyone who had been employed by an American business or the U.S. government. Hundreds of people climbed onto the roof of the American embassy to reach departing helicopters. Others scrambled into boats that met American naval ships farther out at sea. Unfortunately, there was not enough room for all the Vietnamese who wanted to leave. In all, 130,000 Vietnamese refugees came to the United States in 1975.

Thousands more escaped in the years that followed, into the 1980s and beyond, usually by boat in the middle of the night. This second wave of refugees became known as the *boat people*. Hundreds perished before they were able to reach safety. Some were executed while trying to escape, others drowned at sea in leaky, overcrowded boats, and many were robbed, hurt, or killed by pirates. The lucky ones made it to refugee camps in neighboring Southeast Asian countries and eventually to the United States and other countries.

Like Vietnam, Laos was evacuated in a haze of confusion; whole villages of Hmong were airlifted out of the country. Over the next few years thousands of members of

the Lao, Hmong, and Mien ethnic groups escaped to Thailand and eventually America.

Most Cambodians were not able to leave until Pol Pot's repressive regime was overthrown in 1979. After suffering four years of persecution, forced labor, beatings, and starvation they straggled across the border to Thailand, and the world became aware of the horror they had endured. They would arrive in the United States in large numbers from that point on.

Refugee Camps

Usually refugees spent some period of time in an Asian refugee camp before coming to the United States; for some it dragged on for years. Refugee camps were set up in places like Thailand, Guam, Hong Kong, and the Philippines. They were operated by the office of the United Nations High Commissioner for Refugees (UNHCR), with help from individual nations and hundreds of charitable organizations. The camps provided only their most basic needs: safety from persecution, shelter, food, and water. Most of the refugees didn't know where they were going, or how they would get there. The camps soon became overcrowded, and the host countries were overwhelmed with the influx of people. Refugees said that the camps were dirty and that disease was widespread.

Reception Centers

The United States set up camps on military bases to give the first wave of mostly Vietnamese refugees a safe place to land after leaving Southeast Asia. These camps were designed to ease the transition to a very different life in America, where language, customs, work, and family life were radically different from what they left behind. The camps were Camp Pendleton in California, Fort Indiantown Gap in Pennsylvania, Fort Chaffee in Arkansas, and Eglin Air Force Base in Florida.

At the camps the refugees were given classes in English, and their children went to school. The refugees were taught the basics of daily life in America, such as how to shop, write a check, apply for a job, and take public transportation. The camps showed American movies and television, and set up games of Frisbee, volleyball, ping-pong, and baseball. From the camps, the refugees were relocated all across America. The camps were closed by the end of 1975.

American Sponsors

It is commonplace for cultures to welcome their own—the Italians welcome the Italians, the Polish welcome the Polish, etc., and they set up institutions to support new immigrants. However, something different happened in the 1970s when refugees from Southeast Asia arrived in America. Native-born American sponsors from California to New York opened their homes and their hearts to these refugees.

Southeast Asian families were matched up with American sponsors across the United States, who helped them adjust to their new lives. The sponsors were churches, charitable organizations, businesses, and families who wanted to help. The sponsors' responsibility was to supply food, shelter, and clothing until a family could provide these things for themselves. Sponsors either offered the refugees jobs or assisted them in finding work. Sponsors enrolled the children in American schools and offered a helping hand in any way they could.

Make a Sponsor Box

Imagine that you are responsible for sponsoring a Southeast Asian family. Set up a plan for how you would introduce American life to them. Make a list of all the things you do in a week and you will begin to understand what a complex task this was. Fill a box with props to represent the items they will need to start a new life in a new land.

What You Need

2 people

Large cardboard box

Some of the following props, or others based on your own ideas:

- A poster with essential American phrases
- Collage of popular American foods you would introduce to the family
- Balls and sporting goods to demonstrate American sports
- A bus or subway schedule
- Fork, knife, and spoon to show how they are used
- Telephone
- Signs and labels, for example: the symbol for poison (skull and crossbones), the stop sign, the circle with a cross through it that tells you *not* to do something (no smoking, no littering, etc.), and various food labels to help with shopping
- Pictures of how to cross in a crosswalk, push the walk button on a traffic light, use an elevator, and walk up an escalator
- Dollars and change to explain how money is used
- American DVDs and CDs
- Thanksgiving and Fourth of July items
- A written explanation of how to use a dishwasher, washing machine, and dryer

What You Do

1. Fill the box with your chosen props.
2. Decide who will be the refugee and who will be the sponsor.
3. The sponsor should greet the refugee and then explain the items in the box and help explain elements of daily life here in America.
4. Switch roles.
5. Ask each other these questions: What did it feel like to be the sponsor? The refugee? Can you imagine how challenging it would be to come to a new land where you don't speak the language and where life is so different from anything you've known? What would it feel like as you struggle to adjust to this new life?

Adjusting to America

Culture shock is the experience people have when they move to or visit a place that is very different from the one they are from. For Southeast Asian refugees, the first shock was usually the weather. Southeast Asia is a tropical jungle, warm like Florida in the summer. Some of the refugees arrived in the middle of winter without warm clothing such as coats, hats, and boots.

Elderly refugees generally had the most difficult time adjusting. In Southeast Asia, large families, including grandparents, lived and worked together. In the United States, husbands, wives, and children all had to leave to go to work and school. The elderly who were left alone at home felt isolated. They could not drive or speak English. Some were too afraid to leave the house.

The U.S. government had purposely scattered the families across the country, so that no one area would have to bear the economic burden. This way of living, however, was completely contrary to village life in Southeast Asia, where families all lived within walking distance of one another, and friends and neighbors formed a tightly knit community. In the United States, refugee families sometimes found themselves to be the only Asians within miles. They had no sense of family or community. When they had saved enough resources and felt confident enough to move away from their sponsors, many refugees settled together in California and in urban areas of the Northeast. Like most ethnic groups, they moved to be close to their own.

A disturbing problem in the Southeast Asian American community has been youth gangs. Many refugees moved to the United States as minors with no adult supervision, arriving as part of the Amerasian migration (see p. 188). They were attracted to gang life to feel as though they were part of a group or family. Youth gangs remain a problem, because families continue to be disrupted by unemployment, lack of education, and difficulties with language.

Vietnamese in America

The transition to American life proved difficult for the Vietnamese, especially those who came with the later waves of refugees. Those who arrived in the first wave were educated professionals, many of whom already knew how to read and write in English. Those in the second and third waves had fewer skills, little education, and little knowledge of English. This hampered them in finding employment, and many had to rely on welfare to support their families.

Overall, Vietnamese Americans have made great strides in the relatively short period of time they have been here. They work hard and encourage their children to excel in school. Vietnamese fishermen have been very successful in Southern California, and a large percentage of Vietnamese Americans are small business owners.

LEE LY HAYSLIP (1949–)
Vietnamese American Writer

Lee Ly Hayslip has written two books about her life in Vietnam and America. *When Heaven and Earth Changed Places: A Vietnamese Woman's Journey from War to Peace*, written with Jay Wurts, tells about her horrible experiences at the hands of the South Vietnamese during the Vietnam War. It was developed into a motion picture, *Heaven & Earth*, in 1993. *Child of War, Woman of Peace*, written with James Hayslip, describes her life in America as a refugee.

In 1988, Lee Ly Hayslip established the East Meets West Foundation. The foundation works to promote peace between Vietnam and the United States.

Amerasian Homecoming Act of 1987

Amerasian children are children whose fathers are American and whose mothers are Asian. Thousands of such children were left behind in Vietnam after the American troops pulled out, the sons and daughters of American servicemen. The children and their Vietnamese mothers were not allowed to leave. Life in Vietnam was particularly hard for

Amerasian children. They were called "bui doi" (boo-ee duhy), which means "children of the dust," because so many of them ended up living on the streets in Vietnam.

In 1987, the U.S. government teamed up with the Vietnamese government to help Amerasians immigrate to the United States. They simplified the paperwork needed to leave Vietnam and to enter the United States and allocated money for the transition process. Their goal was to reunite families torn apart by war.

Little Saigons: Vietnamese American Communities

Little Saigons have blossomed in areas such as California, Texas, and Florida. These communities offer a glimpse into what life was once like in Vietnam. They have businesses that cater to Vietnamese Americans such as noodle shops, Vietnamese delis, and bakeries that offer delicious breads and pastries reflecting the colonial French influence. Grocery stores sell Vietnamese foods such as fish sauce, rice noodles, rice paper, dried fish, and Vietnamese coffee; tanks are filled with live crab, lobster, tilapia, sea snails, Vietnamese black eels, catfish, and octopus. There are stores that carry traditional Vietnamese clothing and home goods such as delicate tea sets. There are acupuncturists, beauty parlors, and karaoke bars that feature Vietnamese music. Vietnamese jewelry stores feature glass boxes of beautiful gold and jade jewelry.

Tet: Vietnamese New Year

Tet (teht) is the largest and most joyous celebration of the year among Vietnamese Americans. It is celebrated at the beginning of the lunar new year, usually between the last half of January and the first half of February. It signals the end of the Vietnamese winter and the promise of spring. Tet is a time to celebrate new beginnings and appreciate family and friends.

The holiday is celebrated in the United States by families cleaning the house and buying new clothes, gifts, and special foods to prepare for the holiday. All of the work must be completed before the new year begins.

The first visitor to the house on Tet is very important, because he or she sets the tone for the new year. Most families invite a person of great integrity or importance in the hope that that person will be the first visitor of the day. Another important part of the Tet celebration is visiting a Buddhist temple to pray. But being with family is the most important part of the holiday. Some Vietnamese Americans even return to Vietnam to celebrate Tet with their families.

In a traditional Vietnamese American home, an altar is set up with offerings to ancestors. Photographs of relatives who have died are displayed alongside candles, incense, flowers, and platters of fresh fruit. The house is decorated with peach blossoms to symbolize rebirth and the coming of spring.

Traditional Tet foods include pickled vegetables and banh chung (pork, beans, and rice wrapped in banana leaves). Banh chung is symbolic of the earth and is sometimes called "earth cakes." Children enjoy candied dried ginger, coconut, and pineapple treats, known as mut (uum-ut), and receive presents of money in red envelopes from relatives.

Prepare a Bowl of Vietnamese Beef Noodle Soup

Pho (fuh) is a delicious Vietnamese noodle soup that is popular in both the United States and Vietnam. Large, hearty bowls of noodles, meat, vegetables, and broth are enjoyed for breakfast as well as lunch and dinner.

5 servings

What You Need
Adult supervision required
1 cup bean sprouts
Colander
4 small bowls for ingredients
1 bunch fresh basil leaves, washed
3 scallions
Cutting board
Knife
8 ounces banh pho, rice sticks that look like long, clear noodles (available in Asian food stores)
Large pot

½-inch slice peeled fresh ginger
1 pound eye round beef roast
2 tablespoons oil
Regular or electric frying pan
Cooking spatula or spoon
1 package of pho (instant Vietnamese beef broth, available at Asian food stores) and 10 cups of water
OR
5 cups low-sodium beef broth and 5 cups water
Ladle
Serving bowls
Vietnamese fish sauce

What You Do
1. Rinse the bean sprouts in the colander and then set aside in a bowl.
2. Rinse the basil leaves in the colander and set in the second bowl.
3. Rinse and chop the scallion into small pieces and place in the third bowl.

4. Place the banh pho in a large pot of cold water to soften for 10 minutes. Rinse in the colander.
5. Bring a pot of water to a boil and add the rice sticks (noodles). Boil for 8 minutes. Drain and rinse with cold water.
6. Chop the ginger into small pieces and set aside.
7. Slice the beef very thinly into strips.
8. Heat the oil in the frying pan. Fry the ginger for about one minute. Put the beef slices into the pan and fry for about 5 minutes. Take the meat and ginger out and place in the fourth bowl.
9. Heat 10 cups of water to boiling in the pot. Stir in powdered pho mix. (Or substitute the low-sodium beef broth and water.)
10. Remove from heat. Add the bean sprouts and noodles, mix. Place the beef on top.
11. Ladle into serving bowls. Garnish with chopped scallions and a few basil leaves. For an authentic Vietnamese taste, add a few drops of fish sauce.

Create a Foam Dragon for Tet

A fun part of Tet celebrations in the United States is the dragon dance. Make a colorful foam dragon. If you are making dragons as a group you can combine them and try to make the world's longest dragon!

What You Need

9 sheets 9-by-12-inch craft foam, in
    different bright colors
Pen
Scissors
Hole puncher
8-inch plate to trace
1 yard elastic bead cord (available at craft
    stores)
Markers, feathers, buttons, pom-poms, pipe
    cleaners, etc., to decorate dragon's face
Glue

What You Do

1. Start with one foam sheet; turn so the short ends are on the sides. Draw a zigzag design along the bottom as shown and cut out.
2. Pull the top of the foam into a tepee shape, so that it forms a cone. Staple together.
3. Punch 2 holes in the back of the cone, one at the top and one at the bottom, as shown.
4. Repeat steps 1–3 with 7 more pieces, leaving one piece aside to make the face.
5. Attach the shapes together with small pieces of bead cord. Tie the bottom of one shape to the top of the next, allowing the pieces to overlap slightly.
6. Use the plate to draw a circle on the remaining piece of foam and cut it out.
7. Punch a hole in the bottom of the circle and attach with cord to the front of the dragon's body to serve as its head.
8. Decorate the dragon's face with markers, or glue on feathers, buttons, pom poms, and pipe cleaners. Use your imagination—anything goes!

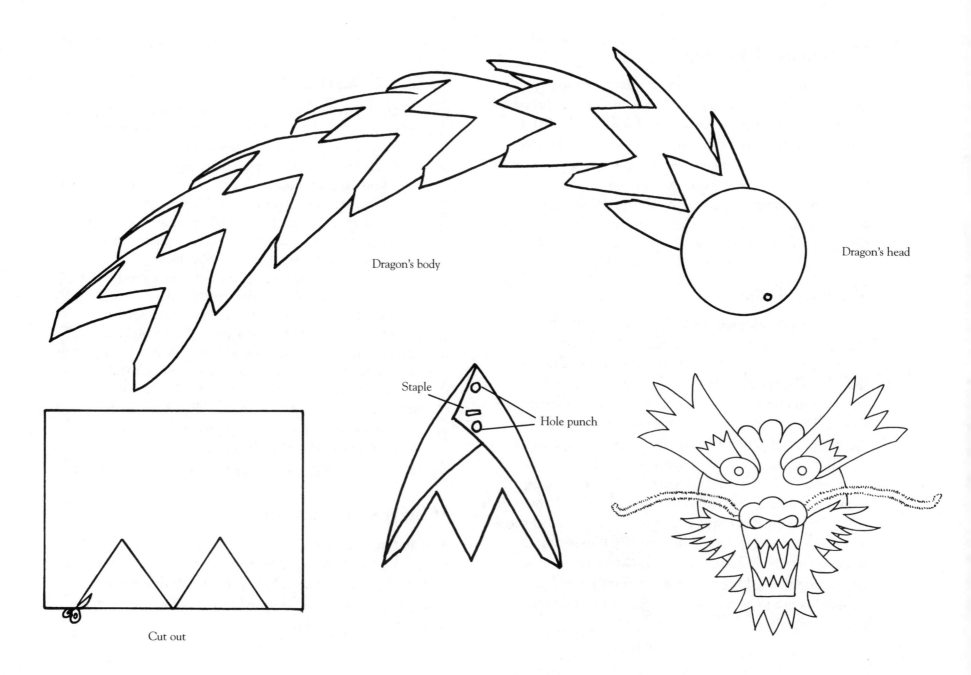

Dragon's body

Dragon's head

Staple

Hole punch

Cut out

193

Vietnamese Clothing

Traditional Vietnamese clothing is usually made of light-weight cotton and accompanied by a conical hat called *non* (known), made of palm leaves and bamboo. The hat works perfectly to shield the face from sun and rain. The traditional Vietnamese women's costume is called *ao dai* (ow zeye). It is a long tunic worn over loose pants. Vietnamese American women enjoy wearing the ao dai for special occasions such as Tet. There is also a similar costume for men that is worn less frequently.

Vietnam Today

The country of Vietnam looks like a long S. It's 1,025 miles (1,653 km) long and only 31 miles (50 km) across at its thinnest point. It is located on the east side of the Indochina Peninsula. Much of the north country is hilly and mountainous. There are many rivers and marshes that thread through the country, especially in the south, and there is a lot of activity on the water. Boats are used for traveling, for homes, and as floating stores!

Vietnam is a very poor country with a growing gap between rich and poor. Most of the workers are farmers. It is still a Communist country, but in recent years the government has encouraged privately owned businesses, and even foreign-owned businesses, to operate in Vietnam. Also, farmers are now allowed to grow crops on private plots (instead of group plots where the government divides the earnings equally).

SOUTHEAST ASIAN FOOD

Southeast Asian food shows a variety of foreign influences, including Chinese, French, and Indian. Southeast Asian food has traditionally depended on fresh local foods: a plentiful supply of fish, rice, and rice products such as rice noodles and rice pancakes, and fresh fruits and vegetables. Pork is a favorite meat. Food is prepared on top of the stove and cut up into small pieces that allow the diner to eat with chopsticks.

Popular Vietnamese foods are pho soup (see p. 190), spring rolls, wraps filled with seafood and vegetables, and French bakery products such as croissants. Dishes found on the Cambodian table include sour soups and spicy seafood salads. Laotians eat sticky rice with every meal. Fermented rice paste called *padek* is used in many Laotian dishes. *Laap* is a dish that is distinctly Laotian, made of fish or meat, lime juice, vegetables, and chilies.

It Started in Vietnam!

The first inhabitants of Vietnam were growing rice by 2000 B.C.E., and they developed advanced irrigation systems as far back as the first century. There is evidence that by 300 B.C.E., the Vietnamese possessed intricate metalwork made in bronze.

Vietnamese water puppetry is a traditional art. It is sometimes performed in the United States as well. Large wooden puppets are moved on poles by puppeteers who stand in water behind a bamboo screen. Their shadows make it appear as if the puppets are dancing on a river or lake. A modern Vietnamese art is filmmaking.

Many of the clothes and shoes that we buy in the United States today are made in Vietnam. You can look for a "Made in Vietnam" label on the inside of the garment. We also buy Vietnamese frozen fish, coffee, and crude oil.

Laotians in America

Laotians arrived in America with even less familiarity with American culture and language than the Vietnamese. In addition, many Laotians were not able to read or write in their own language, so schooling became a difficult issue. They had to learn their own language first and then English, which made their adjustment more complicated.

In Laos, most families earned their living through farming. When they came to the United States, they had trouble finding jobs that they were qualified to do. As a result many of the first-generation immigrants had to rely on welfare to support their families. In addition, men and boys who had been soldiers in Laos suffered from memories of war that caused depression and even sudden death syndrome, a condition in which healthy men suddenly die.

The second generation of Laotians raised in America are doing well in work and in school. Many don't remember Laos, or were born here as Laotian Americans.

Hmong: An Oral Tradition of Communication

For most of their history, the Hmong had only a spoken language. There was no written language until the 1950s! At that time a team of French and American missionaries devised a system that made Hmong sounds using the letters of the English alphabet.

Hmong Clothing

Traditionally the Hmong made their clothing from the hemp plant. The cloth was colored with flower petals to make brilliant colors such as hot pinks, oranges, reds, blues, yellows, and greens. The pride of the Hmong is in the elaborate embroidery they use in clothing and ceremonial costumes. Their clothes and fabrics, like jewels, are the wealth of the family. In traditional Hmong society, the embroidering abilities of a young woman are very important in finding a mate. Girls begin to learn embroidery at about six years of age.

Because the Hmong left their homeland with so few possessions, it has been a blessing that their skill with handicrafts can be taught for generations to come. Each region and sect of Hmong wear their own traditional clothes. Special clothing is made weeks in advance for the Hmong New Year.

Play Pov Pob: A Hmong Ball-Toss Game for New Year's

Hmong New Year is celebrated in much the same way as Tet. The holiday lasts for at least a week in Laos, but usually just for a weekend in the United States. It is a celebration of the harvest, when the farming was over for the season. During the festivities, teenagers play *pov pob* (baw baw), a ball-toss game. It was originally designed to give unmarried teens an opportunity to meet before marriage.

Rows of boys faced girls dressed in their finest embroidered clothes and threw the ball back and forth over a period of days. In that way they had an opportunity to meet other teens, without dating, which is not allowed. Parents would sit by the side to watch the games and laugh at the funny songs. Today in the United States, it is practiced as a fun game and not a courting ritual, as in Hmong celebrations.

What You Need
Even number of players (at least 4)
1 tennis ball for every 2 players

What to Do
1. Divide the players up into two rows of equal number. Line up the groups about 10 feet apart, facing each other in pairs.
2. Throw the ball underhand back and forth.
3. If you drop the ball you must pay for it by singing a song. You can make up songs and ask questions in the songs.

Color a Hmong Flower Cloth: Paj Ntaub

Paj ntaub (pahn dah-oh) means "flower cloth." Brilliantly colored geometric designs are used to decorate clothing, baby carriers, purses, hats, burial cloths, and more. To be able to make paj ntaub is very much a part of being Hmong.

What You Need

2 sheets graph paper
Colored pencils or markers

What You Do

1. Make Hmong designs on the graph paper as shown. The Xs represent the overlapping stitches that would be used to create actual paj ntaub designs. In embroidery terms this is called *cross-stitching*. A cross-stitch is made by bringing a threaded needle from the back of the fabric through the lower left-hand corner of a stitch, going to the upper right-hand corner, then back down to the back of the fabric and back up through the lower right-hand corner and finishing the stitch by putting it through the upper left-hand corner.

For the snail house design:

2. Use a black pencil to make the Xs as shown. Choose one color other than black to fill in the blank spaces with Xs. Traditional Hmong colors include pink, red, blue, purple, green, or yellow.

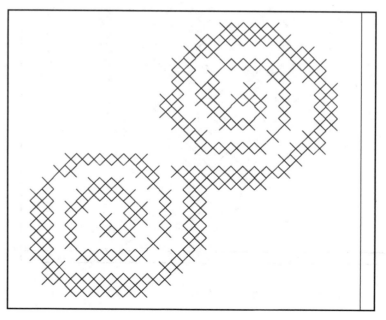

Snail house design

197

For the tiger's face design:

3. Use a black pencil or marker to make the Xs as shown. Choose a color other than black to fill in the blank spaces with Xs. You may use one color for all, or use one for the inside of the heart and another for the outside of the heart.
4. Look at the designs from a distance and you will see the Xs disappear.

Tiger face design

Design a Storytelling Cloth

The *storytelling cloth* is a recent form of tapestry that developed as part of the refugee experience. While waiting in refugee camps in places like Thailand, the Hmong developed story cloths to preserve their history. They include traditional designs as well as drawings of people, animals, trees, rice, water, and homes to depict scenes from life.

The storytelling cloths and flower cloths have become a source of income for the Hmong. Men draw the pictures and women embroider over them.

What You Need
Plain bandanna in denim-colored blue
   (this is the color of most story cloths),
   gray, or ivory*
Fabric markers*

*Regular paper and regular colored markers may be used instead.

What You Do
1. Make a storytelling cloth that tells the story of the Hmong people:

   The Hmong lived thousands of years ago in China. They were driven out, and migrated to different countries in Southeast Asia, including the mountains of Laos. In the 1970s, war broke out in their villages between the Pathet Lao and United States–backed troops. The soldiers gave the Hmong men guns to fight the Pathet Lao. Laos fell to the Pathet Lao Communists after the U.S. troops left. The Pathet Lao hunted the Hmong to punish them for cooperating with the United States. Many Hmong were sent to forced labor camps, or executed. They escaped by floating on bamboo life rafts and boats across the Mekong River to Thailand. They found shelter in the refugee camps in Thailand. Finally they crossed the ocean to life in America.

2. Your story cloth should include a border of traditional Hmong designs as shown. Hmong men are depicted wearing long, baggy black pants and a black shirt tucked in at the waist. Around the waist, a colorful red band is worn. Hmong women are shown with a black or multicolored shirt and skirt (more like a tunic) over black pants, which are also held in place with a red band. Words are sometimes included as well, especially the names of countries.

Laos Today

Laos is a small landlocked country surrounded by Thailand, Vietnam, China, and Cambodia. The country is extremely mountainous and rugged; only 10 percent of the land is fertile enough to use for living and farming. There are no railroads, and roads are not reliable because they are not maintained. There are few telephones, and electricity is available only in limited areas. It is an extremely poor, developing country, and it has remained Communist. In 1986, to help the country grow, the government began a program to encourage private business, but most farmers still earn less than one dollar a day.

It Started in Laos!

Needlework is the Hmong cultural gift to the world. It is the bright light in the bleak refugee experience that they can now share these lovely textiles with others.

Batik is another textile craft from Laos, in which melted wax is painted onto cloth and then dipped in dye. When the wax is removed it leaves softly blending geometric designs.

Recently the government of Laos has promoted tourism. Visitors enjoy visiting the Buddhist temples, cruising down the Mekong River to see Laotian fishing villages, and going to the *Plain of Jars*, a plateau in the northern mountains of Laos where hundreds of enormous stone jars are scattered among the grasses and trees. The mystery is that no one knows how the ancient vessels got there or why! Archaeologists believe that they could be funeral urns, because there was jewelry and burial artifacts in them when they were first discovered in the 1930s. These artifacts are now gone, either lost or stolen. The jars are believed to be about 2,000 years old.

Cambodians in America

It has been a tremendous struggle for Cambodians to adjust to life in America. More than half of Cambodian Americans live below the poverty level, most in inner-city neighborhoods. Lack of language skills and education, cultural differences, and the trauma of living through Pol Pot's terrible regime have taken their toll on Cambodians who managed to flee to America.

In spite of their hardships many Cambodians are succeeding. A high number of working Cambodians have gravitated toward owning their own small businesses such as doughnut shops, restaurants, and convenience stores.

Cambodian Court Dance: Learn the Hand Gestures

Cambodian court dances were originally performed only for royalty. Today the dances are performed for everyone to celebrate traditional holidays. They are highly stylized, meaning every small movement holds a meaning. The dancers wear very ornate clothing and headdresses. Sometimes the costumes must be so tight that they are sewn onto the dancers before a performance!

What You Need

Southeast Asian music CD (you can borrow at your library)

CD player

What You Do

1. To warm up, bend your hand up at the wrist and then gently bend your fingers back.
2. Try these different hand gestures:
   - Index finger pointing up and back: Represents spring buds
   - One hand open, fingers spread back: Represents a leaf
   - Index finger and thumb pinched together, fingers spread: Represents a flower
   - Middle finger and thumb together in a circle, other fingers back: Represents fruit
3. Make up a story/dance using the hand gestures.
4. Move to the Southeast Asian music.

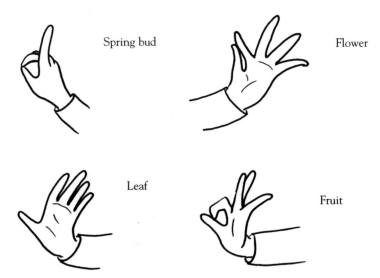

Spring bud

Flower

Leaf

Fruit

Mold a Khmer Theater Mask

When Pol Pot was dictator of Cambodia, all arts were forbidden. If you were caught painting, dancing, singing, or performing, you would be killed. The traditional arts of the *Khmer*, an ethnic group that makes up 90 percent of the Cambodian population, were nearly wiped out during his reign. Many Cambodian dancers, some of whom learned to dance in Southeast Asian refugee camps, now live in the United States, where they perform and teach others to perform in the traditional Cambodian style.

A classic tale of Cambodian dance theater is the Khmer version of the Indian story *Ramayana*. The main character is the monkey god Hanuman, who always wears a white mask. Make this mask and help keep Cambodian artistic traditions alive.

What You Need
Adult supervision required
Thick newspaper surface
1 roll plaster cloth (available in craft
    stores)
Scissors
6 paper cups, 1 filled halfway with warm
    water

Plain plastic mask (available in craft
    stores)
Acrylic paint in white, red, gold, and black
    (to be poured into paper cups as
    needed)
Paintbrush
Gold glitter
Polyurethane gloss varnish (available in
    craft stores, to be poured into paper
    cup as needed)

What You Do
1. Lay out the newspaper work surface.
2. Cut pieces of the plaster cloth, a few at a time. Dip each piece in the warm water and lay across the mask, until the mask is covered in four or five layers. Use the picture as a guide.
3. Cut additional pieces and scrunch them up to make the monkey god's nose, ears, crowning points, and headband. The plaster cloth will stick almost like clay when it is wet. Dispose of the leftover water by stuffing newspaper in it and throwing it away. *Do not pour it down the drain, because it could clog up the pipes.* Let dry for 24 hours.

4. Remove the plastic mask from underneath. The mask can be used again and again to make other masks.
5. Paint the mask all over with the white paint. Let dry.
6. Paint the lips and swirl marks red. Let dry.
7. Paint the ears and headband gold. Sprinkle the gold parts with glitter. Let dry.
8. Paint the eyebrows, crowning points, inner mouth, and outline of the lips and teeth in black. Let dry.
9. Paint the mask all over with gloss varnish. Let dry.

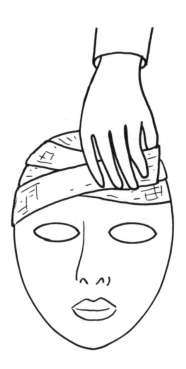

DITH PRAN (1942–)
International Photojournalist

Dith Pran was working as a guide and interpreter for international journalists during the Vietnam War and the takeover of Cambodia by the Khmer Rouge. His four-year ordeal in Cambodia's slave labor camps was dramatically told in the motion picture *The Killing Fields* in 1984.

In 1979 Pran escaped to Thailand and then to the United States, accompanied by the *New York Times* journalist Sydney Schanberg, who had worked for years to get Pran out of Cambodia. In 1980, Pran was given a job to work as a *New York Times* photojournalist.

He has established the Dith Pran Holocaust Awareness Project to educate students in the United States and the rest of the world about the Cambodian tragedy.

Say It in Khmer

The official language of Cambodia is Khmer. Here are some words for you to try.

Hello:	*johm riab sua* (zhoem rih-yahb swah)
Good-bye:	*lia sun hao-y* (lih-yah suhn hah-wee)
Please:	*sohm* (sawm)
Thank you:	*aw kohn* (aw koen)

Cambodian Clothing

Traditional Khmer clothing includes the *sarong* (suh-rawng), a wraparound skirt for men and women; a scarf worn over the head or shoulders called a *krama* (kih-rah-muh); and the women's long dress called *phamuong* (faw-mwahng). Cambodian Americans usually dress in American clothes, and save traditional clothes for holidays and special occasions.

Cambodia Today

Cambodia is located in the southwest of the Indochina Peninsula, with Thailand and Laos to the north and Vietnam to the south. Its coast borders the Gulf of Thailand. Ninety-five percent of Cambodians are Buddhist, and most live and work in the countryside.

The Khmer, who represent 90 percent of the people in Cambodia, are an ethnic group who originally migrated from China. In Cambodia's early years merchants from India came and set up kingdoms. These early Hindu kingdoms spread Indian culture to the Khmer. The Cambodian language, ancient temples, music, dance, and cuisine all reflect this early Indian influence.

In 1993, Cambodia abandoned Communism and established a constitutional monarchy. They have a king who is largely a figurehead. The real power lies in democratically elected officials led by a prime minister and a legislature. The government is still rebuilding the country since the devastation of Pol Pot's regime. The country remains one of the poorest in the world. Most people are farmers and grow just enough food to survive. This is called *subsistence farming*.

It Started in Cambodia!

Cambodia has an ancient center of 100 magnificent temples. They were built by Khmer kings who ruled between the 9th and 15th centuries, and who were believed to be gods. The most famous of these temples is Angkor Wat (ang-koer waht), which is full of ornate carvings from Hindu folklore. It had been abandoned for more than 500 years before being refurbished by a team of historical renovators in the 1980s. In 1992 it was declared a World Heritage Site by the United Nations.

Cambodian traditional dance is considered a national treasure. It began as entertainment for the Khmer god-kings and has survived war and the near destruction of the country.

Recently Cambodia has begun promoting tourism, which will be a good source of revenue for the country in the future.

Make Cambodian Spring Rolls

Try these delicious spring rolls, which Cambodians have brought to America. In Cambodia you might buy these from a street vendor for an afternoon snack.

What You Need

Adult supervision required

1 carrot, peeled
½ onion
2 cloves peeled garlic
4 scallions
Food processor or chopper
Large bowl
Fork
1 pound ground pork
1 egg
½ teaspoon salt

Pepper
½ teaspoon sugar
Paper towels
2 cookie sheets
12–15 spring roll
 wrappers
Tablespoon
Electric frying pan
2 cups vegetable oil
Tongs

What You Do

1. Chop carrot, onion, garlic, and scallions in the food processor.
2. Mix chopped vegetables, ground pork, egg, salt, a few shakes of pepper, and sugar in a large bowl. Set aside.
3. Place several damp paper towels on the cookie sheet. Put 2 spring roll wrappers at a time between them like a sandwich. This is to keep them soft. Put a heaping tablespoon of the pork mixture like a log in the middle of the spring roll wrapper on the top of the pile. Wrap the sides in first and then wrap from the bottom up like an egg roll. Keep moist under the paper towels. Repeat until all the mixture is gone.
4. Take the second cookie sheet and put a few layers of dry paper towels on it. Set aside.
5. Heat the oil in the electric frying pan. Put the spring rolls in and cook, turning on all sides until nicely browned, about 15 minutes. The oil should be bubbling but not cracking.
6. Place cooked spring rolls on the second cookie sheet. To keep warm until serving, place the cookie sheet in the oven with the heat turned low.

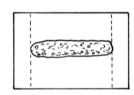 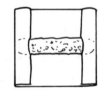

◆ Conclusion ◆

The Challenges of Becoming American

Nowadays sometimes I feel like a frog jumping from one world to the other: school, my family, being American, being Khmer. In a way, to be assimilated into another culture, you have to give up your own culture. With one foot in each culture, the wider you have to spread your legs, the more you could lose your balance. I'm at a point in my life where for the first time I feel vulnerable, and it's scary.

> —Sathaya Tor, a Cambodian refugee who spent four years at a child labor camp in Cambodia. In 1979, at 12 years old, he crossed minefields to escape to Thailand. He immigrated to the United States in 1981 and later enrolled as a student at Stanford University. From *Strangers from a Different Shore: A History of Asian Americans* by Ronald Takaki

The Balancing Act

Trying to keep your balance with a foot in each culture is a good image to keep in mind when trying to understand the challenges of Asian Americans. Age seems to be a large factor in how heavily the immigrant leans toward his or her original culture or toward American culture. Older immigrants usually cling to the language, culture, and attitudes of their homeland. In a way they try to re-create, in this new country, the life they had in their old country.

It is the young immigrants who fully embrace American culture. They quickly learn to speak English, love hamburgers and french fries, watch American movies, listen to American music, and learn how to send instant messages over the Internet. But in the process they lose something as well. They speak less and less of the language of their parents and grandparents, don't learn how to cook traditional Asian food as much, and over time lose the cultural connections of their heritage.

With each succeeding generation, fewer traditional holidays are celebrated. For instance, Diwali in India is a magical celebration. The streets are filled with people, the sounds of firecrackers burst through the air, and hundreds of oil lights glow. People are happy, exchanging gifts and sweets; the air is thick with celebration and festivity. In the United States, celebrations are much more subdued. They take place in isolation—a home here or there, or in a church or community hall. The second and third generations have no memories of celebrations in the old country because they were born in the United States.

Asian Features

As Asian Americans mix into American society, they are more likely than other immigrant groups to still be seen as "different," because they show their heritage with their faces. Asian Americans who were born in the United States, speak perfect English, and have never even been to Asia may be asked where they are from. Or they may be referred to as "the Asian kid" or "the Chinese boy." You never hear someone refer to an Irish American as "the Irish kid," because people who look European are automatically considered Americans.

Language

One of the most difficult hurdles for new Asian immigrants is language. Asian languages are dramatically different from English. In Chinese, you write in characters that must be memorized. They have no letter-sound relationship. Spoken Chinese is just that, a language that you hear only. The sounds are never translated into letters. So to learn English, someone who reads and writes in Chinese must first learn how letters represent sounds. Also, since some Asian languages are tonal, the meaning of the words changing as your voice rises, falls, or stays the same, some Asian immigrants must adjust to the fact that there are no such tones in English.

The first child born in the United States may act as an interpreter for his or her parents or grandparents. This turns the parent/child relationship around, making the parent dependent on the child. Sometimes the grandchildren in an Asian American family cannot speak the family's original language and the grandparents can't speak English. This disrupts traditional family relationships, in which grandchildren are expected to go to their elders for advice and guidance.

Individualism Versus the Group

One of the most striking differences between Asian and American cultures is the Asian value of cooperation within a group, whether it is your family or your community. Asian children are brought up with the knowledge that they are forever in debt to their parents and family. They are taught that the family comes before the individual. Being cooperative, helping others, and putting other people first are very highly valued principles.

In American culture, the opposite values are rewarded. Parents, teachers, employers, and American society in general reward independent thinking. Americans are encouraged to ask questions, challenge authority, be their own people, forge their own paths, go it alone. This kind of thinking does result in a particular type of American ingenuity; for example, more Nobel Prize winners are from the United States than any other country. The downside is that children may live hundreds of miles away from parents and grandparents and may not offer the type of family support that Asian families can count on.

Expectations at School

In most Asian countries, students listen quietly and passively to their teachers. They spend hours taking notes, reading, and taking tests to prove that they have learned a certain set of facts. In American classrooms, teachers expect totally different behavior. Learning in the United States involves asking questions, participating in lively debates, doing independent research, and engaging in innovative thinking. Passive behavior that is rewarded in Asian classrooms can result in bad grades in the United States. Asian students often say that they must act one way at home and another way at school to succeed.

Dating

Dating seems to be one of the most heated issues dividing Asian immigrant parents and their children. In most Asian countries, there is no such thing as dating. When young adults reach marriageable age, their parents or a matchmaker chooses a mate for them. Even if they choose their own marriage partner, it would be disrespectful to openly date in front of their family. Hugging and kissing is never done in public.

In the United States, the children of Asian immigrants are exposed to American dating habits. They are invited to parties and dances and places where young men and women are encouraged to pair up. Many Asian families forbid this behavior, and it makes being an Asian teenager very difficult. The young person has to choose between being an average American teen and a traditional Asian son or daughter.

Other Cultural Differences

There are many hidden examples of cultural differences that people don't even realize are there until cultures interact. For example, in most Asian cultures, looking someone directly in the eyes is seen as being disrespectful or confrontational. In the United States it is seen as a sign of confidence and honesty.

Asian immigrants often have trouble saying no in a direct way. Let's say for example you ask an Asian immigrant if he or she would like to attend a concert next week. That person might reply by answering "maybe" or "perhaps" or "I will get back to you about that" and then not speak about it again. To an American who wants a yes or no answer, this might seem rude. To the Asian person, this is a polite way to say no without offending you.

"Oriental" Is for Rugs

For many years, Americans referred to people from Asia as "Orientals." Many people don't realize that this is really an offensive term. It was originally used by 19th-century people to mean other, exotic, or different. To put it in plain terms, it's like saying "weird" or "freaky," and it is not a term that most people want applied to them. Today the acceptable term is "Asian" or "Asian American."

Asian Pacific American Heritage Month

Asian Pacific American heritage has been celebrated in May every year since 1979. The holiday originated in a congressional bill, and in May 1990 President George H. W. Bush expanded it into a month-long celebration. May was chosen because on May 10, 1869, the transcontinental railroad was completed—largely due to the labor of thousands of Chinese immigrants. Asian Pacific American Heritage Month also celebrates the heritage of Pacific Americans, who are from Guam, Samoa, Fiji, Tonga, the Marshall Islands, and other islands in the Pacific Ocean.

Design a Poster to Celebrate Asian Pacific American Heritage Month

Here's one final activity to honor the tapestry of cultures that help color our country and contribute to the richness of our lives.

What You Need

Posterboard
Markers
Pictures from magazines and the Internet
Scissors
Glue stick

What You Do

1. Find out what the theme of the year will be for the next Asian Pacific American Heritage Month and create a poster to draw awareness. You can find the theme listed yearly with other information about Asian Pacific American Heritage Month on the Web at www.infoplease.com/spot/asianhistory1.html. Previous themes include "Breakthrough," which explored advances that Asian Pacific Americans have made in different aspects of life, "Freedom for All," and "Salute to Liberty."

2. Decide what kind of collage you'd like to create to represent the Asian American experience. You can create a collage of pictures with words or pictures and drawings or all three.

3. You may elect to choose your own theme, such as "Asian Pacific American Music," "Asian Pacific American Literature," "Asian Pacific American Holidays," or "Notable Asian Pacific Americans."

4. If you would like to make your poster about the past, look at some historical photographs available online from the Library of Congress Prints and Photographs Online Catalog. Go to www.loc.gov/rr/print/catalog.html, read and agree to the viewing terms on the opening page, then type in "Chinese children in Olympia" to view the image you see here from 1919. You can search by keywords such as "Chinese American" or "Chinatown" or "relocation camps."

Asian Pacific American
Immigrant Children
"Remembering the Past,
Looking to the Future"
Celebrate Asian Pacific
American Heritage Month

5. Look carefully at the photographs to see if they give clues to the past such as ethnic clothing, food, homes, work, transportation, and more.

6. Ask permission to hang your poster (or a class group of posters) at school, in your local library, or in a museum, restaurant, or store.

A Shared History, A Bright Future

Thousands of Asian immigrants came to America in the mid-1800s to search for work and better opportunities for themselves and their families. Sadly, what they often found was backbreaking labor and racial prejudice. In spite of these difficulties, Asian Americans built railroads, mined ore, cut sugarcane, ran laundries, farmed fields, fished, started businesses, and fought in wars to defend America.

Along the way they have shared the richness of their culture by bringing with them beautiful silks and porcelain, brush-stroke art and calligraphy, new spices and methods of cooking such as stir-fry, different forms of spirituality including Buddhism and Hinduism, and alternative ways to nurture our health such as meditation and acupuncture. We take lessons in taekwondo and yoga, eat dim sum and drink green tea, use computers that run with Asian Indian American–designed Pentium chips, listen to the music of Yo-Yo Ma, and watch golfer Michelle Wie.

There are Asian American leaders in every aspect of American society: scientists, doctors, athletes, politicians, entertainers, entrepreneurs, writers, architects, inventors, artists, and more. Asian Americans fight in our wars, sit on our courts, represent us in Congress, and design our software. Their contributions to American life are tightly woven into the fabric of our country. They are Asian and they are American, and their history is American history.

◆ Resources ◆

ASIAN AMERICAN QUICK FACTS

- According to the United States Census there are 13.1 million Asians living in the United States, which is 5 percent of the total population.
- It is predicted that by the year 2050 there will be 33.4 million Asians in the United States, a 213 percent increase!
- As of 2004 the United States was home to 2.7 million Chinese, 2.4 million Filipinos, 1.9 million Asian Indians, 1.2 million Koreans, 1.2 million Vietnamese, 1.1 million Japanese, 206,000 Cambodians, 199,000 Laotians, and 190,000 Hmong.
- 75 percent of all Asian people live in 10 states: California, New York, Hawaii, Texas, New Jersey, Illinois, Washington, Florida, Virginia, and Massachusetts.

◆ Glossary ◆

Alaskeros: Filipino immigrants who worked in the salmon canneries of Alaska in the early 1900s

alien: a person who is not a citizen of a particular country

Amerasians: the children of American servicemen and Asian women

Angel Island: a processing center for mostly Asian immigrants in San Francisco, California, that operated from 1910 to 1940

anime: Japanese animated films

animism: a nature-based religion, practiced by some people in the Philippines

ao dai: the traditional Vietnamese women's costume, a long tunic worn over loose pants

Asian American: a person who immigrated to the United States from Asia, or who has a parent, grandparent, or great-grandparent from Asia

Ati: the first inhabitants of the Philippines, who traveled there over land bridges from Asia during the ice age

auspicious: lucky or likely to be favorable

ayurvedic medicine: an ancient Asian Indian practice that treats the mind and body as one

balikbayan box: a box containing food, gifts, and clothes that Filipino immigrants in America send home to their families in the Philippines

bandalores: a centuries-old toy from the Philippines that became the basis for the yo-yo

barong tagalog: the national dress for men in the Philippines; it is a long-sleeved buttoned shirt made of pina cloth or cotton, with intricate embroidery, which is worn over trousers

bento: an old Japanese-style boxed lunch that is still made today

bibingka: a sweet rice dessert, the traditional Christmas treat of the Philippines

bindi: a circle of red powder that is worn on the foreheads of Hindu women and girls, for religious ceremonies and special occasions

boat people: refugees who flee, without adequate food and supplies, to another country in small boats

Bon Odori: a Japanese folk dance that shows one's appreciation for family and ancestors

bonsai: the Japanese art of cultivating miniature trees

caste system: hereditary levels of social groups based on wealth, rank, or occupation

Chanoyu: the Japanese tea ceremony, a centuries-old tradition designed to purify your mind and put you in touch with nature

characters: the symbols used to make words in certain Asian languages; unlike letters, which match particular sounds, these symbols represent whole words or ideas

child prodigy: a young person with extraordinary talents

Communist country: a country in which the government owns all the property and businesses and makes most of the decisions for the people

Confucianism: A system of moral behavior and ethics taught by the philosopher Confucius

constitutional monarchy: a form of government led by a king, whose powers are restricted by a constitution

credit-ticket system: the Chinese system in which brokers bought tickets for people who wanted to immigrate to America; the immigrants paid the brokers back along with interest (additional money) after earning money in America

cross-stitching: an embroidery technique, used in the Hmong art of paj ntaub, in which X-shaped stitches are used to form larger designs

culture shock: the experience one has when one moves to or visits a place that is very different from the place one is from

daruma: Japanese dolls believed to be good luck charms

dhoti: an article of clothing worn by men in India; it is a piece of cloth that is wrapped around the bottom half of the body

dim sum: a Chinese brunch; in Cantonese "dim" means "a little bit" and "sum" means "heart"

Diwali: the Asian Indian holiday that celebrates the victory of light over darkness and goodness over evil

diyas: shallow earthenware pots filled with oil and lit to celebrate the Asian Indian holiday Diwali

domino theory: the idea that countries would fall to Communism one after another, like a row of domino tiles, and that if one country went Communist, then the bordering countries were likely to go Communist, too

double happiness: the Chinese character that represents love and the destiny of a man and woman to go through life together

Ellis Island: the primary immigration center for immigrants entering America from 1892 to 1943, located in New York City

emigrate: to leave one's country and move elsewhere. When you say *emigrate* you are talking about the country you are leaving

enlightenment: in Buddhism, it is the understanding that life is suffering and ignorance and desire causes suffering

feng shui: practitioners of feng shui believe that there are two types of energy in the world: chi, a gentle and helpful form of energy that travels in winding ways, and sha, a negative, bad energy that can only move in straight lines

Filipina: a woman from the Philippines

Filipino: a person from the Philippines; also, the primary language of the Philippines

folk art: an art or craft made by ordinary people as well as artists that reflects the country or region where these people live

Four Noble Truths: the teachings of Siddhartha Buddha that form the basis of Buddhism

furoshiki: a square cloth used by Japanese immigrants to carry small possessions

Gam Saan: the name that the Chinese of the 19th century used for California; it means "Gold Mountain"

ghungroos: anklets of jingling bells worn by classical Asian Indian dancers

gyotaku: Japanese fish printing

gyoza: Japanese pan fried dumplings

haiku: a popular type of Japanese peom. Traditional haiku are three lines and have 17 syllables: 5 in the first line, 7 in the middle line, and 5 in the last line

hanbok: the traditional clothing of Korea

Hangul: the Korean alphabet created under King Sejong in the year 1446

Hina Matsuri: Girls' Day, the Japanese holiday that celebrates the health and happiness of girls

Hinduism: a religion that originated in India in about 1500 B.C.E.; Hindus believe that life is a series of births and rebirths called reincarnation

Hmong: ethnic group from the mountains of Laos and other parts of Southeast Asia

ikebana: Japanese flower arranging

immigrate: to move from one country to another where one is not native. When you *immigrate* you are talking about your new country or destination

internment camps: holding facilities for Japanese Americans in World War II

isolationist: a government that chooses not to have international relationships

Issei: the first generation of Japanese immigrants that arrived in the 1800s

jai choy: a vegetarian dish also known as Buddha's Delight, which represents all the wishes for the Chinese New Year

Jainism: a religion that originated in India that preaches nonviolence toward all living creatures

Jan, Ken, Pon: the original Japanese version of the Rock, Paper, Scissors game, which was brought to Hawaii and the United States with the first immigrants from Japan

jeepney: a Filipino vehicle originally made from old U.S. Army jeeps

jegi-chagi: a traditional Korean game similar to hacky-sack

jiaozi: a steamed dumpling eaten to celebrate Chinese New Year; also known as yuen bow

jumoni: a good luck purse into which children tuck the money they receive on Korean New Year

junk: a Chinese sailboat

Kabuki: a traditional Japanese form of theater brought to America with the Issei generation

kadomatsu: a pine and bamboo arrangement placed at the front door of a traditional Japanese home in honor of New Year's

kana: the sound-based forms of Japanese writing, in which symbols represent different syllables

kanji: the character-based form of Japanese writing, in which symbols represent whole words or ideas

Khmer: an ethnic group that makes up 90 percent of the Cambodian population

kimchi: Korean pickled vegetables (usually cabbage or radishes) seasoned with hot pepper flakes, garlic, and other spices

kimono: a loose-fitting Japanese garment that is worn by men, women, and children

Komodo No Hi: Children's Day, the Japanese holiday that honors children and encourages participation in traditional Japanese culture

krama: a scarf traditionally worn over the head or shoulders by the Khmer in Cambodia

kurta: a traditional long shirt worn by men and women in India

laap: a distinctly Laotian dish made of fish or meat, lime juice, vegetables, and chilies

lacquer: a hard, shiny coating that has been used in China for hundreds of years

lai see: Chinese red envelopes filled with money and given to children on holidays

lassi: an Asian Indian yogurt drink

lily feet: bound feet, which was a thousand-year-old custom in China; little girls would have their feet bound in tight bandages to prevent them from growing more than three or four inches long

lotus shoes: beautifully ornate tiny slippers worn by Chinese women with bound feet

lunas: field bosses on sugar plantations in Hawaii who watched the workers from horseback

Mandarin: the official language of China

manga: Japanese comic books

Manilamen: Filipinos who jumped from Spanish slave ships in the 1700s and settled in the marshlands of the Louisiana Territory

Maria Clara dress: the formal woman's dress of the Philippines; it includes a full skirt and butterfly sleeves, and is worn with a scarf called a panuelo over the shoulders

mehndi: Asian Indian hand painting using the crushed leaves of the henna plant, worn on special occasions, especially for weddings

menko: the original Japanese version of the milk-cap game, which was brought to Hawaii by the first Japanese immigrants

miso soup: a flavorful and healthy Japanese soup made from miso (soybean paste) and tofu

mochitsuki: a popular demonstration at Japanese American New Year's celebrations, in which rice is pounded to make mochi cakes

moon cakes: Chinese pastries made with a variety of fillings such as salted egg yolk, sweet bean paste, and coconut. The outside is inscribed with the Chinese insignia of the baker

nian gao: a sticky rice cake eaten on Chinese New Year

nirvana: liberation, freedom from worldly ties, an end to suffering

Nisei: the American-born children of the first generation of Japanese immigrants

nitroglycerine: a powerful and dangerous explosive used in the construction of the transcontinental railroad

Noh: Japan's oldest form of theater, in which the actors wear distinctive white wooden masks

Nobel Prize: an international award that is given yearly for achievements in physics, chemistry, physiology or medicine, literature, and peace

non: a conical hat made of palm leaves and bamboo, traditionally worn in Vietnam

Obon Festival: a time when Japanese Americans honor their ancestors and remember loved ones who have died

onigiri: Japanese rice balls

origami: the Japanese art of paper folding

Oshogatsu: Japanese New Year

otedama: Japanese beanbag game

paj ntaub: Hmong flower cloths that are decorated with brilliantly colored geometric designs and used on clothing, baby carriers, purses, hats, burial cloths, and more

pandango sa ilaw: a colorful, lively Filipino dance in which performers balance lamps on their heads and the backs of both hands while dancing

paper sons: Chinese immigrants who got around exclusionary immigrations laws by paying Chinese men in the United States to sign papers saying that they were their fathers

parol: a star lantern that is the symbol of the Filipino Christmas season; parols are made of bamboo and paper with a light inside and can be as tall as 100 feet

Pasko: The Filipino Christmas season

pensionados: Filipino immigrants who came to the United States through an American sponsorship

phamuong: a long dress traditionally worn by Khmer women in Cambodia

pho: a beef noodle soup that is the most popular Vietnamese food in the United States as well as Vietnam

picture brides: Asian women who married Asian men living in America before meeting them

pina: a beautiful, silky sheer fabric from the Philippines, made from the fiber of the pineapple plant

placer mining: a painstaking type of mining, practiced by Chinese immigrants during the California gold rush, in which you sift sand and water to find gold nuggets and dust

Plain of Jars: a plateau in the northern mountains of Laos where hundreds of enormous stone jars are scattered among the grasses and trees

pojagi: Korean patchwork cloth used to wrap presents, carry things, and store things

pov pob: a Hmong ball-toss game; it was originally designed to give unmarried teens an opportunity to meet before marriage

pulgogi: the most well-liked Korean dish in America; it is made from barbecued strips of beef

queues: long braids worn by early Chinese male immigrants

ramen: Japanese wheat noodles

rangoli: an Asian Indian tradition of drawing chalk designs on the floor or front step

refugee: a person who has left his country and is afraid to return for fear of persecution

Rizal Day: Philippine Independence Day, celebrated on June 12 of every year by Filipinos all over the world

samosa: an Asian Indian flaky pastry filled with a tasty vegetable or vegetable-and-meat stuffing

samurai: the ruling warrior class in Japan

sari: the traditional costume of Asian Indian women

sarong: a wraparound skirt traditionally worn by Khmer men and women in Cambodia

scribe: a professional letter writer hired by early Chinese immigrants, many of whom could not read and write in their own language, to communicate with their families in China

Seol: Korean lunar New Year

Shintoism: a native Japanese religion that worships nature and ancestors

shoguns: warriors who ruled Japan from the end of the 12th century to 1868

shoulder yoke: a device that early Chinese immigrants used to carry heavy loads; they stretched a stick across their shoulders and hung a basket on each end of it

Sikhism: see *Sikhs*

Sikhs: followers of a religious group from India, who were among the first Asian Indians to settle in America

sitar: traditional Asian Indian instrument that is similar to a guitar but with two levels of strings and a droning sound

soba: long, unbroken noodles traditionally eaten on the Japanese New Year's Eve

sojourner: a person who leaves home to seek fortune in another place, with the intention of returning home within a short time

stake a claim: during the California gold rush, to hammer a wooden stake into the ground in places where gold was likely to be found and declare that you owned the gold mined there

stir-frying: the centuries-old Chinese tradition of chopping food into small pieces and cooking it quickly at high temperatures

storytelling cloth: a recent form of Hmong tapestry that developed as part of the refugee experience; while waiting in refugee camps in places like Thailand, the Hmong developed story cloths to preserve their history

subcontinent: a large landmass (such as India or Greenland) that is separate in some way, either through geography or a political division

subsistence farming: growing just enough food to survive

sungka: a very old Filipino game similar to mancala

sushi: fish, usually raw, with vegetables, wrapped in rice and seaweed

syllabaries: in certain sound-based writing systems, symbols that stand for complete syllables rather than individual sounds like the letters in our alphabet

taekwondo: Korea's martial art; it uses the whole body but in particular the hands and feet

tai chi: Chinese martial art that increases strength and balance with slow, measured moves

taiko: Japanese percussion instruments

tandoori: an Asian Indian dish that features a spring chicken marinated with herbs and spices

tempura: batter-fried meats and vegetables

tenant farmers: farmers who have an arrangement with landowners by which they farm the owner's land in exchange for part of the profits

Tet: Vietnamese New Year

Three Perfections: In China, the three highest arts: calligraphy, brush painting, and poetry

Tiger Brigade: the all-Korean unit from the California National Guard that fought in World War II

tiger hat: an elaborately embroidered hat worn by Chinese children; the purpose of these hats is to frighten off bad spirits and attract good luck to the child

tinikling: a traditional Filipino dance performed in bare feet; the dancers move inside and outside of bamboo sticks tapped at floor level

tol: a celebration that marks the first birthday of Korean children

tonal language: a language in which the same word can have different meanings depending on whether your voice rises, falls, or stays the same when you say it

transcontinental railroad: the first railroad to connect the East and West coasts of the United States, which thousands of Chinese immigrants helped to build

tray of togetherness: an eight-section platter shared with guests on Chinese New Year; it holds various sweet dried fruits and seeds such as coconut, ginger, and sweet lotus seed

ttok-kuk: Korean rice cake soup, enjoyed on the first day of the year

Tumbang Preso: a Filipino version of the game kick the can

tuho: a traditional game from Korea in which participants take turns throwing arrows into a narrow pot

ukiyo-e: "pictures of a floating world"; woodblock art prints from Japan

war brides: foreign wives of U.S. servicemen

wok: the large, curved cooking pot that is used for stir-frying

yin and yang: the Chinese believe that in all things, yin and yang must be balanced; yin is feminine, dark, negative, cold, and passive, while yang is masculine, light, positive, warm, and active

yuen bow: gold ingots, ancient Chinese money

yut: a Korean game played with sticks

◆ Bibliography ◆

FOR CHILDREN

Books

Bandon, Alexandra. *Filipino Americans.* New York: New Discovery Books, 1993.

"Cambodia." In *Peoples of Eastern Asia.* Vol. 2. New York: Marshall Cavendish, 2005.

Carpenter, Francis. *Tales of a Chinese Grandmother.* Garden City, NY: Doubleday, Doran and Co., 1944.

Cha, Dia. *Dia's Story Cloth.* New York: Lee and Low Books, 1996.

Cooper, Michael L. *Remembering Manzanar: Life in a Japanese Relocation Camp.* New York: Clarion Books, 2002.

Donegan, Patricia. *Haiku: Asian Arts and Crafts for Creative Kids.* Boston: Tuttle Publishing, 2003.

Gordon, Susan. *Asian Indians.* New York: Franklin Watts, 1990.

Grapes, Brian J., ed. *Japanese Internment Camps.* San Diego, CA: Greenhaven Press, 2001.

Grolier Educational. *Cambodia.* Fiesta! series. Danbury, CT: Grolier Educational, 1999.

Harbin, E.O. *Games of Many Nations.* New York: Abington Press, 1976.

Hoobler, Dorothy, and Thomas Hoobler. *The Chinese American Family Album.* New York: Oxford University Press, 1994.

Hoobler, Dorothy, and Thomas Hoobler. *The Japanese American Family Album.* New York: Oxford University Press, 1995.

Krasno, Rena. *Kneeling Carabao and Dancing Giants: Celebrating Filipino Festivals.* Berkley, CA: Pacific View, 1997.

Lee, Lauren. *Korean Americans.* New York: Marshall Cavendish, 1995.

Mamdami, Shelby. *Traditions from India.* Austin, TX: Raintree Steck-Vaughn, 1999.

McGuire, William. *Southeast Asians.* New York: Franklin Watts, 1991.

McLenighan, Valjean. *International Games.* Milwaukee, WI: Raintree Children's Books, 1978.

Murphy, Nora. *A Hmong Family.* Minneapolis, MN: Lerner Publications, 1997.

Nickles, Greg. *Philippines: The Culture.* New York: Crabtree Publishing, 2002.

Olson, Stuart Alve. *Tai Chi for Kids: Move with the Animals.* Rochester, VT: Bear Cub Books, 2001.

Shalant, Phyllis. *Look What We've Brought You from Korea: Crafts, Games, Recipes, Stories, and Other Cultural Activities from Korean Americans.* Morristown, NJ: Julian Messner, 1998.

Simonds, Nina, and Leslie Swartz. *Moonbeams, Dumplings, and Dragon Boats: A Treasury of Chinese Holiday Tales, Activities, and Recipes.* San Diego, CA: Gulliver Books, 2002.

Springstubb, Tricia. *The Vietnamese Americans.* San Diego, CA: Lucent Books, 2002.

Stepanchuk, Carol. *Exploring Chinatown: A Children's Guide to Chinese Culture.* Berkeley, CA: Pacific View Press, 2002.

Takaki, Ronald. *From the Land of the Morning Calm: The Koreans in America*. New York: Chelsea House, 1994.

Takaki, Ronald. *In the Heart of Filipino America: Immigrants from the Pacific Isles*. New York: Chelsea House, 1994.

Takaki, Ronald. *India in the West: South Asians in America*. New York: Chelsea House, 1995.

Takaki, Ronald. *Issei and Nisei: The Settling of Japanese America*. Adapted by Rebecca Stefoff. New York: Chelsea House, 1994.

Takaki, Ronald. *Journey to Gold Mountain: The Chinese in Nineteenth-Century America*. New York: Chelsea House, 1994.

"Vietnam." In *Peoples of Eastern Asia*. Vol. 10. New York: Marshall Cavendish, 2005.

Viswanath, R. *Teenage Refugees and Immigrants from India Speak Out*. New York: Rosen Publishing Group, 1997.

Westridge Young Writers Workshop. *Kids Explore America's Japanese American Heritage*. Santa Fe, NM: John Muir Publications, 1994.

FOR ADULTS

Books

Avakian, Monique. *Atlas of Asian American History*. New York: Checkmark Books, 2002.

Bautista, Veltisezar. *The Filipino Americans 1763–Present: Their History, Culture and Traditions*. Naperville, IL: Bookhaus Publishers, 2002.

Berliner, Nancy Zeng. *Chinese Folk Art*. Boston: Little Brown and Co., 1986.

Bowes, Olive Scofield. *Ikebana (Japanese Flower Arranging) Simplified*. New York: Sterling Publishing, 1969.

Cassettari, Stephen. *Chinese Brush Painting Techniques*. London: Angus and Robertson Publishers, 1987.

Clark, Donald N. *Culture and Customs of Korea*. Westport, CT: Greenwood Press, 2000.

Faurot, Jeannette, ed. *Asian-Pacific Folktales and Legends*. New York: Touchstone, 1995.

Fawdry, Marguerite. *Chinese Childhood*. New York: Barron's, 1977.

Gong, Rosemary. *Good Luck Life*. New York: HarperCollins Books, 2005.

"Han-gul, the Korean Alphabet." In *Korean Heritage Series*. Vol. 1. Republic of Korea: Korea Overseas Information Series, 1995.

Hansen, Barbara Joan. *Barbara Hansen's Taste of Southeast Asia: Brunei, Indonesia, Malaysia, the Philippines, Singapore, Thailand, and Vietnam*. Tucson, AZ: HP Books, 1987.

Henderson, Carol E. *Culture and Customs of India*. Westport, CT: Greenwood Press, 2002.

Hepinstall, Hi Shoo Shin. *Growing Up in a Korean Kitchen: A Cookbook*. Berkeley, CA: Ten Speed Press, 2001.

Houston, Jeanne Wakatsuki. *Farewell to Manzanar*. New York: Bantam Books, 1995.

Ingram, Scott, and Christina M. Girod. *The Indian Americans*. San Diego, CA: Lucent Books, 2004.

Iyengar, B.K.S. *Yoga: The Path to Holistic Health*. London: Doring Kindersley, 2001.

Kessler, Lauren. *Stubborn Twig: Three Generations in the Life of a Japanese American Family*. New York: Random House, 1993.

Kim, Elaine H., and Eui-Young Yu, eds. *East to America: Korean American Life Stories*. New York: New Press, 1996.

"Kimchi." *Korean Heritage Series*. Vol. 20. Republic of Korea: Korea Overseas Information Series, 1995.

McLeod, Alexander. *Pigtails and Gold Dust*. Caldwell, OH: Caxton Printers Ltd., 1947.

Mitra, Kalita S. *Suburban Sahibs: Three Immigrant Families and their Passage from India to America*. New Brunswick, NJ: Rutgers University Press, 2003.

Novas, Himilce, and Lan Cao with Rosemary Silva. *Everything You Need to Know About Asian American History*. New York: Plume Group, 2004.

O-Young, Lee. *Things Korean*. Rutland, VT: Charles E. Tuttle Co., 1999.

"Pojagis, Wrappings Cloths." *Korean Heritage Series*. Vol. 9. Republic of Korea: Korea Overseas Information Series, 1995.

Qin, Lei Lei. *The Simple Art of Chinese Calligraphy: Create Your Own Chinese Characters and Symbols for Good Fortune and Prosperity*. New York: Watson Guptill Publications, 2002.

Sakade, Florence. *Origami: Japanese Paper Folding*. Rutland, VT: Charles E. Tuttle Co., 1957.

Shimbo, Hiroko. *The Japanese Kitchen*. Boston: Harvard Common Press, 2000.

Sinnott, Susan. *Extraordinary Asian Americans and Pacific Islanders*. New York: Children's Press, 2003.

"Taekwondo." *Korean Heritage Series*. Vol. 18. Republic of Korea: Korea Overseas Information Series, 1995.

Takaki, Ronald. *Strangers from a Different Shore: A History of Asian Americans*. New York: Penguin Books, 1990.

Tanaka, Seno. *The Tea Ceremony*. New York: Harmony Books, 1977.

Tateishi, John. *And Justice for All: An Oral History of the Japanese American Detention Camps*. New York: Random House, 1984.

Toita, Yasuji. *Kabuki: The Popular Theater*. Translated by Don Kenny. New York: Weatherhill, 1970.

Too, Lillian. *Lillian Too's Easy-to-Use Feng Shui: 168 Ways to Success*. London: Collins and Brown Ltd., 1999.

Tran, Diana My. *The Vietnamese Cookbook*. Sterling, VA: Capital Books Inc., 2000.

Wyndham, Robert. *Tales the People Tell in China*. New York: Julian Messner, 1971.

Yang, Jeff, Dina Gan, Terry Hong, eds., and the staff of A. Magazine. *Eastern Standard Time: A Guide to Asian Influence on American Culture from Astro Boy to Zen Buddhism*. Boston, MA: Houghton Mifflin Co., 1997.

Yates, Keith D. *Tae Kwon Do Basics*. New York: Sterling Publishing Co., 1992.

Internet

American Memory. "The Chinese in California, 1850–1825." Library of Congress. www.memory.loc.gov/ammem/award99/cubhtml/cichome.html.

Americans.net. "World War II Congressional Medal of War Recipient Jose Calugas." www.medalofhonor.com/JoseCalugas.htm.

Asian American Net. "Sergeant Tran Quoc Binh." *Who's Who of Young Asian Americans*. www.asianamerican.net/bios/Tran-Binh.htm.

Barboza, Rick. "Strict Rules Govern the Kadomatsu." *Honolulu Star-Bulletin*, December 31, 2004. www.starbulletin.com/2004/12/31/features/garden.html.

CBBC Newsround. "Kids Ditch Computers for Board Game." July 31, 2002. news.bbc.co.uk/cbbcnews/hi/world/newsid_2163000/2163584.stm.

Henderson, Ed, and Poof Magoo. "Otedama: A Fading Japanese Juggling Tradition." *Juggler's World* 43, no. 4 (Winter 1991). www.juggling.org/jw/91/4/otedama.html.

Japanese American National Museum. "Family Activity Guide: Big Drum; Taiko in the United States." July 14, 2005. www.janm.org/exhibits/bigdrum/BigDrum_FamilyGuide.pdf.

Ning, Anna Luan Li. "A Magic Paint Brush." Retelling of a Chinese folk tale. TOPICS Online Magazine. www.topics-mag.com/folk-tales/folk-tale-good-greed-ch.htm.

Otake, Gary T. "A Century of Japanese American Baseball." National Japanese American Historical Society. www.nikkei heritage.org/research/bbhist.html.

Sadiq, Sheraz. "Sophiline Shapiro: The Dancer." *Cambodian Americans Speak.* FRONTLINE/World, October 2002. www.pbs.org/frontlineworld/stories/ cambodia/shapiro.html.

U.S. Census Bureau. "Asian Pacific American Heritage Month: May 2004." Press release, April 19, 2004. www.census.gov/ Press-Release/www/ releases/archives/facts_for_features_special_editions/ 001738.html.

Periodicals

Barbas, Samantha. "I'll Take Chop Suey: Restaurants as Agents of Culinary and Cultural Change." *Journal of Popular Culture,* Spring 2003, 669–87.

Brightman, Marcia. "Fighting with Honor." *Cobblestone,* April 1996, 20–23.

Crown, DiAnne. "Wrapped in Beauty: Simple or Elaborate Saris Fit Every Moment of an Indian Woman's Life." *State Journal-Register* (Springfield, IL), August 14, 2005.

McCollum, Sean. "'Barbarians' Open up Japan: Commodore Perry Broke Through Japan's Secret World 150 Years Ago." *New York Times Upfront,* April 18, 2003, 18–22.

Videos

The Art of Chinese Dance. Performed by Nai-Ni Chen Dance Company. Brooklyn, NY: China Sprout, 2002.

✦ Asian American Museums ✦

CALIFORNIA

Angel Island
The Immigration Station Barracks Museum
San Francisco, CA 29237
www.angelisland.org/immigr02.html

The museum recreates and preserves the Asian immigration experience at Angel Island. Of special interest is poetry that was carved into the walls by immigrants. Closed for renovation through mid-2007.

The Asian Art Museum of San Francisco
200 Larkin Street
San Francisco, CA 94102
(415) 581-3500
E-mail: pr@asianart.org
www.asianart.org

The museum offers demonstrations and workshops in Asian arts, including Chinese calligraphy, Japanese Noh masks, taekwondo, and storytelling.

Chinese American Museum in Los Angeles
425 North Los Angeles Street
Los Angeles, CA 90012
(213) 485-8567 or (213) 485-8484
E-mail: curator@camla.org
www.camla.org

Museum dedicated to the Chinese American experience. Revolving exhibits feature topics such as Chinatown through postcards; "Journeys," about Chinese immigration; and "Footsteps through Time," a family history project.

The Chinese Culture Center of San Francisco
750 Kearny Street, 3rd floor
San Francisco, CA 94108-1809
(415) 986-1822
E-mail: info@c-c-c.org
www.c-c-c.org

Educational and cultural programs about Chinese culture. Recent exhibits include Chinese folk art, Chinese opera, and the winning entries of a youth painting competition to celebrate Chinese New Year. The center also offers walking tours of San Francisco's Chinatown.

The Chinese Historical Society of America
965 Clay Street
San Francisco, CA 94108
(415) 391-1188
E-mail: info@chsa.org
www.chsa.org

Oldest and largest organization dedicated to Chinese American history. Recent exhibits include "Earthquake:

The Chinatown Story," about the San Francisco earthquake of 1906, and "Dragons, Drums, Fireworks, and Floats: A Chinese American Tradition." Workshops feature activities such as lantern making, storytelling, and children's crafts.

Hakone Gardens
21000 Big Basin Way
Saratoga, CA 95070
(408) 741-4994
E-mail: hakone@hakone.com
www.hakone.com
    The oldest surviving Japanese gardens in North America, including a bamboo garden. Museum offerings include the annual Matsuri spring festival and classes in Japanese art forms such as ikebana, the tea ceremony, and Zen meditation.

Japanese American Cultural and Community Center
244 South San Pedro Street, Suite 505
Los Angeles, CA 90012
(213) 628-2725
www.jaccc.org
    The center is committed to preserving Japanese heritage in America through performances such as taiko and traditional Japanese dance, festivals observing Japanese New Year and Children's Day, and more. A sampling of exhibits includes presentations of Kabuki theater, anime and manga, and Japanese instruments and costumes from the sixth century.

Japanese American National Museum
369 East First Street
Los Angeles, CA 90012
(213) 625-0414
www.janm.org
    The museum has the largest collection of Japanese American materials in the world, including the kimono of a picture bride made from the silk of homegrown silkworms. Recent exhibits include taiko drumming, student murals, and the sculptural art of Isamu Noguchi.

Pacific Asia Museum
46 North Los Robles Avenue
Pasadena, CA 01101
(626) 449-2742, ext. 10
www.pacificasiamuseum.org
    Art and artifacts from Asia and the Pacific Islands. Holdings include Chinese tomb treasures, Indian silk sari cloth, and a Korean horsehair hat.

DISTRICT OF COLUMBIA

National Museum of Asian Art
Sackler Gallery
1050 Independence Avenue SW
and
Freer Gallery of Art
Jefferson Drive at 12th Street SW
Washington, D.C. 20081-0001
(202) 633-4880
E-mail: asiainfo@asia.si.edu
www.asia.si.edu

The Sackler and Freer galleries are connected by an underground exhibition space. Visit exhibits such as "Beyond Brushwork: Symbolism in Chinese Painting," "Freer and Tea: 100 Years of the Book of Tea," and "Arts of the Indian Subcontinent and the Himalayas."

Smithsonian Institution
Asian Pacific American Program
Arts and Industries Building, Room 2467
900 Jefferson Drive SW
Washington, D.C. 20560-0440
(202) 786-2409
E-mail: fodo@op.si.edu (Franklin Odo, director of
   the program)
www.apa.si.edu/home.html
   A sampling of exhibits and events include "Korean American Contemporary Art: Celebrating 100 Years of Korean Immigration to the U.S.," "Head to Toe: Vietnamese Americans in the National Museum of American History Collections," and "Jamming with Yo-Yos," about the toy invented by Filipino immigrant Pedro Flores.

FLORIDA

The Morikami Museum and Japanese Gardens
4000 Morikami Park Road
Delray Beach, FL 33446
(561) 495-0233
E-mail: morikami@co.palm-beach.fl.us
www.morikami.org

Japanese art and cultural exhibitions, workshops, and classes. The collections include Japanese dolls, kimonos, woodblock prints, calligraphy, haori (kimono coat) linings, and kites. The Japanese gardens rate among the best in the world outside of Japan.

HAWAII

Bishop Museum
1525 Bernice Street
Honolulu, HI 96817
(808) 847-3511
www.bishopmuseum.org
   Artifacts, documents, photographs, and special exhibits that illustrate the immigrant history of Hawaii and the Pacific Islands. Current and past exhibitions include "Celebrating Chinese Women," "Celebrating the Achievements of Filipino Americans in Hawaii," and "From Bento to Mixed Plate: Americans of Japanese Ancestry in Multicultural Hawaii."

Hawaii's Plantation Village
94-695 Waipahu Street
Waipahu, HI 96797
(808) 677-0110
E-mail: hpv.waipahu@verizon.net
www.hawaiiplantationvillage.org
   This outdoor history museum recreates multicultural Hawaii during the days of the sugar plantations in the early 1900s.

Honolulu Academy of Arts
900 South Beretania Street
Honolulu, HI 96814
(808) 532-8700
www.honoluluacademy.org
Art classes, gallery tours, school programs, and film and performance series celebrating multicultural Hawaii. Examples of the academy's exhibits include "Chinese Painting of the Shanghai School" and "Through My Father's Eyes: The Filipino American Photographs of Ricardo Ocreto Alvarado."

Lyman Museum and Mission House
276 Haili Street
Hilo, Hawaii 96720
(808) 935-5021
E-mail: info@lymanmuseum.org
www.lymanmuseum.org
Natural and cultural history of Hawaii and Asian art. A major feature of the library here is the Shipman Gallery of Chinese Art. Rotating exhibits feature titles such as "Grandfather's House: An Exhibit on Korea," and "Huī Panalā'au: Hawaiian Colonists, American Citizens."

ILLINOIS

Chinese-American Museum of Chicago
238 West 23rd Street
Chicago, IL 60616
(312) 949-1000
E-mail: office@ccamuseum.org

http://ccamuseum.org/Index.html
Celebrating the Chinese American cultural heritage of the Midwest. Samplings of exhibits include "Tofu: The Wonder Food," "Silk and Wood," and "Paper Sons."

MASSACHUSETTS

Peabody Essex Museum
East India Square
Salem, MA 01970
(978) 745-9500
www.pem.org
Featuring Asian art and cultural exhibits, events, workshops, and performances. The Yin Yu Tang House is a 200-year-old Chinese merchant's house that was dismantled piece by piece in China and reassembled at the museum.

NEW YORK

Museum of Chinese in the Americas (MoCA)
70 Mulberry Street, 2nd floor
New York, NY 10013
(212) 619-4785
E-mail: info@moca-nyc.org
www.moca-nyc.org/MoCA/content.asp
A museum of Chinese life in America, featuring artifacts, photographs, and oral histories. The museum offers exhibits such as "Where Is Home? Chinese in the Americas" and "Mapping our Heritage Project," as well as weekly walking tours of Chinatown.

OREGON

Kam Wah Chung and Co. Museum
250 Northwest Canton Street
John Day, OR 97845
(541) 575-0028

The store of a Chinese herbalist has been preserved and restored. It includes hundreds of Chinese artifacts, including medicinal herbs, clothes, furniture, account books, store merchandise, and letters that tell about immigrant Chinese culture in the West.

TEXAS

The Trammell and Margaret Crow Collection of
    Asian Art
2010 Flora Street
Dallas, TX 75201
(214) 979-6430
www.crowcollection.org

The museum is dedicated to the arts of China, Japan, India, and Southeast Asia. Offerings include the exhibits "Touching the Mekong: A Southeast Asia Sojourn" and "News from Abroad: Japanese Woodblock Prints from Yokohama, Japan," and a series of workshops called "Adventure Asia! Art Experiences for Everyone."

WASHINGTON

The Wing Luke Asian Museum
407 Seventh Avenue South
Seattle, WA 98104
(206) 623-5124
E-mail: folks@wingluke.org
www.wingluke.org

Art, history, and culture of Asian Pacific Americans. Permanent exhibits include "One Song, Many Voices," about the 200-year immigration of Asians to America; "Camp Harmony D-4-44," which features a replica of the assembly center in Puyallup, Washington, where Japanese Americans were brought for incarceration during World War II; and "Portrait of a Community," about Seattle's Chinatown.

◆ Suggested Reading List for Kids ◆

Kadohata, Cynthia. *Kira-Kira*. New York: Atheneum, 2004.
The story of how two Japanese American sisters move with their family from Iowa to Georgia in the 1950, and have to deal with one sister's terminal illness.

Lord, Bette Bao. *In the Year of the Boar and Jackie Robinson*. New York: Harper Trophy, 1984.
The humorous story of 10-year-old Shirley Temple Wong's adjustment from China to Brooklyn, New York, in the 1940s.

Mochizuki, Ken. *Baseball Saved Us*. New York: Lee and Low, 1993.
How baseball helped a Japanese American boy cope with life behind the barbed wire fences of a World War II relocation camp.

Park, Linda Sue. *Project Mulberry*. New York: Clarion Books, 2005.
Julia Song, a Korean American girl, reluctantly agrees to grow silkworms for the state fair.

Warren, Andrea. *Escape from Saigon: How a Vietnam War Orphan Became an American Boy*. New York: Farrar, Straus and Giroux, 2004.
The true story of Long, an Amerasian boy who was evacuated from Vietnam during "Operation Babylift" in 1975 and adopted by an American family.

Yep, Lawrence. *Dragonwings: Golden Mountain Chronicles; 1903*. New York: HarperCollins, 1975.
The story of a young boy who travels from China to America to reunite with his father and start a new life in San Francisco's Chinatown.

Yin. *Coolies*. Illustrated by Chris K. Soentpiet. New York: Philomel, 2001.
Picture book that dramatically illustrates the role of the Chinese in building the transcontinental railroad.

◆ Asian American Movies and Videos ◆

MOVIES

Dim Sum: A Little Bit of Heart. Orion Pictures, 1985. PG.
Featuring Laureen Chew, Kim Chew, and Victor Wong, this is a heartwarming picture about a Chinese mother and her Chinese American daughter, set in San Francisco's Chinatown.

Flower Drum Song. Universal Pictures/MCA, 1961. Not rated.
Starring Nancy Kwan, James Shigeta, and Benson Fong, *Flower Drum Song* is the film version of Rodgers and Hammerstein's Broadway play about a Chinese picture bride and her father in San Francisco.

Go for Broke, MGM (Warner) Studios, 1951. Not rated.
Featuring Van Johnson, Lane Nakano, and George Miki, this movie is about the 442nd Regimental Combat Team of Japanese American soldiers who fought in World War II.

A Great Wall (originally *The Great Wall Is a Great Wall*). Orion Pictures, 1986. PG.
Starring Peter Wang, Sharon Iwai, and Kelvin Han Yee, this is the story of a Chinese American family who go back to China to discover their roots. It is a humorous film showing how American a Chinese American can be when in China.

VIDEOS

American Cultures for Children: Chinese American, Japanese American, Korean American, Vietnamese American. Schlessinger Videos.
These videos introduce various Asian American cultures to children in a fast-paced, lively fashion. They feature tours of ethnic neighborhoods, music, folktales, language, arts and crafts, and more.

• Web Sites •

Asian-Nation, www.asian-nation.org/index.shtml
   An information resource and overview of issues involving the Asian American community.

"Asian Pacific American Heritage Month," Infoplease, www.info please.com/spot/asianhistory1.html
   The histories of fortune cookies and tea, feng shui tips, notable Asian Americans, and more.

The Asia Society, www.askasia.org
   Count in Chinese and use an online student atlas.

Camp Harmony Exhibit, www.lib.washington.edu/exhibits/ harmony/Exhibit
   Online presentation describes life at a Japanese American relocation camp during World War II.

Central Pacific Railroad Photographic History Museum (Chinese American Contribution), www.cprr.org/Museum/ Chinese.html
   A photographic history of the transcontinental railroad and the Chinese contributions toward building it.

The Chinese Historical and Cultural Project, www.chcp.org/ games.html
   Learn how to play traditional Chinese games.

"The Chinese in California, 1850–1825," American Memory, Library of Congress, http://memory.loc.gov/ammem/ award99/cubhtml/cichome.html
   A wealth of primary source materials regarding Chinese immigration, including more than 8,000 photographs, original art, cartoons, letters, diaries, business records, and more.

"Echoes of Freedom: South Asian Pioneers in California, 1899–1965," the Library, University of California, Berkeley, www.lib.berkeley.edu/SSEAL/echoes.html
   The story of early Indian immigrants told through photographs.

Enchanted Learning, www.enchantedlearning.com/crafts/ chinesenewyear
   Crafts and activities for Chinese New Year.

"Family Activity Guide: Big Drum; Taiko in the United States," Japanese American National Museum, www.janm.org/ exhibits/bigdrum/BigDrum_FamilyGuide.pdf
   Information and how-tos on taiko percussion instruments.

Japan-guide.com, www.japan-guide.com/e/e2039.html
   Guide to using chopsticks.

Kids Domain, www.kidsdomain.com/holiday/chineseny.html

Many fun links to Chinese New Year celebrations, including recipes, activities, games, and history.

Korean American Museum, www.kamuseum.org/community/
base.htm
An exploration of Korean American history.

Lao Family Community of Minnesota, www.laofamily.org
Stories, history, culture, and crafts from the Hmong and Lao American communities.

"Virtual Japanese Culture," Kids Web Japan, web-japan.org/
kidsweb/virtual.html
Online activities in sumo wrestling, origami, bonsai, wood-block prints, and more.

The Virtual Museum of the City of San Francisco,
www.sfmuseum.net/hist1/index0.html#chinese
Articles about Chinese immigration, Chinatown, foot binding, and more.

• Teacher's Guide •

ACTIVITIES BY GRADE LEVEL

A Kid's Guide to Asian American History was written with the classroom teacher in mind. Most of the activities are inexpensive, can be made with classroom materials, and can be completed in a short period. Although the activities are suitable for all grade groupings, this guide will help you decide which activities are more appropriate for younger or older students. Ideas for adapting activities and extending learning opportunities are included as well.

ELEMENTARY: K–THIRD GRADE

Activity: Create a Japanese Folding Fan, p. 4

Activity: Create a Tiger Hat, p. 13

One grocery bag cut down the middle makes two tiger hats. You may precut the grocery bags for younger students.

Activity: Construct an Evil Spirit Apron, p. 15

To simplify the activity for younger students, you may precut the aprons and/or have them draw the insects directly on the apron with markers.

Activity: Write Chinese Characters, p. 23

Make a photocopy of the characters in the book for each student to copy.

Activity: Make a Lai See: Chinese Red Envelope, p. 40

Activity: Make a Chinese Lion, p. 43

Activity: Perform the Lion Dance, p. 45

Choose two students at a time to be the lion until everyone has had a turn. Substitute scraps of green paper for the lettuce. Accompany with a CD of traditional Chinese music.

Activity: Paint a Chinese Calligraphy Banner, p. 47

Activity: Practice Tai Chi, p. 57

This is a great activity to do outdoors.

Activity: Chase the Dragon's Tale, p. 59

Activity: Try the Chinese Ribbon Dance, p. 63

Activity: Craft a Furoshiki, p. 77

Activity: Fold an Origami Dog and Cat, p. 81

Activity: Create Gyotaku: Japanese Fish Printing, p. 84

If possible, bring in one fish for every four children. Fish with a lot of scales make better prints. Call the fish store ahead of time and ask if they can set some whole fish aside for you.

Activity: Join in a Bon Odori Dance, p. 90

Activity: Play Jan, Ken, Pon (Rock, Paper, Scissors), p. 102

Activity: Make a Korean Flag, p. 109

Activity: Enjoy Yut: A Game Played with Sticks, p. 127

Activity: Practice the Pandango Sa Ilaw, p. 152

Activity: Create Your Own Jeepney, p. 156

Use recycled materials so the students can make Jeepneys the way the Filipinos do.

Activity: Play Snakes and Ladders, p. 171

Photocopy one game for every two students to play.

Activity: Create a Chalk Rangoli: An Asian Indian Welcome, p. 177

The class can make designs to decorate the school playground or school entrance.

Activity: Do Mehndi: Asian Indian Hand Painting, p. 178

To adapt for the classroom, have students trace hands onto paper and decorate with markers.

Activity: Play Pov Pob: A Hmong Ball-Toss Game for New Year's, p. 196

Students can choose to answer in a song or a rhyme.

Activity: Cambodian Court Dance: Learn the Hand Gestures, p. 202

ELEMENTARY: FOURTH AND FIFTH GRADES

Activity: Put on a Chinese Shadow Puppet Show, p. 52

You may extend the activity by breaking the class into groups and inviting each group to find their own traditional Chinese folk tale to write a script and make shadow puppets for. Picture books are an excellent source for this.

Activity: Write Haiku, p. 82

Activity: Make a Carp Streamer for Children's Day, p. 91

For a dramatic presentation, hang several streamers from a pole in front of the school.

Activity: Make a Milk-Cap Game, p. 103

Activity: Join in Tuho: Arrow Throwing, p. 111

Activity: Have Fun with Jegi-chagi: Tassel Kicking, p. 112

Students can have jegi-chagi contests to see who can keep it in the air the longest.

Activity: Make a Jumoni: Good Luck Bag, p. 126

Activity: Construct a Korean Kite, p. 129

Activity: Try Sungka: A Cowrie Shell Game, p. 145

Activity: Try Yoga, p. 168

Activity: Make a Sponsor Box, p. 186

Work in small groups and then present to the class.

Activity: Design a Storytelling Cloth, p. 199

Read the picture book *Dia's Story Cloth* by Dia Cha (New York: Lee and Low Books, 1998), which tells the author's true-life story of her flight from Laos as a child. Pictures of her family's story cloth, stitched by her aunt and uncle in a refugee camp, illustrate the book.

MIDDLE SCHOOL: SIXTH–EIGHTH GRADES

Activity: Create a Chinese Brush Painting Greeting Card, p. 26

Activity: Try Chinese Paper Cutting, p. 30

Make two (same color) copies of the goldfish for each student in a rainbow of colors.

Activity: Put Together a Balikbayan Box, p. 147

This would make a good classroom community service project.

Activity: Color a Hmong Flower Cloth: Paj Ntaub, p. 197

Make a copy of each graph for every student.

Activity: Design a Poster to Celebrate Asian Pacific American Heritage Month, p. 211

This could make an impressive school-wide presentation for Asian Pacific American Heritage Month.

ADDITIONAL RESOURCES FOR TEACHERS

Books

These books will be particularly useful to teachers.

Merrill, Yvonne. *Hands-On Asia: Art Activities for All Ages*. Salt Lake City, UT: Kits Publishing, 1999.

Simonds, Nina, and Leslie Swartz. *Moonbeams, Dumplings, and Dragon Boats: A Treasury of Chinese Holiday Tales, Activities, and Recipes*. San Diego, CA: Gulliver Books, 2002.

Terzian, Alexandria M. *The Kids' Multicultural Art Book: Art and Craft Experiences from Around the World.* Williamson Kids Can! series. Charlotte, VT: Williamson Publishing, 1993.

Videos

Becoming American: The Chinese Experience. PBS, 2003.
Excellent nonfiction series from Bill Moyers, covering the Chinese American experience from the gold rush to today. Program 1: "Gold Mountain Dreams"; program 2: "Between Two Worlds"; program 3: "No Turning Back." Online teaching guide available at www.pbs.org/teachersource/thismonth/mar03/index2.shtm.

"Daughter from Danang." *The American Experience.* PBS, 2003.
The story of Mai Thi Kim, who was a part of "Operation Babylift" at the end of the Vietnam War. The child of an American serviceman and a Vietnamese mother, she was adopted by an American family. The video documents her difficult reunion with her birth mother in Vietnam. Online teaching guide available at www.pbs.org/wgbh/amex/daughter/tguide/

Web Sites

AskAsia.org, www.askasia.org/teachers/
Lesson plans on: Angel Island; Asian American experiences in America; Chinatowns; Chinese inventions; Hangul; Indo-Americans (East Asian Indian Americans); Japanese American internment; Tet; Truyen, a Vietnamese game; and more.

Asian Pacific American Heritage Teaching Resources, Smithsonian Education, www.smithsonianeducation.org/educators/resource_library/asian_american_resources.html
Lesson plans, resources, and exhibits on Asian Pacific American history and culture.

Asian Pacific American Heritage teaching guide, Scholastic Books Online, teacher.scholastic.com/activities/asian-american/
Asian Pacific American stories, Asian immigration, Asian author interviews, Asian American arts and crafts, and more.

History Standards and Learning Objectives

A *Kid's Guide to Asian American History* is a useful resource to support history-learning standards in the classroom. You may use your own state's social studies frameworks and/or the national standards below. These standards were developed by the National Center for History in the Schools at the University of California, under the guidance of the National Council for History Standards. The project was funded by the National Endowment for the Humanities and the U.S. Department of Education.

HISTORY STANDARDS FOR GRADES K–4

Topic 1: Living and Working Together in Families and Communities, Now and Long Ago

Standard 1: Family life now and in the recent past; family life in various places long ago.

Standard 1B: The student understands the different ways people of diverse racial, religious, and ethnic groups, and of various national origins have transmitted their beliefs and values.

Standard 2: The history of students' own local community and how communities in North America varied long ago.

Topic 2: The History of the Students' Own State or Region

Standard 3B: The student understands the history of the first European, African, and/or Asian/Pacific explorers and settlers who came to his or her state or region.

Standard 3C: The student understands the various other groups from regions throughout the world who came into his or her own state or region over the long-ago and recent past.

Standard 3D: The student understands the interactions among all these groups throughout the history of his or her state.

Topic 3: The History of the United States: Democratic Principles and Values and the People from Many Cultures Who Contributed to Its Cultural, Economic, and Political Heritage

Standard 5: The causes and nature of various movements of large groups of people into and within the United States, both now and long ago.

Topic 4: The History of Peoples of Many Cultures Around the World

Standard 7: Selected attributes and historical developments of various societies in Africa, the Americas, Asia, and Europe.

Standard 7B: The student understands great world movements of people, now and long ago.

United States History Standards for Grades 5–12

Era 4: Expansion and Reform (1801–1861)

Standard 2: How the industrial revolution, increasing immigration, the rapid expansion of slavery, and the westward movement changed the lives of Americans and led toward regional tensions.

Standard 2C: The student understands how antebellum immigration changed American society.

Era 6: The Development of the Industrial United States (1870–1900)

Standard 2: Massive immigration after 1870 and how new social patterns, conflicts, and ideas of national unity developed amid growing cultural diversity.

Era 8: The Great Depression and World War II (1929–1945)

Standard 3: The causes and course of World War II, the character of the war at home and abroad, and its reshaping of the U.S role in world affairs.

Era 9: Postwar United States (1945 to early 1970s)

Standard 2: How the Cold War and conflicts in Korea and Vietnam influenced domestic and international politics.

Standard 4: The struggle for racial and gender equality and for the extension of civil liberties.

Era 10: Contemporary United States (1968–the present)

Standard 2: Economic, social, and cultural developments in contemporary United States.

Standard 2B: The student understands the new immigration and demographic shifts.

Standard 2C: The student understands changing religious diversity and its impact on American institutions and values.

Standard 2D: The student understands contemporary American culture.

Index

A

abacus (Chinese)
  constructing, 60
  using, 60
Acohido, Byron (1997 Pulitzer Prize winner), 154
acupuncture, creation by Chinese, 22
Alaskeros, Filipino Americans as, 136
Alien Land Law (1913), 106, 158
All-American Girl TV program (Margaret Cho), 115–116
Amerasian Homecoming Act of 1987, 188–189
America, voyage of Asians to, 1–2
America Is in the Heart (Carlos Bulosan), 143
American citizenship
  attainment by Wonk Kim Ark, 25
  balancing with native culture, 207–208
  challenges of, 207
  of Japanese, 66
Angel Island
  arrival of Asian immigrants on, 5
  and paper sons, 21
Angkor Wat temple (Cambodia), 205
anime (Japanese animation films), 72, 79
animism religion, practice by Filipino Americans, 148
aprons, constructing evil spirit apron, 15
Ark, Wong Kim (civil rights activist), 25
arrow throwing (tuho) game, playing, 111
Asian American movies and videos, 231

Asian American museums
  in California, 225–226
  in District of Columbia, 226–227
  in Florida, 227
  in Hawaii, 227–228
  in Illinois, 228
  in Massachusetts, 228
  in New York, 228
  in Oregon, 229
  in Texas, 229
  in Washington, 229
Asian Americans
  definition of, 1
  population of, 214
Asian immigrants
  balancing cultural differences of, 209–210
  and dating, 209
  and expectations at school, 209
  features of, 208
  individualism of, 208–209
  languages of, 208
  shared history and bright future of, 213
Asian Indian American communities (Little Indias), 163
Asian Indian Americans
  immigration of, 157–158
  racism and discrimination against, 158–159
Asian Indian clothing, 163–164
Asian Indian dancing bells (ghungroos), making, 167

Asian Indian Festival of Lights (Diwali), 175–176
Asian Indian food, 169
Asian Indian hand painting (mehndi), doing, 178
Asian Indian men, relationship to Mexican American women, 159–160
Asian Indian welcome (rangoli), creating, 177
Asian Indians
  as American citizens, 158
  considering as Caucasians, 158–159
  immigration to United States, 160
Asian Pacific American Heritage month, celebration of, 210–212
Asian-Indian religions
  Hinduism, 161–162
  Jainism, 162–163
  Sikhism, 162
Asians, voyage to America, 1–2
Asiatic Barred Zone law (1917), 158
ayurvedic medicine, 173–174

B

bachelor societies, participation of Chinese men in, 24
balikbayan (return home) box, making, 147
banana lassi (yogurt drink), making, 170
bandalores (Filipino toy), 155
barong tagalog (Filipino dress), 154
batik (Laos), 201

baw baw (Hmong ball-toss game), playing, 196
Bellingham, Washington, racism against Asian Indian Americans in, 158
Bemis, Charlie, 17
Bemis, Polly (Chinese American frontier woman), 17
Bento lunch, making, 67
Bhatia, Sabeer (Hotmail inventor), 169
bibingka (Filipino Christmas treat), making, 151
bindi (Asian Indian symbol), 164
Bing, Ah (Bing cherries), 9
Binh, Tran Quoc (Vietnamese sergeant), 182
boat people (Southeast Asians), 184
Bodhidharma (Indian Buddhist priest), 73–74
Bollywood, 174
Bon Festival, 89
Bon Odori (Japanese folk dance), 89–90
bonsai (miniature-tree cultivation), 79
book, printing of first book, 22
Bose, Amar (speaker system), 173
bound feet, 12
brahmin sect of Hinduism, 161
brush painting greeting card, creating, 26–27
bubble tea, making honeydew bubble tea, 11
Buddha
  Mokuren as student of, 89
  relationship to lunar calendar, 31, 33

Buddha's Delight, eating for Chinese New Year, 36
Buddhism, basis of, 10
bui doi (children of the dust), Amerasian children as, 189
Bulosan, Carlos (Filipino writer), 143

C
calendar, Chinese lunar calendar, 31, 33
California
    Asian American museums in, 225–226
    exodus of Chinese from, 9
calligraphy banner, painting, 47
Calugas, Jose (army sergeant), 137
Cambodia
    contributions of, 205
    in current time, 205
    official language of, 205
    takeover by Communists, 183–184
Cambodian clothing, 205
Cambodian Court Dance, learning gestures of, 202
Cambodian spring rolls, making, 206
Cambodians, presence in America, 201
Cantonese food, 58
carp, role in Japanese Children's Day, 89
carp steamer, making for Children's Day, 91–92
caste system, sects of, 161–162
"Caucasian" versus "white," 158
celadon ceramics, creation by Koreans, 131
Central Pacific Railroad, construction by Chinese, 17–18
chalk rangoli (Asian Indian welcome), creating, 177
Chandrasekhar, Subrahmanyan (1983 Nobel Prize for Physics), 161
Chang, Leonard (Korean American novelist), 124
Chang, Michael (tennis player), 34
Chang, Sarah (Korean American violinist), 113
Chanoyu (Japanese tea ceremony), 94–95
chapati (Asian Indian food), 169
Chase the Dragon's Tail game, playing, 59
Chawla, Kalpana (Asian Indian astronaut), 166

Cherry Blossom Festival, 93
chi energy, 32
child prodigy, Sarah Chang as, 113
Children's Day (Komodo No Hi), 89, 91–92
chima (Korean women's clothing), 113
Chin, Fee Har (nian gao cake), 35–36
China
    as Communist country, 22
    current population of, 22
    in current time, 22
    flowers originating in, 18
    immigration of males from, 24
    reasons for emigration from, 8
Chinatowns, emergence of, 9–10
Chinese, current immigration of, 62
Chinese abacus
    constructing, 60
    using, 61–62
Chinese American weddings, 55
Chinese Americans
    construction of transcontinental railroad by, 17–18
    contributions of, 22
    contributions to West, 7
    development of rice in Hawaii by, 9
    exodus from California, 9
    as farmworkers, 8–9
    in laundry cleaning industry, 18
    as paper sons, 21
    population between 1880 and 1920, 21
    practice of placer mining by, 8
    racism and discrimination against, 20
    treatment in gold mines, 8
    use of irrigation techniques by, 8–9
Chinese brush painting greeting card, creating, 26–27
Chinese calligraphy banner, painting, 47
Chinese characters, writing, 23
Chinese clothing, 10, 12
Chinese culture, significance of food in, 37
Chinese dragons, 50. See also dragon lantern
Chinese Exclusion Act, 20
Chinese foods, 10
Chinese jiaozi, wrapping, 38–39
Chinese lion, making, 43–44
Chinese New Year, 33–34, 36–37
Chinese nian gao cake, cooking, 35–36
Chinese opera face painting, 16

Chinese paper cutting, 30
Chinese red envelope (lai see), making, 40–41
Chinese restaurants, 58
Chinese ribbon dance, 63
Chinese school, 53
Chinese shadow puppet show, putting on, 52–53
Chinese zodiac and lunar calendar, 31, 33
Cho, Margaret (Korean American comedian), 115–116
Chopra, Deepak (Asian Indian doctor and author), 159
chou in Chinese opera, 16
Choy, Herbert (U.S. Court of Appeals), 114
Christianity, impact on Korean Americans, 117
Christmas, celebration by Filipino Americans, 148–150
Chung, Eugene (National Football League draft pick), 117
clothing, 10, 12
Coal Miners' Japanese dance, 89
Columbia shuttle, participation of Kalpana Chawla on, 166
Communism, abandonment by Cambodia, 205
Communist countries
    China, 22
    governments of, 181–182
Communists, takeover of Vietnam, Cambodia, and Laos by, 183–184
compass, invention by Chinese, 22
Confucianism, 24
cowrie shell game (Sungka), playing, 145–146
credit-ticket system, explanation of, 7
Cruz, Philip Vera (1965 Filipino farmworkers' strike), 134
culture shock, experience by Southeast Asian Americans, 187
cultures, balancing, 207–208

D
daruma doll, painting, 73–74
dhal (Asian Indian food), 169
Dham, Vinod (Pentium processor), 164
dhoti (Asian Indian clothing), 164
Diem, Ngo Dinh (Communist leader), 182

dim sum, 55
Dinh, Viet D. (assistant attorney general of U.S.), 183
discrimination
    against Asian Indian Americans, 158–159
    against Chinese, 20
    against Filipino Americans, 136
    against Japanese, 70
    against Korean Americans, 106
District of Columbia, Asian American museums in, 226–227
Diwali (Asian Indian Festival of Lights), 175–176
diya, making for Diwali, 176
dog, year of, 33
domino theory, 182
double happiness character, including in Chinese American weddings, 55–56
dragon
    creating for Tet (Vietnamese New Year), 192
    significance of, 56
    year of, 33
dragon lantern, lighting up, 48–49. See also Chinese dragons
Draves, Victoria Manalo (Olympic diver), 138
dumplings (jiaozi), wrapping, 38–39

E
Ellis Island, relationship to Angel Island, 5
emigrate, definition of, 8. See also immigrate
Endo, Mitsuye (Japanese internment camps), 98–99
energy, relationship to feng shui, 32
enlightenment, finding in Buddhism, 10
Er, Lady Chang (Moon Festival), 50
evil spirit apron, constructing, 15
Excelsiors (Japanese baseball league), 97

F
fa mein, role in Chinese opera, 16
fan, creating Japanese folding fan, 4
farmers in China, immigration to America, 7–8
farmworkers
    Chinese immigrants as, 8–9
    Filipino Americans as, 135–136
fat choy (sea moss), eating for Chinese New Year, 36

Feast of Lanterns, 89
feng shui, 32
filial piety, relationship to Confucianism, 24
Filipino Americans. *See also* Little Manila (Stockton, California)
  as Alaskeros, 136
  celebrations of, 148–150
  discrimination against, 136
  as migrant farmworkers, 135–136
  religions of, 148
  Watsonville attacks on, 135–136
  and World War II, 136–137
Filipino clothing, 154
Filipino dances
pandango sa ilaw, 152
tinikling, 154
Filipino farmworkers' strike, 134
Filipino food, 141
Filipino immigrants (pensionados), 135
Filipino language, 134
Filipino respect, 143
Filipino shell crafts, 139
Filipino vocabulary examples, 141, 143
Filipinos
  immigration after 1965, 155
  immigration to America, 133–134
fish printing (gyotaku), 84
Flores, Pedro (yo-yo manufacturer), 155
Florida, Asian American museums in, 227
flower arranging (ikebana), 93, 101–102
flower face, role in Chinese opera, 16
flowers, origins in China, 18
foam dragon, creating for Tet (Vietnamese New Year), 192
folding fan, creating Japanese folding fan, 4
folk art, Chinese paper cutting as, 30
fook, painting on Chinese calligraphy banner, 47
foot binding, 12
fortune cookies, 58
442nd Regimental Combat Team and 100th Battalion, participation in World War II, 96
Four Noble Truths of Buddha, 10
front kick in Taekwondo, trying, 121
fun see (bean threads), eating for Chinese New Year, 36
furoshiki (square cloth), crafting, 77

G
Gam Saan, definition of, 7
games
  Chase the Dragon's Tail, 59
  origin of pachisi, 174
  otedame beanbag game, 68–69
  pov pob (Hmong ball-toss game), 196
  Snakes and Ladders, 171
  Sungka (cowrie shell game), 145–146
  Tumbang Preso (kick the can game), 144
Gandhi, Mahatma, 162
gardens, building Japanese rock garden, 100
gayageum (Korean instrument), 131
Gentlemen's Agreement, impact on Japanese, 70
geta (wooden sandal), 76
ghagra choli (Asian Indian clothing), 164
ghungroos (Asian Indian dancing bells), making, 167
Gim Gong, Lue (frost-resistant orange), 9
Girls' Day (Hina Matsuri), 92–93
Go (Japanese game), 72
gold mines, treatment of Chinese in, 8
gold rush, 7–8
good fortune, Chinese character for, 47
good-bye
  in Filipino, 141
  in Hindi, 166
  in Japanese, 80
  in Khmer, 205
  in Korean, 108
  in Mandarin Chinese, 25
Guangdong, 7
gyotaku (Japanese fish printing), 84
gyoza, 72

H
haiku poem, writing, 82
halo-halo (Filipino treat), 142
hanbok (Korean clothing), 113
hangul (Korean scientific alphabet), 131
Harijan, renaming of untouchables to, 162
Harkness, Ruth (giant panda bear arrival), 27
Hawaii
  as 50th United State, 69
  annexation to United States, 69

  Asian American museums in, 227–228
  development of rice in, 9
  immigration of Filipinos to, 134–135
  immigration of Japanese to, 66, 69
  in late 1900s, 66
  Senator Daniel K. Inouye from, 99
  U.S. Representative Mink from, 93
Hayslip, Lee Ly (Vietnamese American writer), 188
hello
  in Filipino, 141
  in Hindi, 166
  in Japanese, 80
  in Khmer, 205
  in Korean, 108
  in Mandarin Chinese, 25
herbal shops, 31
herring rice, eating for Japanese New Year, 87
Heungshan poetry, example of, 5
Hina Matsuri (Girls' Day), 92–93
Hindi vocabulary examples, 166
Hinduism, practice by Asian Indians, 161
history standards and learning objectives, 237–238
Hmong, oral tradition of, 195
Hmong ball-toss game (pov pob), playing, 196
Hmong clothing, 195
Hmong flower cloth (paj ntaub), coloring, 197–198
Hmong storytelling cloth, designing, 199
Ho Chi Minh Trail, 182
Holt Bill, relationship to Korean adoptees, 118
honeydew bubble tea, making, 11
horse, year of, 33
ho-see (dried oysters), eating for Chinese New Year, 36
humaneness, relationship to Confucianism, 24
Hyundai (Korean automobile manufacturer), 131

I
ikebana (Japanese flower arranging), 93, 101–102
Illinois, Asian American museums in, 228
immigrant trunk, packing, 3
immigrants, current Chinese immigrants, 62

immigrate, XI. *See also* emigrate
Immigration Acts (1924 and 1965), 20, 106, 118, 158
immigration of Filipinos after 1965, 155
India
  contributions of, 173–174
  crops produced by, 174
  in current time, 173
  religions of, 160
  rule from 1858-1947, 157
  as subcontinent, 173
Indochina War (1947), 182
Inouye, Daniel K. (senator from Hawaii), 99
Internet resources, 223–224. *See also* Web sites
internment camps, placement of Japanese Americans in, 95–99
Interpreter of Maladies (Jhumpa Lahiri), 174
irrigation techniques, use by Chinese, 8–9
isolationist policy, relationship to Korea, 105
Issei generation of Japanese, 71

J
jai choy, eating for Chinese New Year, 36
Jainism, practice by Asian Indians, 162–163
Jaisohn, Philip (Korean medical doctor), 107
Jan, Ken, Pon (Rock, Paper, Scissors) game, playing, 103
Japan
  in 1853, 65
  contributions of, 79
  in current time, 79
  main islands of, 79
  plantation life in, 66
Japanese
  as American citizens, 66
  immigration to Hawaii, 66, 69
  invasion of Korea by, 105
  on mainland, 69
  picture brides, 70–71
  racism and discrimination against, 70
  schoolboys, 74
  vocabulary examples, 80
  writing, 80
Japanese Americans
  in internment camps, 95–99

participation in World War II, 96
    as wartime interpreters, 99
Japanese baseball leagues, 97
Japanese clothing, 76
Japanese fish printing (gyotaku), 84
Japanese flower arranging (ikebana), 93, 101–102
Japanese folding fan, creating, 4
Japanese folk dance (Bon Odori), 89–90
Japanese food, 76
Japanese immigrants, generations of, 71
Japanese New Year (Oshogatsu), celebrating, 87
Japanese rock garden, building, 100
Japanese tea ceremony (Chanoyu), 94–95
Japantowns, 71–72
jeepney (Filipino transportation), creating, 156
jegi-chagi (tassel kicking) game, playing, 112
jiaozi (steamed dumplings)
    eating for Chinese New Year, 36
    wrapping, 38–39
Jong-II, Kim (North Korean leader for life), 130
jumoni (Korean good luck purse)
    eating for Lunar New Year, 124
    making, 126
junk, definition of, 7

K
kabuki actor, painting face like, 86
kadomatsu (pine and bamboo arrangement), 87–88
kaht (Korean man's hat), 113
kami (living spirit), 80
kana symbols, 80
kanji (Japanese characters), 80
Kenjinkai picnic, 79
Khmer people, presence of, 205
Khmer Rouge, 183–184
Khmer theater mask, molding, 203–204
Khmer vocabulary examples, 205
kick in Taekwondo, trying, 121
kick the can game (Tumbang Preso), 144
The Killing Fields (Dith Pran), 204
Kim, Harry (Sun Grand nectarine), 106
kimchi (Korean pickled vegetables), 114
kimono (garment), 76
king, character for, 13
King Sejong (Korea), 131
kite-flying for Seol (Korean Lunar New Year), 124, 129

Komodo No Hi (Children's Day), 89
Korea
    contributions of, 131
    in current time, 130–131
    invasion by Japanese, 105
    isolationist policy of, 105
Korean adoptees, 118
Korean Americans
    discrimination against, 106
    impact of Christianity on, 117
    and Los Angeles riots of 1992, 116–117
    as small business owners, 116
    as war brides, 117
    and World War II, 114–115
Korean barbecued beef (pulgogi), 113–114
Korean birthday celebration (tol), 118–119
Korean board game (yut), playing, 124, 127–128
Korean camps, 120
Korean clothing, 113
Korean cultural centers, 120
Korean flag, making, 109
Korean food, 113–114
Korean good luck purse (jumoni), 124, 126
Korean immigration, great wave of, 118
Korean independence movement, 108
Korean kite, constructing, 129
Korean Lunar New Year (Seol), celebrating, 124
Korean pancake (pindaettok), eating for Lunar New Year, 124
Korean pickled vegetables (kimchi), 114
Korean rice cake soup (ttok-kuk)
    eating for Lunar New Year, 124
    preparing, 125
Korean schools, 120
Korean scientific alphabet (hangul), 131
Korean Taekwondo Association, founding of, 121
Korean vocabulary examples, 108
Korean War, 115–116
Korean wrapping cloth (pojagi), creating, 122–123
Koreans
    educational drive of, 107
    immigration to America, 105–106
    industries worked in, 106–107
    women immigrants, 108
Koreatowns, 120

Korematsu, Fred (activist), 97
kshatriya sect of Hinduism, 161
Kwan, Michelle (figure skating champion), 34

L
lacquer box, crafting, 28–29
Lahiri, Jhumpa (Pulitzer Prize–winning author), 174
lai see (Chinese red envelope), making, 40–41
Lakshmi (Asian Indian goddess of prosperity), 175
Laos
    contributions of, 201
    in current time, 201
    groups fighting for control of, 183
    takeover by Communists, 183–184
Laotians, presence in America, 195
laundry cleaning industry, Chinese involvement in, 18
learning objectives and history standards, 237–238
Lee, Sammy (Korean American Olympic medalist), 120
letter writers, 9
Liang, Ma (The Magic Paintbrush), 52
lily feet, 12
Lin, Maya (architect/sculptor), 29
lion, making Chinese lion, 43–44
lion dance, 42, 45
Little Indias (Asian Indian American communities), 163
Little Manila (Stockton, California), 137–138. See also Filipino Americans
Little Saigons (Vietnamese American communities), 189
Little Tokyo, 72
Locke, Gary (Chinese American governor), 54
Los Angeles riots of 1992, impact on Korean Americans, 116–117
lotus shoes, 12
lunar/solar calendar, use by Chinese, 31, 33
lunas (field bosses), role in Hawaiian plantation life, 66

M
Ma, Yo-Yo (cellist), 33
The Magic Paintbrush Chinese folktale, 52
Malay, 141

males, immigration from China, 24
Manchus, 10, 12
Mandarin, 25
manga (Japanese comic book), 72
Manilamen (Filipino immigrants), 133
Maria Clara dress (Filipino), 154
Massachusetts, Asian American museums in, 228
McCarran-Walter Act (1952), 66
Medal of Honor, receipt by Sadao S. Monemori, 92
mehndi (Asian Indian hand painting), doing, 178
Meng Liang character, using face paint with, 16
menko game, playing, 104
Mexican American women, relationship to Asian Indian men, 159–160
migrant farmworkers, Filipino Americans as, 135–136
milk-cap (POG) game, making, 104
miners, claims staked by, 7–8
Minh, Ho Chi (Communist leader), 181–182
mining, practice of placer mining, 8
Mink, Patsy Takemoto (U.S. representative from Hawaii), 93
miso soup, 72, 75
mochitsuki (pounding rice), performing for Japanese New Year, 87
Mokuren (student of Buddha), 89
monkey
    pushing away in tai chi, 57
    year of, 33
moon cakes, eating during Moon Festival, 50
Moon Festival, 50–51
Moua, Mee (Hmong American state representative), 198
movable type, creation by Chinese, 22
Mu Ke (Stockaded Village) opera, 16
Mumbai, India (film industry), 174
Munemori, Sadao S. (private first class), 92
Murao, Helen (release from internment camp), 98

N
naan (Asian Indian food), 169
Nanak, Guru (Sikhism), 162
Nathoy, Lalu (Polly Bemis), 17
needlework (Laos), 201

New Year (Chinese), 33–34, 36–37
New York, Asian American museums in, 228
Nguyen, Dat (Vietnamese American NFL player), 184
nian gao (Chinese), cooking, 35–36
1906 San Francisco earthquake, effect on Chinese, 21
Nisei, 71
  Japanese spoken by, 80
  volunteering in World War II, 96
Nisei Week, 93
nitroglycerine, use in railroad construction, 18
no, saying in Hindi, 166
Nobel Prize, award to Subrahmanyan Chandrasekhar, 161
Noh (theater), 79
North Korea (Democratic People's Republic of Korea), 130

O
Obon Festival, 89
100th Battalion, participation in World War II, 96
onigiri (rice balls), making, 78
opera face painting (Chinese), 16
oranges, development of frost-resistant orange, 9
Oregon, Asian American museums in, 229
"Oriental," 210
origami dog and cat, folding, 81
Oshogatsu (Japanese New Year), celebrating, 87
otedame beanbag game, creating, 68–69
otoso (spiced sake), drinking for Japanese New Year, 87
ox, year of, 33
Ozawa, Seiji (conductor), 87

P
pachisi game, origin of, 174
paj ntaub (Hmong flower cloth), coloring, 197–198
panda bear, arrival in United States, 27
pandango sa ilaw (Filipino dance), practicing, 152
paper, creation in China, 22
paper cutting, 30
paper sons, Chinese men as, 21
Par, Chan Ho (Korean American major league baseball player), 116

parol (Filipino Christmas symbol), making, 149–150
Pasko (Filipino Christmas), 148
PATRIOT Act (Viet D. Dinh), 183
Pearl Harbor, bombing of, 95
Pei, M. (architect), 31
pensionados (Filipino immigrants), 135
Perry, Matthew C. (storming Edo Bay in Japan), 65
Philippine Independence Day (Rizal Day), celebrating, 152
Philippines
  colonization by Spanish, 134
  contributions of, 154–155
  in current time, 154
  population of, 134
  relationship to United States, 133–134
pho (Vietnamese noodle soup), preparing, 189–190
phoenix, 36, 56
picnics
  Kenjinkai picnic, 79
  Moon Festival picnic, 51
picture brides, practice by Japanese, 70–71
picture frame, making as Filipino shell craft, 139
pig, year of, 33
pina (Filipino fabric), 154
pindaettok (Korean pancake), eating for Lunar New Year, 124
pine and bamboo arrangement (kadomatsu), 87–88
placer mining, practice by Chinese, 8
Plain of Jars (Laos), 201
plantation life in Japan, 66
please
  in Hindi, 166
  in Khmer, 205
POG (milk-cap) game, making, 104
pojagi (Korean wrapping cloth), creating, 122–123
porcelain, origination in China, 22
Pot, Pol (dictator of Khmer Rouge), 183–184
pot cover gong, making, 46
pov pob (Hmong ball-toss game), playing, 196
Pran, Dith (international photojournalist), 204

Presidential Medal of Freedom, receipt by Fred Korematsu, 97
pulgogi (Korean barbecued beef), 113–114
puppet show , putting on, 52–53

Q
Qing Dynasty, duration of, 12
queues
  definition of, 9
  wearing of, 10

R
rabbit, year of, 33
racism
  against Asian Indian Americans, 158–159
  against Chinese, 20
  against Filipino Americans, 135
  against Japanese, 70
  against Korean Americans, 106
railroad, construction by Chinese, 17–18
raita (Asian Indian food), 169
ramen, 72
rangoli (Asian Indian welcome), creating, 177
rat, year of, 33
recipes
  banana lassi (yogurt drink), 170
  bibingka (Filipino Christmas treat), 151
  Cambodian spring rolls, 205
  halo-halo (Filipino treat), 142
  honeydew bubble tea, 11
  ttok-kuk (Korean rice cake soup), 125
  Vietnamese beef noodle soup, 189–190
red color, significance of, 12, 164
reeducation camps, setup in South Vietnam, 183
refugee camps, establishment for Southeast Asians, 184–185
refugees, Southeast Asians as, 181, 184. See also Southeast Asians
reparations, awarding to Japanese Americans, 99
restaurants (Chinese), 58
ribbon dance (Chinese), 63
rice, development in Hawaii, 9
rice balls (onigiri), making, 78
rice pounding (mochitsuki), performing for Japanese New Year, 87

ritual, relationship to Confucianism, 24
Rizal, José (Filipino medical doctor), 152
Rizal Day (Philippine Independence Day), celebrating, 152
Rock, Paper, Scissors (Jan, Ken, Pon) game, playing, 103
Rokusei generation of Japanese, 71
rooster, year of, 33

S
sake (otoso), drinking for Japanese New Year, 87
Salonga, Lea (Tony Award–winning actress), 146
salwar kameez (Asian Indian clothing), 164
Samsung (Korean company), 131
samurai, definition of, 4
San Francisco
  Chinese restaurants in, 58
  Japantown in, 72
San Francisco earthquake (1906), effect on Chinese, 21
Sansei generation of Japanese, 71
sari (Asian Indian clothing), 163–164, 165
Saund, Dalip Singh (Asian Indian elected to U.S. Congress), 163
Scott Act (1888), 20
scribe, definition of, 9
Sejong, King (Korea), 131
Seol (Korean Lunar New Year), celebrating, 124, 129
sha energy, 32
shadow puppet show, putting on, 52–53
Shankar, Ravi (sitar performer), 160
sheep, year of, 33
shell crafts (Filipino), 139
sheng in Chinese opera, 16
Shen-Nung (emperor), relationship to tea drinking, 22
Shin Issei generation of Japanese, 71
Shintoism, 80
shogun, definition of, 65
shoulder yoke, making, 19
shudra sect of Hinduism, 161
Shyamalan, Manoj "Night" (movie director and screenwriter), 158
Sierra Nevada, construction of railroad across, 17
Sik jor fan meh ah?, 37
Sikhism, practice by Asian Indians, 162

Sikhs, appearance of, 157
sitar (Indian musical instrument), 174
The Sixth Sense (Manoj "Night"
    Shyamalan), 158
snake, year of, 33
snakes and ladders game, playing, 171
sojourners, Chinese as, 7
South Korea (Republic of Korea),
    130–131
South Vietnam, reeducation camps in,
    183
Southeast Asia, fleeing, 184
Southeast Asian Americans, immigration
    to United States, 181–182
Southeast Asian food, 194
Southeast Asians. *See also* refugees
    adjustment to America by, 187–188
    American sponsors of, 185
    reception centers for, 185
Spanish, colonization of Philippines by,
    134
sponsor box, making for Southeast Asian
    family, 186
SS *Gaelic*, Korean immigrants on, 106
stake a claim, relationship to gold rush,
    7–8
steerage, transport of Asians in, 1
stir-frying, 37
Stockaded Village (*Mu Ke*) opera, 16
Stockton, California (Little Manila com-
    munity in), 137–138
storytelling cloth (Hmong), designing,
    199
subsistence farming, practice in
    Cambodia, 205
sugar plantations
    Filipino laborers on, 134–135
    Japanese laborers on, 66
Su-Lin (giant panda bear), 27
Sun Grand nectarine (Harry Kim),
    106
sungka (cowrie shell game), playing,
    145–146
sushi, 72
syllabaries, kana symbols as, 80
Syngman, Rhee (South Korean presi-
    dent), 115

T
tabi (sock), 76
Taekwondo, front kick in, 121
tai chi, practicing, 57
taiko drumming, practicing, 83
Tan, Amy (author), 30
tandoor, 169
Tanko Bushi Bon Odori Japanese dance,
    89
tassel kicking (jegi-chagi) game, playing,
    112
tax for mining, imposition of, 8
tea
    categories of, 10
    discovery in China, 22
tea ceremony (Chanoyu), 94–95
Teacher's Guide, 234–236
tempura, 72
tenant farmers, Chinese as, 8–9
Tet (Vietnamese New Year), 189, 192
Texas, Asian American museums in, 229
thank you
    in Filipino, 141
    in Hindi, 166
    in Japanese, 80
    in Khmer, 205
    in Korean, 108
    in Mandarin Chinese, 25
The King and I (Lea Salonga), 146
Three Perfections (China), 47
tiger, year of, 33
Tiger Brigade, Korean Americans in, 115
tiger hat, creating, 13–14
tinikling (Filipino dance), 154
tol (Korean birthday celebration),
    118–119
tonal language, Mandarin as, 25
Tor, Sathaya (Cambodian refugee), 207
transcontinental railroad, construction by
    Chinese, 17–18
tray of togetherness
    creating, 42
    eating for Chinese New Year, 36–37
trunk, packing immigrant trunk, 3
ttok-kuk (Korean rice cake soup)
    eating for Lunar New Year, 124
    preparing, 125

tuho (arrow throwing) game, playing,
    111
Tumbang Preso (kick the can game), 144
Tydings-McDuffie Independence Act of
    1934, 136
type, creation of movable type by
    Chinese, 22

U
Uchida, Yoshiko (children's book
    author), 98
ukiyo-e (pictures of a floating world), 79
union Pacific Railroad, construction by
    Chinese, 17–18
untouchable sect of Hinduism, 162
U.S. Court of Appeals, appointment of
    Herbert Choy to, 114
USA PATRIOT Act (Viet D. Dinh), 183

V
vaisya sect of Hinduism, 161
Vardhamana, Nataputta (Jainism),
    162–163
Viet Cong, 182
Vietnam
    contributions of, 194–195
    in current time, 194
    split into North and South, 182
    takeover by Communists, 183–184
Vietnam Veterans Memorial (Maya Lin),
    29
Vietnam War, 182–183
Vietnamese American communities
    (Little Saigons), 189
Vietnamese beef noodle soup, preparing,
    189–190
Vietnamese clothing, 194
Vietnamese in America, 188
Vietnamese New Year (Tet), 189, 192
Villa, Pancho (Filipino flyweight cham-
    pion), 155

W
"The Wall" (Vietnam Veterans
    Memorial), 29
Wang, An (computer inventor), 62
Wang, Vera (fashion designer), 12
wang character, 13

war brides, Korean Americans as, 117
Washington, Asian American museums
    in, 229
water puppetry (Vietnamese), 195
Watsonville attacks on Filipino
    Americans, 135
Web sites, 232–233, 236. *See also*
    Internet resources
weddings (Chinese American), 55
welcome
    in Filipino, 141
    in Hindi, 166
    in Japanese, 80
    in Korean, 108
    in Mandarin Chinese, 25
West, contributions of Chinese to, 7
"white" versus "Caucasian," 158
Wie, Michelle (Korean American golfer),
    108
wong character, 13
World War II
    Filipino American participation in,
        136–137
    Japanese American participation in, 96
    Korean Americans in, 114–115

Y
Yamaguchi, Kristi (Olympic figure
    skater), 76
yang foods, examples of, 37
yes, saying in Hindi, 166
yin and yang, 31
yin foods, examples of, 37
yoga, trying, 168
yogurt drink (banana lassi), making, 170
Yonsei generation of Japanese, 71
yo-yo, manufacturing of, 155
yu (fish), eating for Chinese New Year,
    36
yuen bow (gold money), 36
yut (Korean board game), playing, 124,
    127–128

Z
Zara, Gregorio (Filipino inventor), 155
Zheng, creation of compass
    by, 22